COMPARATIVE SOCIOLOGY AND SOCIAL THEORY

Comparative Sociology and Social Theory

Beyond the Three Worlds

Graham Crow

St. Martin's Press
New York

St. Martin's Press, Scholarly and Reference Division,
175 Fifth Avenue, New York, N.Y. 10010

First published in the United States of America in 1997

This book is printed on paper suitable for recycling and
made from fully managed and sustained forest sources.

Printed in Hong Kong

ISBN 0–312–17311–3 (cloth)
ISBN 0–312–17312–1 (paper)

Library of Congress Cataloging-in-Publication Data
Crow, Graham
Comparative sociology and social theory : beyond the three worlds
/ Graham Crow.
p.   cm.
Includes bibliographical references and index.
ISBN 0–312–17311–3 (cloth).   ISBN 0–312–17312–1 (paper)
1. Sociology—Comparative method.   I. Title.
HM51.C887   1997
301—dc21   96–51081
                                                                        CIP

For Rose

Contents

Acknowledgements

Thanks are due to many people for the assistance which they gave me in the course of writing this book. My undergraduate tutor, Gavin Williams, first pointed me in the direction of comparative sociology, and my erstwhile colleague John Hall later nurtured my developing interest. The Department of Sociology and Social Policy generously provided a period of leave in 1995, which allowed an uninterrupted spell during which the greater part of the first draft was written. Various colleagues in the Department also took time out from their busy schedules to read and comment on draft material and to discuss the underlying ideas; Graham Allan, Waltraud Ernst, Roger Lawson and Tony Rees deserve special thanks in this regard. In addition, useful feedback has come from the several cohorts of undergraduates who have taken my final-year course on comparative sociology. The secretarial staff in the Department, Doreen Davies, Glynis Evans, Gwen Gordon and Eileen Upward, also made valuable contributions to improving the quality of the final product. The library staff at both the University of Southampton and the London School of Economics helped in securing access to the wide range of material which work of this sort requires. At the publishers, the project has been speeded along at various points by timely and supportive editorial guidance from Frances Arnold, Catherine Gray and Nicola Young; the comments on the draft which were made by the publisher's anonymous reader were an important part of this process. Friends and colleagues at other universities gave further constructive advice and encouragement when responding to my requests for them to cast a critical sociological eye over draft chapters; Fiona Devine (who read every draft chapter), Will Medd and Claire Wallace are all owed a debt in this respect. Finally, special appreciation is due to Rose Wiles, whose contribution has been quite literally beyond comparison; this book is dedicated to her.

Introduction

Comparative Sociology and the Sociological Imagination

In 1960, towards the end of his life, the sociologist C. Wright Mills visited South America for the first time. At a seminar there on 'the problem of industrial development', he urged his audience to 'imagine all the range of alternatives that might exist' (1967, p. 156) to the state of underdevelopment in which they found themselves. The need for this exercise of sociological imagination arose because, in Mills' view, none of the existing patterns of development pioneered in Europe, North America and the Soviet Union offered an appropriate model for underdeveloped societies to follow. Characteristically, Mills was at odds with the conventional wisdom of his time in which the range of options for poor countries seeking to escape underdevelopment was restricted to mimicry of either capitalist or state socialist paths of industrialization. Mills saw neither option as ideal, since both were variants of what he called 'the overdeveloped society' in which *the style of life is dominated by the standard of living*' (1967, p. 150, emphasis in original) and where the course of change threw up serious obstacles to the attainment of reason and freedom in social relations. Following either the USA or the Soviet Union held out the prospect of the material poverty of 'the underdeveloped society' being replaced by the waste, alienation and other irrationalities of 'the overdeveloped society' in which individuals degenerated into 'cheerful robots'. For Mills, the choice between capitalism and state socialism did not exhaust the full range of possibilities, and he argued passionately for consideration to be given to further options, including that of 'the properly developing society' in which people have the freedom to make 'a choice among various styles of life' (1967, p. 150) and in which the democratic framework exists to allow the realization of their choices.

Comparative sociology is concerned with the sorts of issue to which Mills drew attention in making the distinction between 'underdeveloped' and 'overdeveloped' societies. The act of comparison is central to the practice of sociology for a number of reasons, of which three are particularly important. To begin with, comparison reveals the enormous diversity of social arrangements, both past and present. By showing the existence of almost infinite variation in the ways in which people relate to each other, comparative sociology can be thought of as 'an exercise in deprovincialization' (Moore, 1984, p. 267), driving home the point that the social relations of our own time and place are in many ways quite distinct. Secondly, comparisons are useful for showing the systematic nature of many of the variations which can be observed, allowing the recognition of broad similarities in the course of social change followed in different contexts. The founders of modern social science worked from the premise that the purpose of comparison of societies, cultures and groups was 'not mainly to describe their unique or distinctive properties but rather to extract from a different set of social arrangements that which was, if not universal, at least generally true of a large number of cases' (Inkeles and Sasaki, 1996, p. xi), and this tradition continues to be important in contemporary analyses. Thirdly, the systematic study of difference in comparative sociology is an essential part of studying not only how social phenomena vary, but also why these variations occur. Durkheim captured the essence of this point in his observation that 'Only comparison affords explanation' (1970, p. 41); it is only by detailed comparative research informed by theoretical analysis that the causes of variation can be properly understood. In sum, comparative sociology allows social phenomena to be placed in perspective and in doing so reveals the existence of general patterns in the ways in which social change takes place, patterns which are at the heart of debates in social theory about diversity and causality. Chapter 1 will be devoted to the elaboration of these general themes of what comparative sociology involves.

The identification of patterns should not be confused with the formulation of deterministic laws of social development. Research in historical sociology has exposed the poverty of crude notions of inevitability by charting the great variety of ways in which change has occurred and the active role played by human agents in bringing about these various changes. If there are patterns to history it is, as Mann says, 'only because real men and women *impose* patterns' (1986, p. 532, emphasis in original) and not because these regularities are in any sense historically necessary and unavoidable. Mills' exhortation to his South American audience to exercise their sociological imagination derived from his conviction that the opportunity exists for people to re-shape the social relationships in which they live, although he was fully aware of how easily the full range of possibilities can become obscured. The belief that history repeats itself underlay the view which was commonly held in Mills' time that underdeveloped societies faced a stark choice between either the capitalist path of industrialization forged in countries like the USA or the state socialist alternative pioneered in the Soviet Union. Comparative sociology will in many instances lead us to draw the opposite conclusion, that options available in one period come to be ruled out in another, at the same time as new opportunities arise. This is the gist of the argument which is examined in greater detail in Chapter 2, where attention is focused on Moore's (1967) suggestion that countries which were not in the first wave of industrializing nations have been forced to construct alternative strategies of development as the route followed by the pioneers became foreclosed.

The essentially conservative idea that history repeats itself can be contrasted with the view that, as Mills puts it, 'sometimes there are quite new things in the world' (1970, p. 173). The emergence during the twentieth century of innovative development strategies is only one of many historical comparisons which bear out the veracity of Mann's observation that 'the most significant problems of our time are novel' (1986, p. 32). Chapters 6 and 7 relate how the peoples of the underdeveloped parts of the world have come to find themselves facing difficulties which conventional models of industrialization and development offer little prospect of resolving. The peoples of the industrialized world also find themselves moving into uncharted territory. Processes of social change have taken the more developed parts of the world to a situation in which the certainties underlying modernist thinking have been brought into question, making it appropriate to speak not only of routes to modernity but also of routes through or beyond it towards a less clear-cut future (Therborn, 1995). The processes currently bringing about the restructuring of contemporary capitalist societies are pushing them in previously unanticipated directions, which few commentators feel able to predict with any confidence, as the discussions in Chapters 3 and 4 reveal. Similarly, in the case of the former state socialist societies which are examined in Chapter 5, the transition may even be seen as comparable in scope to the great transformation of the nineteenth century which ushered in industrial societies, as Bryant and Mokrzycki (1994) have noted. The question of whether these changes add up to 'post-modernity' is considered in Chapter 8 at the end of the book.

Making sense of these developments as they unfold in the various parts of the world requires the adoption of a perspective which is both imaginative and systematic. What Mills called the sociological imagination is necessary if analyses are to be sensitive to the possibility of social arrangements alternative to those which exist at present. Mills' insistence that 'These systems can be changed' (1960, p. 184) was voiced in criticism of the unimaginative fatalism which he felt pervaded the intellectual climate of his day. History played an integral part in freeing the imagination, according to Mills, who argued that 'we must study the available range of social structures, including the historical as well as the contemporary'(1970, p. 163). At the same time, an unbridled imagination can lead to wildly unrealistic conclusions, and Mills himself was not immune from flights into utopianism, as his biographer Horowitz (1983) points out. For the most part, however, Mills recognized the need to harness the sociological imagination within an analytical framework which approached the subject under investigation in a disciplined, methodical fashion. Mills treated systematic comparisons as vital in attempting to answer most sociological questions, since 'Comparisons are required in order to understand what may be the essential conditions of whatever we are trying to understand' (1970, p. 163). Put another way, comparisons allow us to discern regularities and to distinguish between broad types of sociological phenomena which are fundamentally the same and which conform to the same general patterns of development despite the presence of innumerable superficial differences between cases.

The division of the countries of the globe into three worlds of industrial capitalist, state socialist and underdeveloped societies is a prime example of a comparative typology generated in order to make sense of the bewildering diversity of reality. Grouping countries into first, second and third worlds has a long and complicated history which can be traced back to the period immediately following the Second World War. Current developments are taking us rapidly beyond the three worlds, and most commentators would agree with Giddens' assessment that 'The term "third world"... has become distinctly threadbare with the virtual disappearance of the "second world", coupled to the emergence of the "newly industrializing countries"' (1992, p. 2). The move beyond state socialism in the Soviet Union and Eastern Europe and the rise to global prominence of Taiwan, South Korea and other 'tiger economies' have intensified the urgency of the need to reconsider the three worlds model, which even at the outset had a number of tensions and contradictions inherent within it. From the very beginning, the danger existed that the three worlds framework would lead to important differences between countries in each of the groupings being overlooked and their homogeneity wrongly assumed. As Chapter 6 details, this was particularly problematic in the case of the third world, which was a remarkably heterogeneous grouping of states held together principally by the fragile bonds of common disadvantage in the global order. It is also important to recognize that significant variations existed between industrial capitalist societies, and that state socialist countries were never a uniform, monolithic bloc. It is a central theme of this book that each of the three worlds was always characterized by internal diversity, however much their heterogeneity may have become more pronounced over time.

In addition to the difficulties which the three worlds perspective faced in dealing with variations within the types of society it identified, uncertainty existed over the precise basis of the classification. As writers such as Worsley (1984) have noted, economic, political, military, geographical and cultural characteristics were run together in the construction of the categories, creating a situation in which it proved problematic to place many countries neatly into any one category. It has been observed that in South Africa 'First-World and Third-World conditions coexist within one state' (Mayo, 1994, p. 128), and while this society's history of apartheid undoubtedly makes it a special case, it is far from being the only country which straddles the division of the globe into developed and underdeveloped regions. Latouche (1993, p. 86) recounts that Brazil has been likened to a fusion of Sweden and Indonesia, or Belgium and India, while Argentina has been imaginatively recast as 'Norwegypta', the combination of Norway and Egypt, in an attempt to highlight its intermediate and contradictory status within the three worlds classification. The fact that such societies contain within them emergent industrial development suggestive of 'first world' membership alongside social phenomena such as poverty on a scale previously thought to be found only in the least developed parts of the 'third world' serves to remind us that societies are heterogeneous and contradictory entities, and are as a result very difficult to classify.

In the light of the increasing difficulties of employing the three worlds classification, some observers have drawn the conclusion that comparison at the level of societies and groupings of societies has become redundant. Awareness of global forces which cross national boundaries has grown enormously in recent years, and the discussion in Chapter 7 of the economic, political and cultural dimensions of globalization emphasizes the increasing interconnectedness of the modern world. Trends such as the growing power of transnational corporations, the spread of democratic political arrangements, and the emergence of global culture have all illustrated the limits of the autonomy which states and societies can exercise. At the same time, the forces of globalization do not usher in a progressively uniform, homogenized world; growing interconnectedness by no means does away with difference, and in important ways it may be considered to have promoted diversity and complexity. The implication of globalization for comparative sociology is that comparisons continue to have a vital role to play in the analysis of the modern world provided it is recognized that societies are not completely self-contained units and that comparisons need not be restricted to analysis at the level of national societies. May's suggestion that globalization 'renders comparative research even more important' is supported by his observation that 'cross-national comparative research is a growing phenomenon' (1993, pp. 153–4). Writing this book would have been considerably harder had this not been the case; indeed, in some of the chapters which follow, the availability of material has far exceeded the space which it is possible to devote to its full discussion, inevitably leading to the coverage being selective.

To say that comparative sociologists are able to draw on extensive sources of material is not, of course, to imply that all issues are adequately researched. In particular, there exists a problem relating to research findings constantly needing to be updated in the context of rapid and sustained social change. Social scientists necessarily take time to catch up with events which unfold with the speed of those relating to the collapse of state socialism, to take an extreme example which prompted Therborn to adopt a certain tentativeness in his analysis on the grounds that 'The Eastern European sphinx still has many secrets to be revealed' (1995, p. 300). This case also illustrates the further point that comparative sociologists take time to adjust to developments because of the need to revise the theoretical perspectives through which they are interpreted. The largely unanticipated character of the rapid transformation of the state socialist world left observers working with analytical frameworks such as 'the transition from communism to capitalism', which were soon revealed as inadequate to the task of describing and explaining the nature of the changes taking place (Bryant and Mokrzycki, 1994; Clarke *et al.*, 1993). Events such as the 1989 revolutions in Eastern Europe illustrate the general point that comparative sociologists periodically have to deal with what Therborn has called 'the recurring importance of the unexpectable' (1995, p. 358), as a result of which their theoretical perspectives are permanently under review.

Comparative sociology's theoretical perspectives are currently in a state of extreme flux. The three worlds framework was never unproblematic but, as Hettne has observed, 'The fact that the "three worlds" are disintegrating and development is becoming a global and universal problem' (1995, p. 266) makes its reassessment imperative. Responses to the analytical limitations of thinking in terms of three worlds have taken several forms. One response has been to continue to generalize but at a lower level of abstraction, and to distinguish between competing types of capitalist societies, various post-communist trajectories and alternative development options. Hutton, for example, emphasizes the point that 'European, American and Japanese capitalism each have distinctive characteristics' (1996, p. 257). In similar fashion regarding Eastern Europe, it has been noted that 'The transition from communist rule took a variety of forms; so too did the construction of a postcommunist order' (S. White, 1993, p. 12). Likewise, the steady differentiation of the countries once grouped together as the third world has increased awareness of their diverse and unequal positions within a hierarchy (Hettne, 1995). In contrast to this approach, which treats the range of types of society as having proliferated, another response to the reappraisal of the three worlds model has been to promote the view that we now live in a world in which alternatives are being closed down. According to Fukuyama, liberal capitalism has become established across the globe to such an extent that 'there are few versions of modernity other than the capitalist liberal-democratic one that look like they are going concerns' (1992, p. 133). The demise of state socialism signals 'the end of history' in the sense that competing visions of the future to that of liberal capitalism have lost their power to convince.

Both of these responses to the breakdown of the globe into three worlds betray a failure to exercise the sociological imagination. Fukuyama's position suffers from being highly speculative, and he fails to establish convincingly that the broad framework of social arrangements is now set. Fukuyama's reference to 'the total exhaustion of viable systematic alternatives to western liberalism' (1989, p. 3) has been hotly contested (Füredi, 1992), not least because, as Therborn says, 'Prophets of one option only are always to be mistrusted' (1995, p. 359). Such figures have been discredited by subsequent events on more than one occasion in the history of social theory. The alternative response of moving beyond the three worlds by identifying several different types of capitalism, post-communism and underdevelopment avoids this pitfall, but taken to excess the proliferation of these types risks losing sight of the analytical purpose of classification. While it is 'tempting to look for finer and finer comparisons' (Tilly, 1984, p. 144), comparative sociology requires that limits be placed on how far things are taken in this direction. As Durkheim's classic statement puts it, classification's 'main purpose should be to expedite the scientific task by substituting for an indefinite multiplicity of individuals a limited number of types' (1982, pp. 110–11), and what is true for the study of individuals also holds for the comparative study of societies. A typology which has as many types as it has cases is of limited analytical value since it has not made the necessary move beyond acknowledgement of the uniqueness of each individual case to identifying key points of similarity and difference. Mills' sociological imagination required that the process of classification 'must be controlled and not allowed to run away from its purposes' (1970, p. 235), and it is instructive that Mills felt that his point about the issue of development mentioned above could best be made employing only three types of society, 'underdeveloped', 'overdeveloped' and 'properly developing'.

It is, of course, the case that much has happened in the world since Mills devised this typology, which was in any event never fully elaborated. The significance of Mills' work for comparative sociology today lies less in the detail of his nascent analytical schema, and more in the fact that Mills possessed the peculiar knack of knowing how to pose the most perceptive and penetrating questions. His insistence on the importance of asking questions about history linked in to his awareness that it is vital that we understand how we have come to be where we are now. The frequency with which he raised doubts about the exercise of power was connected to his conviction that alternative futures have to be fought for. Also, his exhortation to exercise the sociological imagination embodied his belief that it is always fruitful to ask whether things could be different, and if so how. These are not always easy questions to ask, but preparedness to ask them has an important part to play if things are to be different from the social arrangements which characterize our current time and place. The adoption of this approach to comparative sociology will on occasion invite criticism for utopianism, but it is worth remembering that key features of our own social arrangements which we now take for granted were once regarded with similar incredulity (Polanyi, 1957). At a time of global crisis, there is a strong case to be made for consideration to be given to what Hettne has called '*realistic Utopias*, such as making a shift towards sustainable development' (1995, p. 267, emphasis in original). It was after all no lesser figure than Max Weber who, after a lifetime of comparative sociological research, concluded that it is only by our forebears having 'reached out for the impossible' (1970a, p. 128) that we have attained that which we now know to be eminently possible.

1

The Theory and Practice of Comparative Sociology

Sociology is in essence a comparative discipline, as Durkheim recognized when he wrote that 'Comparative sociology is not a special branch of sociology; it is sociology itself' (1982, p. 157). As soon as we go beyond purely descriptive accounts into the realms of analysis and explanation, sociologists are necessarily involved in making comparisons, since it is only through comparisons that the particular characteristics of different social situations and relationships can be distinguished from their more general, universal features. In this enterprise, social theory plays a central role by providing frameworks through which comparisons can be made and analyses and explanations developed. It was in the course of developing her critique of atheoretical, descriptive accounts that Stacey argued that 'The most valuable researches in the field of sociology are those which can be used comparatively' (1969, p. 138). Stacey emphasized the need to be clear about what it is that is being compared, and what methods of comparison are being employed, if comparative sociologists are to contribute to the development of the discipline.

It is significant that Stacey went on to highlight the importance of the dimensions of time and space for comparative sociology. Sociological comparisons are often framed in historical terms, as in the contrast between industrial societies and their pre-industrial antecedents by which sociologists from the 'founding fathers' onwards have attempted to make sense of their changing social worlds. Alternatively, sociological comparisons may focus on differences which have geographical expressions, as when the rich countries of the North of the global system are contrasted with the poor countries of the South. Giddens (1981, 1984), Harvey (1989) and Wallerstein (1991) have been prominent among those contemporary social theorists who have directed attention to the

9

ways in which social relationships need to be placed into appropriate time and space contexts, because while time and space are not in themselves sociological variables, they are crucial dimensions of sociological accounts. Temporal and spatial expressions of social structures and processes are at the heart of comparative sociology, and as we attempt to understand the broad types of social relationship in which we find ourselves engaged, we confront the need to locate them in time and space. In this sense, historical sociology and area studies can be seen as key points of departure for comparative sociology.

In historical sociology, comparisons are frequently made between different types of society which form part of developmental series. Classic sociological accounts drew upon distinctions between feudal and capitalist societies, or agrarian and industrial societies, but while contemporary sociologists continue to add to the range of types of society which can be identified, their approaches are less likely than those of their predecessors to be framed in terms of overarching theories of 'progress'. Among the types of society recently designated are 'the castaways' society' (Latouche, 1993), 'the classified society' (Cohen, 1985), 'complex societies' (Melucci, 1989), 'the exclusive society' (Lister, 1990), 'fragmented societies' (Mingione, 1991), 'the metronomic society' (Young, 1988), 'post-military society' (Shaw, 1991), 'quantum society' (Zohar and Marshall, 1994), 'risk society' (Beck, 1992), 'surveillance society' (Lyon, 1994), 'the transparent society' (Vattimo, 1994) and 'the unplanned society' (Wedel, 1992), all of which in different ways raise doubts about the overall nature and direction of social development.

Comparative sociology is not, however, concerned only with different types of society. Indeed, the very notion of 'society' is itself problematic, as various observers have been at pains to point out. In the context of globalization, the boundaries of nation states have become increasingly attenuated, leading to speculation that we are moving towards a 'global society' (McGrew, 1992a). At the same time, forces have been at work weakening the internal cohesion of societies and prompting uncertainty about precisely what constitutes 'society'. Mann's description of human society as a 'patterned mess' (1993, p. 4) captures the thrust of much current thinking which recognizes that regularities in social relationships are less orderly and organized than they were portrayed as being by earlier generations of sociologists. It can certainly no longer be assumed that people sharing a particular geographical space will also have the common social ties and culture by which 'society' has conventionally been defined.

In the light of these changes, the legacy of the classical sociologists to contemporary comparative sociology has been subjected to profound reassessment. Many of the certainties held by eminent socio-logical forerunners are open to question, if not fundamental re-exami-nation. From the standpoint of the late twentieth century, faith in 'progress' in its many guises needs to be challenged, not only because it has been 'mis-measured' (Twine, 1994), but also because of the frequency with which what Mies (1986, p. 77) calls 'retrogressive progress' occurs. The consequent re-thinking has been particularly extensive in the field of development studies, where fixed ideas about development processes have been undermined by an awareness of the diverse routes taken by societies passing through the transition to modernity, and by concerns over 'maldevelopment' (Amin, 1990a) and the various problems of 'post-development' (Latouche, 1993). Similar re-thinking has accompanied the unexpected nature of the on-going transformation in former state socialist societies. More prof-oundly still, comparative sociology has been forced to recognize the limits of the whole canon of beliefs held by the classical sociologists about modernity in general.

Yet if the answers provided by classical sociologists have proved unsatisfactory on a number of counts, the core questions which they posed remain highly pertinent for contemporary comparative soci-ology. The relationship between economic and political processes which so concerned Marx and Weber are central to current debates over democratization (Rueschemeyer *et al.*, 1992), while the manage-ment of the tensions between economic change and social order to which Durkheim's attentions were directed is of continuing impor-tance in the context of the upheavals accompanying economic restructuring and globalization (Robertson, 1992). The social signifi-cance of military matters and violence has been the subject of renewed interest in the wake of the end of the Cold War, and even if few people now read Spencer's works, his suggestion of a connection between militarism and social evolution still has contemporary relevance (Mann, 1986). The continued importance for comparative sociology of the classical sociologists is due in no small part to their conviction that systematic comparisons are crucial to the investigation of how and why social orders are reproduced or transformed.

Contemporary debates in comparative sociology revolve around a set of linked issues. The first of these concerns the question of precisely what it is that is being compared. The conventional focus of compara-tive sociology has been on 'societies', but globalization and the internal fragmentation of nation states have made such comparisons increas-ingly problematic. It is also important not to lose sight of other comparisons besides those made between societies. Skocpol's (1979) work comparing states and social revolutions, Collins' (1981) 'comparative sociology of violence', Charles' (1993) comparative analysis of gender divisions of labour and Esping-Andersen's (1990) comparisons of different welfare-state regimes all illustrate the point that comparisons do not have to be framed only in terms of 'societies', but can examine social phenomena from different angles and at different levels. Thus debates about contrasts between the 'first world' and the 'third world' (or the 'North' and the 'South' of the global system) benefit from being able to range more broadly than comparisons between individual societies (South Commission, 1990). At a more micro level, much can be learned from comparisons between groups within societies, such as the contributions to the understanding of the process of social polarization which comparisons between localities and their populations can provide (Byrne, 1989). Such comparisons reveal that social processes are characterized by uneven development which has local as well as national and global expressions. Comparisons periodically throw up 'astonishing parallels' (Szelenyi, 1988, p. 21), such as that between the state socialist *kolkhoz* system of agricultural production and the semi-feudal Junker estates, and such discoveries are all the more likely to emerge where comparisons are not restricted to a focus on 'societies'.

The related issue of the methods employed in making comparisons is a second focus of attention in contemporary debates, since it is vital to ensure that like is compared with like if legitimate conclusions are to be drawn. There are practical as well as conceptual difficulties involved in this process, and comparative sociologists need to bear in mind what Øyen (1990) has called 'the imperfection of comparisons'. One practical consideration is that the data necessary for global and historical comparisons are rarely available in forms which are easily compatible, and this problem has a major bearing on which measures of contested concepts are used. In the sociology of development, for example, data on life expectancy (which are widely available) have been used as an indicator of quality of life, but critics have pointed out that quality of life is a more elusive entity than quantity of life (Barnett, 1988). In similar fashion, comparative analysis of welfare states can be said to have suffered from over-reliance on 'analysis of the easily available data' (Cochrane, 1993, p. 8). It is also important to recognize that there needs to be some theoretical basis on which comparisons can be made. Wallman's observation that 'it is as impossible to compare items that contrast too much as it is to compare items that match too closely' (1985, p. 194) brings out the dual nature of the limits in operation here.

Further grounds for caution arise from the diverse theoretical traditions from which ideas and concepts are drawn. The impact of feminist writers in redirecting attention towards the global feminization of poverty (Scott, 1984), 'housewifization' (Mies, 1986) and the gender-biased nature of social developments more generally (Pearson, 1992a, 1992b), which were previously neglected, provides one example of the potential for 'blind spots' to which social theorists are prone where blinkered perspectives are adopted. Comparative sociology is characterized by long-standing debates about the most appropriate focus and analytical framework to adopt. This phenomenon is common to all branches of the discipline, but because of the breadth of comparative sociology's subject matter, the dangers of individuals' standpoints leading to partiality are arguably more far-reaching. It is, of course, impossible for people's ideas to be completely divorced from their positions and experiences in the world. It is not surprising to find divergence between 'first world' and 'third world' views of 'development', for example, with one person's 'globalization' being another's 'Westernization' or even 'Westoxication' (Featherstone, 1990, p. 11). For Minh-ha, 'Whether "Third World" sounds negative or positive... [in part] depends on *who* uses it. Coming from you Westerners, the word can hardly mean the same as when it comes from Us members of the Third World' (1993, p. 608, emphasis in original). Many other instances of contested concepts could be cited, all of which reinforce the case for paying careful attention to the methods, concepts and theories employed in the practice of comparative sociology.

Comparative sociology: comparisons of what?

Defining precisely what it is that comparative sociologists compare is a problem to which many researchers have devoted considerable energies. It is not surprising to find historical sociologists prominent among them, for without some sense of bounded units between which comparisons could be made, the detection of the patterns of history and social development would be unfeasible. Mann's panoramic analysis of the history of power recognizes the ubiquity of the concept of 'society' in various schools of historical sociology, and points out the looseness and flexibility of the term which emerges as a result. He notes that a more precise definition would emphasize the importance of treating society as 'a unit with boundaries' (1986, p. 13), although it does not follow that the various boundaries of a particular society will necessarily be located together. Indeed, Mann argues, it is historically exceptional for the boundaries of the ideological, economic, military and political networks of social interaction which make up 'society' to coincide neatly. The more usual situation in which these networks of interaction have an overlapping character makes answering the question 'In which society do you live?' (1986, p. 16) far more difficult than it appears at first sight.

The discrepancy between the boundaries of the nation states to which we belong and the economic networks in which we are engaged may have been heightened by the process of globalization, but it has long historical roots. While it is tempting to equate societies with nation states on the grounds that 'For some important purposes, the nation state represents a real interaction network with a degree of cleavage at its boundaries' (Mann, 1986, p. 16), this would, Mann suggests, be a serious oversimplification. The cost of adopting the alternative conception of societies as 'confederal, overlapping, intersecting networks rather than as simple totalities' (1986, p. 17) is that social theory becomes more complex, but at the same time it becomes a more powerful analytical tool. Social relationships are in a process of constant development and flux, and have a tendency to escape from institutional structures set up to contain them. As a result there is no neat correspondence between the state and political relations, nor is economic life the sole preserve of what are conventionally thought of as 'economic' organizations; rather, Mann concludes, 'Organizations and functions weave across each other in the historical process, now separating clearly, now merging in varying forms' (1986, p. 18). Mann thus rejects a unitary conception of society, and with it the approach to comparative sociology which treats societies as 'self-contained units to be simply compared across time and space' (1986, p. 30). Instead, he treats societies as 'organized power networks', with the specific configuration of ideological, economic, military and political organizations and the related distribution of power in any one society having many unique features. This leads directly to the conclusion that 'The chances for comparative sociology are very limited when there are so *few* comparable cases' (1986, p. 30, emphasis in original). In order to maximize these opportunities, Mann argues against exclusive concentration on modern, industrial societies and for a broad historical sociology which draws on all types of society.

A similar set of conclusions is reached by Runciman in his discussion of the question 'What are societies made of?' (1989, p. 1). Starting from the premise that 'the study of societies is the study of people in roles, and the study of people in roles is the study of the institutional distribution of power' (1989, p. 3), Runciman recognizes that such a definition requires that attention be paid to the matter of whom it is appropriate to treat as a member of a society, since it is by no means certain that what he calls 'institutional catchment areas' (1989, p. 5, emphasis in original) will coincide with territorial frontiers. If it is the case that the boundaries of societies are 'fluid and tenuous', and that 'many roles and institutions either overlap or transcend them' (1989, p. 5), then the issue of whom to treat as a member of any particular society is clearly problematic. An individual may have only weak links to the central institutions of a society, or alternatively may have affiliations with more than one society; as Runciman expresses it, 'the possibilities of both multiple and partial membership are in practice very wide' (1989, p. 5). Historically, there have been great variations in the degree to which individuals and groups have been integrated as members of particular societies, and this has a direct bearing on the extent to which relations of power are characterized by either 'domination' or 'co-operation'.

In Runciman's view, the problematic nature of delineating the boundaries of societies in social space and also in historical time makes the conventional sociological treatment of societies as 'social systems' misleading. Social processes such as migration across frontiers undermine the case for regarding societies as self-contained, bounded entities, as the whole issue of the contested citizenship rights of migrant workers amply demonstrates. Similarly, the notion of society as a system is questionable for its implication that the reproduction of social cohesion is an automatic process. In contrast to the certainties of the approach which views society as a system, Runciman suggests a more contingent analysis in which 'the continuity of a society is subject to both the openness of its boundaries and the mutability of its institutions' (1989, p. 7). It follows that if the spatial and temporal boundaries of societies are treated as fluid rather than rigid, in the process of defining societies 'there will always be borderline cases which cannot be settled by fiat' (1989, p. 7). In other words, it is not possible to produce a hard and fast definition of what constitutes a society which would be universally applicable.

Runciman's suggested solution to this problem is framed in terms of the process of differentiation. The patterns of interaction between individuals within a society's set of institutions are constantly changing, and this leads to social differentiation and new relationships of domination or co-operation. The roles of the members of a society may become increasingly incompatible, leading in the extreme to that society splitting into two, or 'fission'. At the other end of the range of possibilities lie 'absorption' and 'fusion', where two formerly separate societies merge as a result of domination or co-operation respectively. These limiting types demonstrate the need for the observer to draw on social theory in order to arrive at a workable classification. Runciman's own social theory leads him to emphasize the centrality of a society's 'patterns of domination' (1989, p. 9) which are embodied in culture as well as in social structures. The three kinds of power which Runciman identifies, economic, ideological and coercive, relate to 'access to or control of the *means of production, means of persuasion* and *means of coercion*' (1989, p. 12, emphasis in original). The three-dimensional conceptualization is put forward as superior to Mann's four-fold classification on the grounds that it is inappropriate to separate out political and military sources of power. In other respects, however, what is striking is the degree of coincidence between the two approaches to the study of comparative sociology in terms of their rejection of unitary conceptions of 'society' and their emphasis on the importance of the institutions of power.

While Mann and Runciman both reject conventional approaches which treat societies as unitary objects with strong boundaries, they nevertheless continue to operate with the concept of 'society'. For Mann, 'societies are constituted by multiple, overlapping networks of interaction' (1993, p. 728), while Runciman's concerns about '"Society" in the abstract' do not rule out analysis at the level of 'societies (and wider and narrower institutional catchment areas) as actually observed and reported' (1989, p. 60). Other writers have taken the critique of the concept of society further on the grounds that it pitches analysis at an inappropriate level. Wallerstein, for example, proposes that 'the basic concept of "society"' inherited from nineteenth-century social science is 'fundamentally offbase' (1991, p. 76). For Wallerstein, the question 'What is a society?' should be dropped in favour of the more illuminating question 'When and where is a society?' (1991, p. 245). He argues that in the modern world 'it is futile to analyse the processes of *societal development* of our multiple (national) "societies" as if they were autonomous, internally evolving structures, when they are and have been in fact primarily structures created by, and taking form in response to, world-scale processes' (1991, p. 77, emphasis in original). Wallerstein's view that the proper subject of study is not societies but the capitalist world-system leads him to operate with very different concepts, framing his comparative analysis in terms of the 'core', 'semi-periphery' and 'periphery' of the world-system (Wallerstein, 1979, Ch. 1). Although Wallerstein's approach recognizes 'only *one* world-system' (1979, p. 35, emphasis in original), there is still scope for comparative analyses of the various parts or 'zones' (Wallerstein and Smith, 1992, p. 4) of this system and its evolving stages. It is also interesting to note in this context that writers employing the world-systems approach find it easier in theory than in practice to escape from the realm of 'societies', as is suggested in Tilly's observations about their use of 'statistical analysis of data for national aggregates' in their investigations. This said, Tilly does favour 'abandoning the notion of "society" and "societies" as autonomous systems' (1984, p. 25) and is sympathetic to attempts to go beyond them.

Wallerstein's allocation of countries to core, peripheral and semi-peripheral statuses within the world-system has been criticized on a number of counts. In terms of the issue of what comparisons it generates, Worsley (1987) has noted its tendency to obscure significant political differences between countries in the same category. For Worsley, the differences between countries according to their political systems matter just as much as economic differences reflecting varying levels of development, and logically this two-dimensional approach generates at its simplest 'four possible categories: developed and underdeveloped capitalist countries, and developed and underdeveloped communist countries' (1987, p. 82). Worsley is aware of this model being a critique not only of Wallerstein's single world-system but also of the more popular division of the globe into 'three worlds', in which the 'third world' operates as a large and heterogeneous residual category into which all non-industrialized countries of whatever political complexion are placed. Recent events in the state socialist world (to be examined in Chapter 5) have led to much of the detail of Worsley's classification being superseded, but his method of comparing societies as members of blocs defined by both political and economic criteria remains as a distinct approach to comparative sociology.

Of course, Worsley's identification of distinct socio-political worlds has not been the last word on the matter. He himself recognized that 'We can all think of many difficulties, exceptions, omissions, etc, for any system of classifying countries, even if we increase the number of worlds' (1987, p. 82). Thus the poorest of the underdeveloped countries may be separated out as the 'Third World's Third World' or the 'Fourth World', although, as Worsley notes, 'One logical end-product of this multiplication of worlds would be the abandonment of the concept of "world" and its replacement by a purely *linear list* of countries ranked in order of level of development' (1984, p. 321, emphasis in original). Two further problems with his model acknowledged by Worsley are that the use of 'timeless, synchronic models... cannot, inherently, capture relationships other than those built into the model', and that the focus on countries leaves out of the picture 'relationships between the major groups within the country (classes, ethnic groups, religious communities, etc.)' (1984, p. 320). The neatness and simplicity of Worsley's approach is achieved at the expense of neglecting dynamic processes and relations between groups within individual countries.

Consciousness of the differences which exist between countries of the advanced capitalist world because of their contrasting internal political and economic relations has provided another point of departure for comparative analysis in recent years. Esping-Andersen's identification of *The Three Worlds of Welfare Capitalism* arises from the recognition that 'welfare states are not all of one type' (1990, p. 3), there being important distinctions between 'liberal', 'conservative' and 'social-democratic' welfare-state 'regimes'. Within these distinct welfare-state regimes, Esping-Andersen identifies the presence of 'qualitatively different arrangements between state, market, and the family', and claims that the USA, Canada and Australia are clustered around the liberal type, Austria, France, Germany and Italy are clustered around the conservative type, while the Scandinavian countries are 'predominantly social democratic' (1990, pp. 26, 28). The detailed assessment of Esping-Andersen's thesis will be left until the consideration of modern capitalism and the state in Chapter 4, but it is important to note here that his comparisons have been faulted for their neglect of gender differences (Cochrane, 1993), differences which have for other writers been sufficient to justify the distinction between 'men's welfare state' and 'women's welfare state' (Bryson, 1992). Along with gender inequalities, Dominelli (1991) has argued that welfare states treat black and white citizens very differently, and that this too is an important (albeit neglected) dimension of international comparisons. It follows that comparative analysis will be deficient if it stays at the level of the state and ignores inequalities 'expressed through "race", gender, class and other social divisions' (1991, p. 9) which exist among citizens, and which make it inappropriate to treat them as a single, homogeneous community.

These debates about the appropriate focus of comparative sociology highlight the importance of the choice of level at which analysis is pitched and the theoretical traditions from which concepts are drawn. Different purposes are served by the comparison of supra-national entities than are served by focusing on divisions within societies. Globalization has heightened awareness of the growing interconnectedness of the contemporary world, although this is not a new phenomenon, as Giddens observes in saying that '*there are very few, if any, societies which have ever existed in isolation from others*' (1981, p. 46, emphasis in original). And if economic and other relations which cross national boundaries make problematic the notion of society, so too do divisions within a country's borders. For example, data on inequalities between women and men lead Abbott and Sapsford to conclude that 'it would appear that modern Britain is to some extent two societies, partitioned by gender' (1987, p. 179). Clearly, there is much in the legacy of the classical sociologists to contemporary comparative sociology which is problematic. The concepts and analytical frameworks which they bequeathed have been drawn upon widely and continue to exert a powerful influence on the direction taken by researchers' enquiries, but it is an equally strong theme of contemporary comparative sociologists that their agenda is a constantly shifting one. Max Weber, who is regarded by many commentators as the greatest comparative sociologist, did not exclude his own writings from his assessment that any scholar's work becomes 'antiquated in ten, twenty, fifty years' (1970b, p. 138). Weber may have been unduly modest in that much of his writing remains unsurpassed three quarters of a century after his death, but he was correct in identifying the suggestion of new questions to be answered as the most enduring legacy of academic enquiry, his own included.

The legacy of the classical sociologists

Comparisons have been a central aspect of sociological analyses since the foundation of the discipline. Pawson has suggested that 'Most sociological theory takes the form of comparison of the probabilities of certain types of action in certain social groupings' (1989, p. 324), and the theories of the classical sociologists provide good examples of this. Much of Marx's work revolves around the contrast between behaviour in capitalist and non-capitalist settings, challenging the notion that what has come to be called 'possessive individualism' (Macpherson, 1962) could be treated as a universal characteristic of all human societies in all historical periods. The distinction made between societies based on mechanical and organic solidarity was equally central to Durkheim's theorizing and explanations of the regularities which he found in human behaviour. The comparisons in Weber's sociological writings are more diverse and multi-faceted than those of either Marx or Durkheim, but it remains the case that his work too is essentially comparative in character. Marx, Durkheim, Weber and their contemporaries played a pivotal role in defining the sociological agenda through their contributions to sociology's 'unit ideas' (Nisbet, 1967), and comparative analysis was crucial to the development of these ideas.

Nisbet's judgement is that the linked antitheses of '*community–society, authority–power, status–class, sacred–secular, alienation–progress...* form the very warp of the sociological tradition' (1967, p. 7, emphasis in original) and epitomize the contrast between tradition and modernity which is the cornerstone of classical sociological thinking.

An indication of the powerful nature of the classical sociologists' legacy is given by the ways in which many contemporary sociologists frame their analyses of present-day trends by reference to the classics. Ritzer's (1993) account of *The Mcdonaldization of Society* is explicit in the acknowledgement of its intellectual debt to Weber's theory of rationalization. Similarly, Therborn's (1989) analysis of the way in which the process of 'Brazilianization' in advanced capitalism is producing 'the two-thirds, one-third society' has its roots in Marx's theory of social polarization. The legacy of Durkheim's focus on the changing division of labour is apparent in Pahl's (1984, 1988) approach to the study of work in all its forms, while the idea of habit is central to Young's (1988) analysis of *The Metronomic Society*, and this takes him back to the writings of Durkheim and his generation of sociologists. Beck's discussion of 'individualization' commences with 'the classical discussion from Marx via Weber to Durkheim and Simmel' (1992, p. 127), although it does go on to doubt the sustainability of classic models of class and status divisions under present-day conditions. Many other contemporary analyses have similar historical roots, even if (like Tiryakian's [1986] account of 'de-differentiation' and Crook *et al.*'s [1992] examination of 'disalienation and debureaucratization') they suggest a reversal of the trends identified by the classics. The substance of sociological comparisons may have shifted significantly over the course of the twentieth century, but the general approaches of the classical sociologists remain important starting points for many contemporary debates.

The significance which the classical sociologists have for contemporary debates can be seen in the debate over the usefulness of the term 'society'. In his critique of the concept of 'society' and its 'profoundly misleading connotations' (1991, p. 245), Wallerstein argues against the inherited wisdom that 'Human beings are organized in entities we may call societies, which constitute the fundamental social frameworks within which human life is lived' (1991, p. 244). He suggests that this legacy of nineteenth-century thought requires 'unthinking' because its underlying assumption of societies and states being coterminous has become increasingly anomalous. There was no simple legacy bequeathed by the nineteenth century, however. The problematic nature of 'society' was a central concern of the classical sociologists (Frisby and Sayer, 1986), and their attempts to grapple with this problem continue to have great contemporary relevance. The debate about the meaning of 'society' has a long history, having (as Wallerstein notes) its origins in the pairing of 'state' and 'society' which allowed the assumption to be made that 'There is a society underlying each state' (1991, p. 246). Williams has traced the distinction between society as 'that to which we all belong' and the state as 'the apparatus of power' (1983, p. 293) back at least as far as the eighteenth century.

The complexities and sociological implications of this distinction were not lost on the classical sociologists. Marx, for example, was mindful of the significance of 'civil society' for the operation of the capitalist mode of production and state, and even if his conception of it can now be judged 'somewhat narrow' (Urry, 1981, p. 25), he recognized the need to address the problem of explaining and not simply assuming the nature of state–society relations. Durkheim's concern with the role of 'occupational groups' and other intermediate associations between the individual and the state offers a different way of approaching the same issue, indicating that he too was wary of using the term 'society' to suggest inevitable coincidence between political and social orders (Giddens, 1971, Ch. 7). Weber was also careful to distinguish between 'society' and the state, and the view of his biographer Bendix is that 'the distinction between *society* and *polity* [stands] as the fundamental theme of Weber's work as a whole' (1966, p. 478, emphasis in original). The conventional model of 'society' as described by Wallerstein was clearly not adopted uncritically by Marx, Durkheim or Weber, all of whom in different ways recognized what Mann (1986, p. 4) refers to as the 'messiness' of societies compared with the neatness of abstract models.

In making the case for discarding the concept of society from the sociological lexicon, Wallerstein recognizes that the debate about the most appropriate mode of analysis remains unconcluded. His own view is that the appropriate unit of analysis is not that of 'society' but that of 'historical system', which can take the form of 'mini-systems, world-empires, and world-economies' (1991, p. 247). These units of analysis highlight the interconnectedness of states, but in doing so world-system theory is open to the criticism of placing too much store on the capacity of economic forces to shape social developments (Harrison, 1988; Robertson, 1992; Skocpol, 1994). Wallerstein's emphasis on the unfolding logic of the world capitalist-system runs into precisely the same problems of economic determinism which were at the heart of Weber's critique of Marx. According to Wallerstein, 'The three presumed arenas of collective human action – the economic, the political, and the social or socio-cultural – are not autonomous arenas of social action. They do not have separate "logics"' (1991, p. 242). Likewise, Wallerstein's claim that 'there is a single "set of rules" or a single "set of constraints" within which these various structures operate' (1991, p. 242) is directly at odds with Weber's approach, which stressed multi-causality and the need to employ an ideal-typical methodology. In contemporary debates, Mann (1986) acknowledges his affinity with Weber's scepticism about necessary connections, and on this basis he can argue that 'capitalism and militarism are both core features of our society but they are only contingently connected' (1988, p. 127). More generally, Mann identifies the question of 'whether we can single out economic power as ultimately decisive in determining the shape of societies' as 'the major point of contention between Marxian and Weberian theory' (1986, p. 30). This issue constitutes a central part of the debate between Wallerstein and his critics about the scope for comparative sociology.

The interconnectedness of the modern world-system leads Wallerstein to adopt the standpoint that 'no useful research model can isolate "factors" according to the categories of economic, political, and social, and treat only one kind of variable, implicitly holding the others constant' (1991, p. 242). This is a direct rebuttal of the position taken by Weber, who saw it as 'a fundamental task of comparative sociology' to compare 'the largest possible number of historical or contemporary processes which, while otherwise similar, differ in the one decisive point of their relation to the particular motive or factor the role of which is being investigated' (1978, p. 10). Mann follows Weber in arguing that while these processes will frequently be economic, it is important to recognize the simultaneous presence of non-economic processes to which they are not necessarily connected. Mann's misgivings about unitary conceptions of society can also be seen to echo Weber's reservations about the use of the term 'society', which according to Kalberg were so great that 'he scarcely uses the term', preferring instead to operate with the concept of 'societal domains' (1994, pp. 23, 53). There is also more than a passing affinity between Weber's 'societal domains' and Runciman's 'institutional catchment areas', while Runciman's broader analytical framework, which distinguishes between production, persuasion and coercion, 'is a conscious attempt to combine... the most valuable insights of both Marx and Weber' (1989, p. 12). Claims that we are witnessing a fundamental revision of the sociological agenda therefore have to be treated with some caution. The suggestion that present-day social processes such as globalization are working to 'render problematic what has long been regarded as the basic subject matter for sociology: society, conceived almost exclusively as the bounded nation-state' (Featherstone, 1990, p. 2) gives too little recognition to the depth of the classical sociologists' work and their awareness of the crucial debates in comparative sociology.

The legacy of the classical sociologists has a bearing on other debates in comparative sociology besides those relating to the questions of what is being compared and the appropriate methods of comparison. A third dimension of this legacy relates to theories of social change, in which the current reassessment of the whole idea of 'progress' can benefit from consideration of where the classical sociologists stood on this issue (Alexander and Sztompka, 1990). From Lyotard's post-modern position, the idea of progress exemplifies the more general point that 'The grand narrative has lost its credibility' in 'postindustrial society' (1990, p. 331). It is doubtless the case that this critique does something other than re-state the views of the classical sociologists on the subject, but the reservations which they expressed about how well the idea of progress captured the complexities of social change refute the suggestion that they were crude social evolutionists. Durkheim's consciousness of the social disorganization brought by the development of industrial society prevented him from sharing the optimism of his contemporaries such as Spencer who believed unambiguously in progress (Nisbet, 1965). Marx too had differences with mainstream nineteenth-century notions of progress, which he found excessively abstract and insufficiently sensitive to the active, conscious role of human agents in the processes of social development and to the possibility that societies could follow different routes (Melotti, 1977; Shanin, 1984). Weber's strictures against the idea of progress were more profound and far-reaching (Giddens, 1971; Kumar, 1978), and his scepticism about this and other grand narratives of his time makes him, for some commentators at least, 'our foremost social theorist of the condition of modernity' (Whimster and Lash, 1987, p. 1). The continuing importance of Weber and the other classical sociologists reflects the fact that the question of the rationality (or otherwise) of modern society and its associated processes of social change were as central to their work as they are to contemporary comparative sociology.

Current issues and contemporary debates

To say that the classical sociologists have a continuing relevance to comparative sociology through the questions which they posed is not to suggest that their answers to these questions have stood the test of time equally well, nor that the agenda of comparative sociologists' research has stayed within the confines of their legacy (Skocpol, 1984). Much current debate has arisen precisely because of the short-comings of the classical legacy. Comparative sociology today has a heightened sensitivity to diversity, emphasizing the range of alterna-tive routes which have been followed in the transition to the modern world, the heterogeneity which exists within societies of a broad type, and the plurality of perspectives which can be adopted towards these phenomena. Many contemporary debates therefore revolve around issues of classification, as can be seen for example in the debates about the utility of the category 'third world' (which will be looked at in Chapters 6 and 7). Comparative sociologists are also trying to escape the methodological legacy in which quantitative and qualitative approaches are conceived of as opposites. As with other comparative analyses in the social sciences, comparative sociology is better under-stood as 'a method not a field' (Higgins, 1981, p. 3), but within the broad approach of making and drawing conclusions from compar-isons there are many options in terms of the analytical tools available. The appropriate choice of methodological tools will in turn depend on the nature of the theoretical problems which are being posed. Garfinkel's puzzle 'If social science is the answer, what is the question?' (1981, p. vi) applies as much to comparative sociology as elsewhere in the discipline. As Sklair has noted, 'all measures are theory laden' (1995, p. 23), and it is over defining the key theoretical questions to be investigated that some of the fiercest debates are taking place.

The history of comparative sociology has not been a story of unbroken progress. According to Merton, in the period after the clas-sical sociologists were writing, 'serious work in comparative sociology dwindled for several decades', only to re-emerge after the Second World War 'on a scale greater than ever before' (1967, p. v). For a time, broadly functionalist perspectives dominated the thinking behind the comparative analyses that were undertaken, and it is appropriate to regard the 1950s and 1960s as the heyday of two variants of func-tionalism, convergence theory and modernization theory. Kerr *et al.*'s (1973) *Industrialism and Industrial Man* (originally published in 1960), with its claim to have uncovered 'the logic of industrialization', exem-plified convergence theory's belief in a global movement towards 'industrial society'. At the same time, Rostow's (1960) *The Stages of Economic Growth: A Non-Communist Manifesto* embodied the thrust of modernization theory by specifying four prior stages through which societies had to pass in order to reach the fifth stage of 'high mass consumption'. At the root of both approaches was the belief spelled out most fully by Parsons (1966, 1977) that an evolutionary process of structural differentiation could be identified, allowing the development of a typology of societies which would be systematic and applicable to all societies, from 'primitive' to 'modern'.

Comparative sociologists are still working through the implications of the demise of this functionalist model's hegemony, which was due in no small part to dissatisfaction with the assumption that 'developments in the United States must somehow mirror or anticipate developments in other nations, other societies, and other social groups' (Inkeles and Sasaki, 1996, p. xi). To begin with, there is a far greater sensitivity to diversity, captured in the shift from thinking about industrial society in the singular to industrial societies in the plural (Scase, 1977, 1989). Not only has it been increasingly problematic to accept the idea that political differences between capitalist and state socialist societies could be overridden by economic and technological pressures towards convergence (Goldthorpe, 1971; Kumar, 1978; Worsley, 1984), but there has also been a proliferation of types of capitalism identified in the literature. The distinction between organized and disorganized capitalism (Lash and Urry, 1987; Offe, 1985) is now well established in the writing which will be examined in more detail in Chapter 3, but alongside this 'advanced capitalism' (Habermas, 1976), 'casino capitalism' (Strange, 1986), 'disaggregated capitalism' (Pahl, 1988), 'fast capitalism' (Agger, 1989), 'global capitalism' (Peet, 1991), 'non-individualistic capitalism' (Abercrombie *et al.*, 1986), 'overmanaged capitalism' (Taylor, 1990), 'peripheral capitalism' (Alavi, 1982) and 'welfare-state capitalism' (Hinrichs *et al.*, 1988) have also been distinguished. This reaction against a generalized model of capitalism may well reflect widespread acceptance of Dore's 'preference for the particular over the general' (1987, p. 114), but it also reflects a broad move away from models in which primacy is given to economic factors. The rejection of the idea that economic forces somehow determine social development has had profound implications not only for liberal convergence and modernization theories, but also for varieties of Marxism which rely on similarly deterministic notions.

Recognition that economic forces do not dictate patterns of development has focused greater attention on the significance of political relations for patterns of social development. This has allowed comparative sociologists to 'bring the state back in' to their accounts (Evans *et al.*, 1985), since it is clear that states have played a crucial role in shaping societies. Moore's (1967) classic study on the different routes to the modern world highlights the contrasting roles of democratic and dictatorial regimes as societies enter the modern world, and has been a key point of reference for much subsequent research in historical sociology (Skocpol, 1994; Smith, 1991). Kerr *et al.* had already recognized that 'Not one... but several roads lead into this new industrial society' (1973, p. 56), but Moore's analysis goes much further in specifying the political dimensions of this diversity and exploring the complexity of economy–state relations. In the field of the sociology of development too, analyses freed from the restrictions imposed by economically deterministic frameworks have been able to explore the scope which exists for states in comparable economic positions to pursue alternative development strategies. As Booth has noted, growing credence has been given by development sociologists to '[t]he notion that differences in developmental outcomes in otherwise similar settings may be more due to differences in state structure and political arrangements than to anything else' (Booth, 1994, pp. 120–1). In similar fashion, the challenge to economic determinism has been strengthened by arguments that while explanation of crises in Western capitalist societies may appropriately be framed in economic terms, 'in state socialist societies the nature of crises are *political*' (Scase, 1989, p. 3, emphasis in original). State socialist societies undoubtedly have economic contradictions, but these cannot easily be said to have been the sole or even major determinants of the course of events there. As a result, the focus of much recent debate about state socialism has been on relations between the state and civil society, a theme which will be explored further in Chapter 5.

The demise of convergence and modernization thinking has also cast doubt on other theories which suggest universalizing tendencies. The growing economic influence of Japan has led to much speculation about whether a trend towards 'Japanization' could be identified (Gould, 1993; Hall and Jacques, 1989; Thompson and McHugh, 1990; Wood, 1991). As part of these debates, the cultural distinctiveness of Japanese society has been emphasized (Robertson, 1992, Ch. 5), and Dore's comparison between Japan and Britain has led to his being 'overwhelmed by a sense of the wide differences in ideology, in patterns of personal relations, in modes of authority between the two countries, in spite of the similarities in formal institutions' (1987, p. 114). If cultural differences within the 'first world' of advanced capitalist countries are this great, global cultural differences are all the greater, and recognition of these has uncovered the strong Western biases which are present in much social theory. The move away from 'Eurocentrism' has been a crucial part of the reorientation of development theory in recent years as 'the voice of the third world' has begun to be heard (Hettne, 1995). At the same time, debates around globalization have further reinforced awareness of the heterogeneity of global culture and exposed the error of thinking about globalization as a 'homogenizing process' which necessarily erodes cultural diversity (Featherstone, 1990). Indeed, it is Latouche's view that the inevitable failure of 'attempts to universalise Western styles and standards of living' (1993, p. 23) necessarily produces (and reproduces) social differentiation between people of different cultures, the most vulnerable of which are pushed to the margins of viability.

Latouche's argument that global developments have led to the uneasy co-existence of 'two planets' (1993, p. 33) is one to which this book will return at various points. A major reason for its importance lies in its implications for the methodology employed in comparative sociology. According to Latouche, the growth in attention paid to measurements of 'development' reflects the broader 'degeneration from a concern with issues of quality to the preoccupation with quantity alone that has come to dominate the Western perspective' (1993, p. 191). In short, the concern with qualitative 'differences in *modes* of living' has been reduced to quantitative 'differences in *levels* of living' (1993, p. 190, emphases in original). Concomitant with this shift is a narrowing of the agenda of debate and the growing 'danger of theoretical myopia' (1993, p. 28), for which no amount of expansion in the amount of data available can compensate. Latouche's warnings about the trend towards the accumulation of 'fabulous supplies of data, without taking the time necessary to make good use of them, let alone to think critically about their interpretation' (1993, p. 28) is reminiscent of Mills' (1970) critique of 'abstracted empiricism' for its neglect of 'the sociological imagination', while being equally conscious of the need to avoid 'grand theory' in which ordinary people's everyday lives are lost from view. Latouche's critique of quantification also carries echoes of Mills' (1967) portrayal of 'the overdeveloped society', which was discussed in the Introduction.

Latouche is far from being the only writer in the field of comparative sociology to express reservations about the limitations of overreliance on quantitative data. Melucci's argument that 'we are entering an era qualitatively different from both the capitalist model of modernity and socialism as we've known it historically' (1989, p. 185) implies that to focus on quantitative indicators of change alone would miss the essence of the transition. A related criticism is that made by Skocpol of scholars who 'believe that only phenomena of which there are a large number of cases can be studied in a truly scientific manner' (1979, p. 33). Skocpol is aware, however, of the dangers of presenting the complex methodological issues which confront comparative sociologists in terms of a stark opposition between quantitative and qualitative approaches, since this does not convey the variety of ways in which comparisons can be made. Historical sociology throws up many examples of phenomena such as revolutions in which the number of instances is 'too few for the use of statistical techniques requiring a large number of independent cases' (1994, p. 13), but which can nevertheless be compared in a rigorous way. Together with Somers, Skocpol (1994, Ch. 3) has identified three distinct approaches to comparative history: parallel comparative history (in which the principal aim is to demonstrate the fruitfulness of certain theoretical arguments to a variety of cases), contrast-oriented comparative history (where contrasting cases are juxtaposed) and macro-analytic comparative history (which aims to make causal inferences about macro-level phenomena). They go on to note that in practice these approaches may be combined, since each of them on its own is open to criticism about how theory and evidence are related within the approach and about the level of generality at which analysis is pitched. The quantitative/qualitative distinction has a bearing on these debates within historical sociology and related debates in other branches of comparative sociology, but when posed as a dichotomy between which a choice has to be made it is of doubtful value.

The quantitative/qualitative distinction has been the basis of comparative sociology's division into 'two radically different research traditions' (Rueschemeyer *et al.*, 1992, p. 12) between which relatively little dialogue took place, but various attempts to go beyond this split have been made in recent years. Rueschemeyer *et al.*'s work on the relationship between capitalist development and democracy is a case in point, attempting as it does 'to develop a theoretically adequate account of the causal conditions of democracy that is sensitive to the insights of comparative historical research and capable of explaining the persistent statistical relationship between development and democracy' (1992, p. 36). Szelenyi's (1988) combination of ethnography and statistical analysis in the study of changes in Hungary's class structure could also be cited as an example of research which is sympathetic to Ragin's (1987) call to move beyond a forced choice between qualitative or quantitative research strategies. Ragin argues that such a choice produces either research which is methodologically rigorous in terms of the use of statistical techniques to generate broad comparisons but which suffers from insensitivity to the specificity of the context in which the phenomena under investigation are located, or research which is more sensitive to 'the social bases and origins of specific phenomena'

(1987, p. ix) but which is open to the charge of limiting the scope for broader generalizations.

The issue of the most appropriate level for analysis to be conducted continues to be a core problem in many contemporary debates, not least those in historical sociology (Tilly, 1984). It is in this field, for example, that Mann's bold attempt to 'quantify' power in support of his argument that 'quantities of power have developed enormously throughout history' (1986, p. 30) is combined with caution concerning the readiness with which some comparative sociologists have been prepared to lump together 'societies from different historical epochs in the same comparative categories and generalizations' (1986, p. 525) as part of grand evolutionary arguments. Similarly, concern to avoid overgeneralization has had a significant impact on the sociology of development, where in many respects 'synthetic and comparative work is lagging well behind the production of detailed empirical studies' (Booth, 1994, p. 15). Much attention has also been devoted to the question of how appropriate it is to regard Germany as typical of capitalist societies more generally (Lash and Urry, 1987). Steering a middle course between the imposition of 'categories which lop off any structural or cultural characteristics which are inconvenient for a theory which claims regularities at a level of generality where they do not in fact exist' (Runciman, 1989, p. 59) and the opposite danger of taking account of differences which are irrelevant to the analysis in hand is a notoriously difficult balance to strike, but one which the comparative sociologist is compelled to attempt to make.

There is, of course, no one solution to the problem of how best to go about practising comparative sociology. Much depends on the question being addressed and, as Rodinson has observed, 'no one has a key to fit all locks' (1977, p. viii). Hettne (1995) suggests that the theoretical agenda in the field of development studies is constantly shifting along various axes. The positive–normative dimension of debates concerns the question of whether studies deal with the world as it is or involve value judgements as to how it should be. The formal–substantive dimension 'contrasts the *formal* approach, where development is defined in terms of a limited number of universally valid principles and quantifiable indicators which can be combined in a predictive model, with the *substantive* approach, where development involves historical change of a more comprehensive, qualitative and less predictable nature' (1995, p. 254, emphases in original). As a result, various combinations can be identified, such as the combination of normative and substantive elements in dependency theory (of which more will be said in Chapter 6). In addition to these dimensions, along which debates tend to run in a cyclical pattern, Hettne argues that there have been long-term, secular trends away from Eurocentric perspectives towards more pluralistic models which recognize the fallacy of taking Western societies as norms, and away from theories of social change which highlight endogenous, internal factors to theories which emphasize the role of exogenous, global forces.

Hettne's argument has a wider applicability. The cyclical loss and recovery of the actor-oriented paradigm of research in the sociology of development described by Long (1992) has parallels throughout other branches of comparative sociology. Equally, the paradigm shift which globalization theory represents has implications far beyond development theory, as does the challenge to Eurocentrism and the classic contrast between 'the West and the rest' (Hall, 1992) which underlies it. Clearly, there are many reasons making it imperative to move beyond theoretical models which rely on the division of the globe into 'three worlds' of Western capitalism, state socialism and developing societies, but it is easier to proclaim 'the end of the third world' (Harris, 1987) than it is to provide an alternative theoretical model which is more coherent and sustainable. In order to do this, it will be vital to consider not only what is happening within contemporary Western capitalist societies, state socialist societies (and their successors) and the poor countries of the South of the global system, but also to consider the origins of these societies and their possible futures. For this task, consideration of social theorists' attempts to make sense of these phenomena will be crucial. Comparative sociologists necessarily ask big questions related to the bases of social order and the sources of social change, and in attempting to answer these questions their researches cover a correspondingly broad range. Arguably, what distinguishes the best comparative sociologists is their combination of this concern to ask big questions with attention to detail in their analysis of their research material. In this respect, as well as because of its subject matter, it is appropriate to turn first to the work of Barrington Moore.

2

The Making of the Modern World: the Historical Sociology of Barrington Moore

One of the central contributions made by historical sociologists to comparative sociology has been to trace the several routes by which societies have entered the modern world. Sociology as a discipline emerged in the context of what Polanyi (1957) called 'the great transformation' which accompanied the spread of the market economy and which undermined explanations of traditional social arrangements as 'natural' phenomena. To those living through this great transformation, the emerging industrial societies of the nineteenth century were clearly different from anything that had gone before, but several of the classical sociologists were careful to distance themselves from the then popular idea of social evolution following a single pathway of development. Marx, for example, insisted that his 'historical sketch of the genesis of capitalism in Western Europe' should not be interpreted as 'a historico-philosophical theory of the general course fatally imposed on all peoples, whatever the historical circumstances in which they find themselves placed' (1982, pp. 109–10). Weber's strictures against theories of progress were even more severe, and his scepticism is well captured in his observation that 'Thus far the continuum of European culture development has known neither completed cyclical movements nor an unambiguously oriented "unilinear development"' (quoted in Gerth and Mills, 1970, p. 51). Unlike many of their contemporaries, Marx and Weber were too mindful of the historical and geographical diversity of social development to accept universal theories of evolution which glossed over differences in the contexts in which social changes took place.

The pitfalls of grand theory in historical sociology do not, however, rule out generalization altogether. Indeed, Marx and Weber stand out because of their awareness that while no universal path of develop-ment can be traced, there are nevertheless identifiable 'patterns of history' (Hall, 1986). It is into this broad tradition of historical sociology that the work of Barrington Moore fits. His *Social Origins of Dictatorship and Democracy* (1967) (hereafter *Social Origins*) is the book for which he is most famous, and rightly so, as the ambitiousness of its project is on a par with the classic writings of historical sociology (Tilly, 1984). Indeed, the central problem of the study can be seen as the same one which so concerned the classical sociologists, namely the connections between social and economic development and political change. In Nisbet's account of the emergence of sociology, the writings of Marx, Weber, Durkheim and others are presented as reactions to 'two revolutions', economic and political, and the relationship between them. For Nisbet, 'The fundamental ideas of European sociology are best understood as responses to the problem of order created at the beginning of the nineteenth century by the collapse of the old regime under the blows of industrialism and revolutionary democracy' (1967, p. 21). With the benefit of hindsight relating to the tumultuous events of the twentieth century which the classical sociologists did not live to witness, Moore develops an argument in which three main alternative routes to the modern world are distinguished. Each of these routes is characterized by contrasting political and economic forms, and each of them has revolutionary implications for traditional social orders.

Moore's work is in the spirit of classical historical sociology, but it also involves departures from the writings of the classics in a number of respects. To begin with, Moore does not focus his attention on social developments in Western Europe to anything like the same extent as do the classical sociologists, and his detailed discussion of the routes to the modern world taken in China, Japan and India (where, Moore argues, the process of modernization is far from complete) puts Asia much more centre stage of the analysis. Of course, Marx had grappled with the idea of an 'Asiatic mode of production', while China, India and countries of the Middle East had figured prominently in Weber's comparative sociology, but both of these projects remained incomplete (Turner, 1981), with many of their wider implications left implicit. In addition to Moore's more truly global geographical perspective, *Social Origins* also contains important re-thinking in relation to time by virtue of its proposition that the various routes to the modern world are sequential rather than being alternatives which are open at every historical period. The description of the American Civil War of 1861–5 as 'the last capitalist revolution' signals Moore's view that from the late nineteenth century onwards the classic modernization route of capitalist democracy was unavailable, leaving only more dirigiste options. Moore was not the first to observe the significance of 'late' development, but his analysis draws out many of the implications for countries and their political systems of being temporally 'behind' others in the industrialization process.

The importance of Moore's work can be gauged by the extent to which it has influenced the agenda of subsequent research in historical sociology. According to Rueschemeyer *et al.*, *Social Origins* 'was without doubt the most important comparative historical research on development and political form, and it achieved paradigmatic influence in the field' (1992, pp. 22–3). Skocpol's (1979, 1994) analyses in the comparative sociology of revolutions owe an obvious debt to Moore's major work, to take just one example. Moore's influence can be seen to be all the greater when it is recognized that his writings extend over a far broader range than the subject matter of *Social Origins*. The theme of the pervasiveness of violence and coercion is central to all of Moore's investigations of power and social change, and this has clear echoes in the work of Mann, who includes Moore among those writers who 'go beyond the economy, adding various political, military, geopolitical and ideological power relations to modes of production and social classes' (1993, p. 17). Echoes of Moore's emphasis on the importance of a sense of injustice in episodes of revolt and periods of political quiescence can also be found in the work of other writers keen to examine the 'moral orders' of societies both past and present (Corrigan and Sayer, 1985; Marshall *et al.*, 1988; Scott, 1985). Moore has not been without his critics, of course. The enormity of the range of subjects he tackles and his preparedness to ask original and awkward questions about them has meant that his work has a bearing on many historical and sociological disputes. The fact that his awareness of the dangers of overgeneralization informed but did not deter his attempt to detect cross-national patterns in the search for 'principles of change that apply to more than a single series of events' (1962, p. 152) supports the case for treating Moore as one of the most prominent and creative comparative sociologists.

Barrington Moore's three routes to the modern world

The identification of patterns of industrialization and modernization which Moore attempts is a truly global undertaking, and one which has continuing relevance to countries currently undergoing the industrialization process as well as having significance to broader historical debates. In *Social Origins*, Moore identifies 'three main historical routes from the preindustrial to the modern world' (1967, pp. xi–xii). These three routes can be distinguished by the nature of the political regimes which have overseen the industrialization process: capitalist democracy and two types of dictatorship, dictatorship of the right (fascism) and dictatorship of the left (communism). These three political systems are presented as alternative frameworks within which industrialization has taken place, emphasizing the point that there is no single, universal path to the modern world. Whereas many nineteenth-century thinkers regarded the pattern of British industrialization as a kind of model which would be followed elsewhere, Moore treats the experience of countries such as Britain, France and the USA, which were the first to industrialize, as exceptional and difficult if not impossible to reproduce. The configuration of social and economic forces characteristic of the early phase of industrialization is 'highly unlikely' to be 'repeated anywhere in the twentieth century' (1967, p. 425). From the late nineteenth century onwards, all countries which have industrialized successfully have done so with much more direct state intervention in economic and social affairs than was the case in the capitalist democracies; they have undergone, in Moore's terms, 'forced industrialization' (1972, p. 30).

Moore's analysis departs from conventional wisdom in a number of other respects besides his rejection of unilinear evolution. He is also sceptical of the idea that a necessary link exists between capitalism and democracy, arguing that the fascist route to the modern world was also a capitalist one, but one which in countries such as Germany and Japan dispensed with the political framework of liberal democracy. For Moore, there is nothing inevitable about the emergence of democracy; indeed, the balance of social forces which allows the development of democratic institutions is in many ways precarious and historically unusual. Neither, Moore argues, should equations be made between democracy and a peaceful transition to the modern world on the one hand and dictatorships and violence on the other. In Moore's view, the movement from the pre-industrial to the modern world is inherently conflictual and violent, and the different routes by which societies make this transition vary only in the degree to which violence is present. Moore reminds us that capitalist democracies have their origins in revolutionary upheavals, even if in crude statistical terms the numbers of people killed during these revolutions were less than those killed in twentieth-century industrialization. Perceptions of the differences between the various routes are prone to distortion because of the greater historical distance between the present day and early industrialization, and also because of the more gradual pace of early industrialization. Moore notes in addition the fact that the principal victims of the industrialization process have been rural populations, whose perspective is progressively lost to view as the norms of the modern, urbanized world become more firmly established. One of the central purposes of *Social Origins* is to show the crucial roles played by rural classes in the passage to modernity, even if they have not turned out to be beneficiaries of that transformation. It is for this reason that the book is subtitled 'Lord and peasant in the making of the modern world'.

It is, of course, impossible to do full justice to the complex and detailed arguments of a book of over five hundred pages within a short space, but it is a testimony to the systematic approach which Moore adopts in *Social Origins* that a summary of the overall case can be attempted which at least conveys its main points. From the experiences of England, France and the USA, Moore is able to find sufficient in common to group them together as countries having undergone 'capitalist revolutions'. Democracy was the outcome in such countries because there was a rough balance between contending groups among the élite. Put another way, no one group held a sufficiently strong position on which absolute power could be based, although this point had to be established through civil wars and revolutions. In each case, the political upheavals of the English Civil War and Revolution of the 1640s, the French Revolution of the late eighteenth century and the American Civil War of 1861–5 were bloody, violent affairs, even by twentieth-century standards. Thus the American Civil War saw over 600,000 people killed, some 2 per cent of the population at the time (Ward, 1991, p. xix). Conventional wisdom contrasts the peaceful and gradual character of the democratic route to modern society with the violence and brutality of the dictatorial routes, but Moore rejects this dichotomy as simplistic, based on a misperception of the standards by which such comparisons should be made and on misinterpretation of the evidence relating to the costs of modernization which is considered.

Moore's account stresses that economic explanations of revolutionary social change are inadequate, not least because economic tensions do not on their own necessarily lead to social upheaval and violence. Rather, Moore suggests, these political conflicts have to be understood in terms of a clash of cultures between which unbridge-able gaps had emerged, like that which existed between the aristocratic southern slave states and the free-market northern 'Yankee' states of the USA. It was not with economics uppermost in his mind that the future President Lincoln had observed in 1858, 'A house divided against itself cannot stand... half slave and half free' (quoted by Ward, 1991, p. 22), but because the two ways of life in the two parts of the pre-Civil War USA were founded on principles which were ultimately irreconcilable. Co-operation between southern plantation owners and northern industrial capitalists would, in Moore's view, 'have been quite possible had strictly rational economic calculations been the only issue' (1967, p. 121). What made such co-operation so difficult to sustain was the impossibility of separating out 'economic differences' from 'moral issues' (1967, p. 123). In short, the resort to violence arose out of conflicting values as much as it did out of opposed economic interests, although there are limits to how far the two can be separated out in practice.

Much of Moore's account of the social and political revolutions through which capitalist democracies came into existence is devoted to the economic changes which preceded them. In particular, Moore directs attention to the commercialization of agriculture, since in his account this process holds the key to the modernization process. The resources required for successful industrialization have come from surpluses generated in the rural economy, and it is for this reason that arriving at a solution to the 'peasant question' is crucial. What Moore calls 'the taming of the agrarian sector' involves political and economic upheavals to social systems built around the interdepen-dence of peasants and a traditional landowning class: 'The political hegemony of the landed upper class had to be broken or transformed. The peasant had to be turned into a farmer producing for the market instead of for his own consumption and that of the overlord' (1967, p. 429). Moore follows Marx and others in emphasizing the length of the period prior to the industrial revolution when agriculture was subjected to increasing commercial pressures. In the countries which followed the route of capitalist democracy, the rural classes were confronted by the growing power of an urban class of merchants and manufacturers, and the strength of this group prevented the exclusive concentration of power in the hands of either the state or the landed upper classes.

Moore presents the presence of a strong bourgeoisie as a necessary (although not sufficient) condition for the development of democratic politics. In countries going through the industrialization process later, the bourgeoisie has tended to be weaker and to play a less prominent role in the development of social and political arrangements. Those countries following the route of 'conservative modernization' (1967, p. 441) were characterized by a politically dependent bourgeoisie; here, 'sections of a relatively weak commercial and industrial class relied on dissident elements in the older and still dominant ruling classes, mainly recruited from the land, to put through the political and economic changes required for a modern industrial society' (Moore, 1967, p. xiii). In countries such as Germany and Japan, the commercialization of agriculture and the process of capitalist industrialization took place with more direct involvement of states which were authoritarian and 'reactionary' in orientation, attempting 'to preserve as much of the original social structure as they could' (1967, p. 438). Moore's account highlights the contradictions inherent in this strategy, and he argues that 'Germany and, even more, Japan were trying to solve a problem that was inherently insoluble, to modernize without changing their social structures' (1967, p. 442). The apparent solution to this problem offered by militarism and the appeal to internal unity against an external threat led to fascism and foreign expansion and ultimately to military defeat in the Second World War, but not before it had been established that 'nondemocratic and even antidemocratic modernization works' (1967, p. 159).

A weak bourgeoisie is also to be found in Moore's other non-democratic route to the modern world, communism, although in this case the key role is played by the peasantry rather than the landed upper classes. In Russia and China, the power of 'great agrarian bureaucracies' tended to stifle progressive commercialization in the countryside and industrialization, with the result that 'in the absence of more than the most feeble steps towards modernization a huge peasantry remained' (1967, p. xiii). Moore argues that the weak bonds which existed between lord and peasant in systems dominated by these agrarian bureaucracies heightened the potential for peasant opposition, in contrast to other rural social arrangements which were more likely to produce political passivity among peasants. The survival into the modern era of the peasantry in terms of both numbers and traditions made Russia and China particularly vulnerable to peasant revolutions, which came when the peasants found themselves 'subject to new stresses and strains' (1967, p. 477). In the context of new economic demands being made upon them plus the impact of the dislocations of war, 'peasant revolutions' swept away the old order. The irony that the peasants themselves became the principal victims of the communist regimes which they, in alliance with urban workers, had helped to bring to power is not lost on Moore, who takes it as further confirmation of his view that 'the poor bear the heaviest costs of modernization under both socialist and capitalist auspices' (1967, p. 410). The observation that 'The main victims of progress were... the ordinary peasants' (1967, p. 11) applies under both systems.

Several conditions are therefore necessary in Moore's view for the prospects for democratic modernization to be favourable. These include '*the development of a balance to avoid too strong a crown or too independent a landed aristocracy*' and '*a turn toward an appropriate form of commercial agriculture*' (Moore, 1967, p. 430, emphases in original), both of which highlight the importance of rural class relations for political developments accompanying the transition to industrialism. Where these and other preconditions for democracy are absent, the modernization process is likely to take place under the direction of an authoritarian political system, or not to take place at all. Those countries which since the late nineteenth century have successfully carried through industrialization have done so in the context of political dictatorships of the left or right. In contrast to the revolutionary events in other Asian countries, India has experienced 'peaceful change', but this has been at the price of its 'prolonged backwardness', explained by Moore in terms of the absence of '*a revolutionary break with the past*' (1967, p. 431, emphasis in original). Modernization necessarily involves social and economic upheavals of the most fundamental kind, and Moore's message for countries yet to modernize is a harsh one, namely that 'a strong element of coercion remains necessary if a change is to be made... Either masked coercion on a massive scale, as in the capitalist model including even Japan, or more direct coercion approaching the socialist model will remain necessary' (1967, p. 410). Stated bluntly, the options for countries in India's position appear to involve a simple choice between forced industrialization under the auspices of an authoritarian state, or permanent underdevelopment. The dilemma for those in positions of political power is that the longer the grasping of this nettle is postponed, the higher the stakes are raised, for to do nothing may lead to the population becoming 'steadily worse off' (1967, p. 410). In such circumstances, academics have a moral duty to expose the cruelties of this dilemma, however politically unpopular this may make them.

Moore's view that the combination of capitalism and Western democracy 'arose out of specific circumstances' (1967, p. 159) is a direct challenge to functionalist theories which posit a necessary link between the two. While broad connections between changing economic and political forms in the industrialization process can be identified, they are not the neat correlations derived from single variable theories. Moore's researches led him to the conclusion that 'No theory emphasising a single factor appears to be satisfactory' (1967, p. 453), whether the factor highlighted by the theory be economic, political, religious or something else. Rather, it is the case that the course of modernization has been influenced by all manner of variables, and the particular configuration in each country is to a degree unique. Moore constructed his three routes to the modern world well aware that 'Within each major type there are also striking differences... as well as significant similarities' (1967, p. 414), the justification for the typology being that for the purposes of analysing and explaining patterns of modernization the significance of the similarities outweighs that of the differences. The problem of determining the degree to which different elements in the complex processes of social change matter is a fundamental one in comparative sociology. It is not surprising therefore to find that one of the most enduring legacies of *Social Origins* is the debate which it sparked on how best to make sense of variations in the routes by which countries have become 'modern'.

The comparative sociology of revolutions

Perhaps the simplest response to Moore's identification in *Social Origins* of three main routes to the modern world came from critics who attempted to reassert the primary importance of economic factors in the development process. Frank, for example, argues that 'the real dichotomy is not capitalist democracy versus capitalist or communist dictatorship but rather capitalism on the one hand, be it "democratic" or "dictatorial", and socialism on the other hand' (1984, p. 29). This interpretation is in tune with his other writings in which he presents the options facing poorer countries as a stark choice between 'capitalist underdevelopment or socialist revolution' (Frank, 1969). There is some congruence with Moore's position here, in that the prospects for democratic capitalist industrialization in the latter part of the twentieth century in countries such as India are agreed to be unfavourable. This said, Frank's preparedness to relegate political differences between countries which have gone through capitalist industrialization to a second-order phenomenon loses sight of one of the central conclusions to be drawn from Moore's analysis, namely that both variants of late industrialization, authoritarian capitalist and communist, have much in common through having been 'forced'.

Countries which have gone through the industrialization process later than the capitalist democracies have been 'forced' to do so in two senses. Industrialization in these countries has been the product of state direction and compulsion to a far greater degree than was the case for the early industrializers, even when the extensiveness of state involvement in early industrialization in countries such as England is acknowledged (Corrigan and Sayer, 1985). For example, Japan's experience differed from that of the early industrializers in that 'the government undertook most of the first steps in industrialization', just as in Germany the state had 'aided industrial construction in several important ways' (Moore, 1967, pp. 270–1, 440). The role of the state was more extensive still in communism's command economies, where industrialization was imposed through central planning, of which the Five Year Plans in the Soviet Union were the prototype. The second sense in which later industrialization is 'forced' is a reflection of the external military threat posed by the early industrializers to countries such as the Soviet Union, whose leader Stalin in 1931 summed up the position in the starkest terms: 'We are fifty or a hundred years behind the advanced countries. We must make good the distance in ten years. Either we do it or they crush us' (quoted in Berliner, 1966, p. 161). Fears of the military threat posed by more industrially advanced nations had earlier led to similar reasoning in Japan, as Moore (1967) notes, just as it was to subsequently in China (Berliner, 1966).

The notion of later industrialization being 'forced' might suggest that it is not so much the distinction between different types of capitalist route which is superfluous as the distinction between different types of dictatorship. Moore makes this distinction by referring to conservative modernization as 'a form of revolution from above' (1967, p. xii), while communism arises out of peasant 'revolutions from below'. This terminology echoes the speech made in 1856 (immediately following the Crimean War) in which Tsar Alexander II heralded the modernization of social relations in the Russian country-side by saying to his gentry audience: 'You yourselves know that the existing order of ruling over living souls cannot remain unchanged. It is better to abolish serfdom from above than to await the day when it will begin to abolish itself from below' (quoted in Emmons, 1968, p. 41). Moore himself raises some doubts about the viability of this distinction between revolutions from above and below, because while peasants are crucial agents of political change in the latter but not the former, their revolutions serve simply 'to make way for the communist version of an industrial revolution from above' (1967, p. 160), of which they become the principal victims. Taking this line of argument further still, Moore later observes that 'At bottom all forms of industrialization so far have been revolutions from above, the work of a ruthless minority' (1967, p. 506). What sustains the distinction between revolutions from above and below is Moore's view that industrialization in Germany and Russia employed 'very different means' (1967, p. 160), together with the fact that the various routes to the modern world have led to very different institutional results, namely capitalist democracy, fascism and communism. Moore's view is that 'it is necessary to group revolutions by the broad institutional results to which they contribute' (1967, p. 417). He believes that these are sufficiently distinct for it to be worthwhile exploring how it is that different class configurations, together with the timing of industrialization, can determine which outcome happens in which country.

In what is arguably the most perceptive assessment of *Social Origins*, Skocpol accepts Moore's distinction between the fascist and communist routes to the modern world as one which is well grounded theoretically. For Skocpol, these two routes 'represent genuine theoretical constructs in that they identify patterns of (a) initial class structure, (b) revolutionary political conflict, *and* (c) ultimate systemic political outcome'. In contrast, the 'bourgeois route' is for Skocpol a 'residual category defined only by the twentieth-century political system ("Western democracy") common to its "members"' (1994, p. 28, emphasis in original). Starting the modernization process with distinct class structures and going through very different patterns of class struggle, England, France and the USA may have become more alike, but they have not really passed through the same processes in the way that countries in Moore's other routes have. Moore accepts that there is a methodological inconsistency in his work in noting that he uses the term 'peasant revolution' when 'speaking about the main popular force behind them', but employs the term 'bourgeois revolutions' to refer to processes in countries which share 'a series of legal and political consequences' (1967, pp. 428–9). In Skocpol's view, Moore's preparedness to lump together disparate cases in the single category 'capitalist democracy' reveals several more general shortcomings in his overall approach, relating in particular to his treatment of social class, his method of comparison and his neglect of external influences on the course of modernization in different countries.

Several commentators have pointed out that Moore is not wholly consistent in his analysis in so far as it relates to social classes. Abrams, for example, shows how the initial focus on the rural social classes of landowners and peasants is broadened as *Social Origins* progresses, so that 'the urban commercial and industrial bourgeoisie make their appearance as a third crucial class formation in the passage to democracy, fascism or communism' (1982, p. 175). At one point, the bourgeoisie is given the role of key variable in the modernization process, when Moore describes it as 'the chief actor in the drama', elaborating on the (uncharacteristically simple) formulation, 'No bourgeois, no democracy' (1967, pp. 422, 418). This thesis has been questioned on the grounds of its relation to the historical record. Hall notes that in the light of Germany's history, 'the critics of Moore's position are... quite correct to say that the bourgeoisie has not always been a friend of liberty' (1993, p. 276), just as Rueschemeyer *et al.* note the strength of 'the case against attributing a subordinate posture to the German bourgeoisie' (1992, p. 108). Skocpol's view is that a reactionary, upper-class, anti-democratic coalition of bourgeoisie and aristocracy similar to Germany's 'marriage of iron and rye' was to be found in some periods in England's history (such as the early nineteenth century), and draws the conclusion that its failure to resist democratization in England's case 'lies as much in class *capacities* as class *interests* (1994, p. 39, emphases in original). The fact that the first industrial nation did not follow the reactionary route to the modern world is for Skocpol a reflection of the more general point that 'state organization importantly affected the capacity of landed upper strata to preserve their interests during modernization' (1994, p. 38). The objectives of classes are frequently not achieved, and in order to explain this it makes sense to consider 'political institutional arrangements as an *independent* constraint on class political capacities' (1994, p. 39, emphasis in original). Skocpol concludes that 'if the times are out of joint, it can matter a great deal who staffs the state, and how it is organized' (1994, p. 44). The revolutionary upheavals accompanying the passage to the modern world are just such periods.

Skocpol's point about the potential autonomy of the state from control by dominant economic interests ties in with her criticism of the comparative methodology which Moore employs in *Social Origins*. Moore's work is recognized as asking many of the central questions of comparative sociology, as happens early on in the book when he wonders why the USA did not have a 'marriage between iron and cotton' (1967, p. xi) similar to that of Germany's reactionary coalition of iron and rye. What he fails to do, Skocpol suggests, is to recognize the crucial distinction between social and political revolutions, a distinction which allows her to conclude that the two are qualitatively different: 'Social revolutions are rapid, basic transformations of a society's state and class structures; and they are accompanied and in part carried through by class-based revolts from below... Political revolutions transform state structures but not social structures, and they are not necessarily accomplished through class conflict' (1979, p. 4). Looking in a very different way at the similarities and differences of processes of modernization in many of the same countries studied by Moore, Skocpol arrives at quite distinct groupings: France, Russia and China 'serve as three positive cases of successful social revolution', while in contrast England, Japan and Germany 'were comparable countries that underwent non-revolutionary political crises and transformations in broadly similar times and circumstances' (1979, p. 37). England and France may have reached the same outcome, namely bourgeois democracy, but according to Skocpol it is inappropriate to say that they arrived there by the same route.

The difficulties encountered by Moore in his account of the various routes to the modern world are compounded according to Skocpol by the focus in *Social Origins* on relations within societies rather than the wider international context in which their transition to the modern world took place. Moore does observe that 'the methods of modernization chosen in one country change the dimensions of the problem for the next countries who take the step' (1967, p. 414), but Skocpol argues that his analysis gives insufficient weight to the 'intersocietal perspective' in which it is recognized that 'no society is free from foreign influences' (1994, p. 44). In her own work on social revolutions, Skocpol emphasizes the importance of international pressures arising from the fact that, prior to their revolutions, France, Russia and China all 'suddenly had to confront more economically developed military competitors' (1979, p. 41). And if economic and military disadvantages in the international arena had profound consequences for these countries which had resisted colonial subjugation, international influences are likely to be even more profound for the course of modernization in countries which were colonized. Moore's account of India does acknowledge the inhibiting influence on that country's development of British colonial administration, but it has little in common with theories of imperialism and dependency which stress the draining effects on colonies of the extraction of resources and their transfer to other parts of the global system (Foster-Carter, 1985).

Three decades after its publication, the influence of *Social Origins* on debates in comparative history remains significant. For Rueschemeyer *et al.*, 'Moore's book represents a towering achievement' (1992, p. 25), despite their disagreement with its thesis on several detailed points. Numerous other critics have also noted flaws and inconsistencies in the argument (Abrams, 1982; Sheehan, 1980; Smith, 1983; Wiener, 1975), but Moore's work continues to be a reference point in a number of debates. It remains, for example, a point of departure for scholars concerned to compare revolutions. Thus, Krejčí's *Great Revolutions Compared* operates with a typology of revolutions which extends Moore's distinction between 'revolution from above' and 'revolution from below' with a third type, 'revolution from abroad' as well as the hybrid type of 'revolution from below and above' (1994, p. 10). His account gives greater weight than Moore did to the impact of external effects on the course of development of particular societies, but the intellectual debt to Moore's work is nonetheless unmistakeable. This is particularly true if all of Moore's writings are considered, since revolutionary movements are often driven by a sense of injustice. The perception of injustice and the wider sociology of the moral bases of social order and disorder have been central concerns of Moore's work throughout his career, and these writings explore in greater depth aspects of his social theory which are more or less implicit in *Social Origins* but which are equally important legacies to contemporary comparative sociology.

Violence and the moral order of society

Much attention has been given to the question of Moore's affinities with the key figures and traditions of historical sociology (Smith 1983, 1991). The association with Marx has been made primarily on the grounds of Moore's employment of class analysis in the search for patterns in the routes by which countries have come to be modern, although Moore is insistent in his attachment of importance to the moral order of societies and to the need to weave this into multi-causal explanations, and these aspects of his work take him closer to Durkheim and Weber respectively. Moore's writings have clearly been influenced by the classical sociologists, but this influence is arguably most profound in terms of the types of question which he poses rather than in the answers at which he arrives. Moore's emphasis on the importance of rural classes in influencing the direction of social change, his identification of the different routes to the modern world constituting in some sense a sequence, each linked to 'successive historical stages' (1967, p. 414), his critique of economic determinism and inevitability, and his theme of the pervasiveness of violence in society all bear a degree of originality and take his analyses beyond those of the classics. Yet Moore's questions remain the fundamental ones of classical sociology, investigating the bases of social order and social change. It is equally pertinent to note that he pursues these questions with the same degree of commitment to systematic comparison as that displayed by the classics.

The titles of some of Moore's other writings besides *Social Origins* give an indication of his approach to questions of social cohesion and conflict. Amongst many other things, Moore is the author of articles or chapters on 'The relation between social stratification and social control' (1942), 'A comparative analysis of the class struggle' (1945) and 'Totalitarian elements in pre-industrial societies' (1962, Ch. 2), and books on *Reflections on the Causes of Human Misery and upon Certain Proposals to Eliminate Them* (1972) and *Injustice: The Social Bases of Obedience and Revolt* (1978). What particularly interests Moore is the question of why it is that some societies are more stable and unchanging than others. At the level of individuals this focus is expressed as an interest in 'why people so often put up with being the victims of their societies and why at other times they become very angry and try with passion and forcefulness to do something about their situation' (1978, p. xiii). It is clear to him that crude economic explanations of social stability and instability just will not suffice, since 'misery does not necessarily bring about a class struggle' (1945, p. 34). Indeed, Moore goes further in observing that 'Those who are the worst off are generally the last to organize and make their voices heard' (1978, p. 143). Put another way, 'Massive poverty and exploitation in and by themselves are not enough to provide a revolutionary situation' (1967, p. 220). Dominated and exploited classes may be politically passive and fatalistic rather than actively challenging their disadvantaged situation, and historically there is no great evidence to support the view that unequal societies are forced to change simply by virtue of being unequal. Indeed, many examples can be found of groups at the bottom of unequal societies which conform to the exercise of social control by dominant groups. The obedience to authority of groups as diverse as the untouchables in the Indian caste system, slaves in the pre-Civil War USA and concentration camp prisoners shows that it takes more than simply inequality to produce social change, and here Moore wants to emphasize the moral dimension, in particular ideas relating to justice and legitimacy. The element of 'felt injustice' (1967, p. 220) is often crucial in the development of challenges to and revolts against unequal social arrangements, since it reflects the absence of the 'sense of common identity' (1978, p. 12) which Moore treats as a defining characteristic of a 'society'.

Of course, Moore is not the first writer to suggest that a society's stability will be greater the more its people perceive the prevailing social arrangements to be fair and just, or, at least, not unfair and unjust. Weber's (1978) typology of the authority of the state was developed to elaborate on this point, with traditional, charismatic and rational–legal authority all in their appropriate settings serving to justify the right of rulers to rule. Moore also concurs with Weber's approach to power as the study of domination (Parkin, 1982), and his work recognizes the several bases of power which can be identified. But while Moore's statement that 'Authority implies obedience on the basis of more than fear and coercion' (1978, p. 17) is consistent with Weber's analysis of legitimacy, Moore's explanation of what else beyond compulsion is involved differs from Weber's in important respects. To begin with, Moore presents a more dynamic analysis than Weber's, which suffered from a tendency in Moore's view to become 'an arid desert of definitions' (1962, p. 122). Weber's theory of rationalization went some way to offsetting this, but Moore's work contains a different view of social change over the longer term, since he holds to a general belief in the possibility of progress in the development of rational social organization which stands in sharp contrast to Weber's pessimism. As Smith puts it, Moore 'assumes that higher forms of rationality become possible with each stage of social evolution' (1983, p. 49). These ideas surface again in another context in the writings of Habermas on legitimation and the movement towards a more rational society which will be examined in Chapter 4, and also in the discussion of democratization in Chapter 7.

Moore's discussion of the moral dimensions of processes of social order and social change differs from Weber's in the further sense that it is written from a politically committed rather than an ethically neutral point of view. Moore was a critic of both dictatorship and democracy in its 'predatory' form, arguing instead for 'liberalism-with-a-difference' (1972, p. 156), in which there is less military expenditure and consumerism and more resources are devoted to publicly provided social welfare, where there is extensive public debate about social goals and science pursues humane ends, and generally misery and injustice are progressively reduced. While Moore recognizes that many attempts to specify in detail the characteristics of the ideal society have come to grief as utopian schemes overtaken by events, he argues that it is possible to identify in broad terms what it is that people are against, and he infers from this that 'human society ought to be organized in such a way as to eliminate useless suffering' (1972, p. 5). Aware that there is a 'range of variations in human willingness to put up with oppressive social relationships' (1978, p. xv), and also that there is historical variation in the ways in which 'rationality' has been understood, Moore nevertheless rejects the relativistic conclusion that no general criteria exist by which societies can be judged. Rather, Moore holds to the belief that 'a rational basis for criticising and evaluating society and moral behavior' (1962, p. 106) can be found. Despite the enormous variations in social arrangements which have been recorded, it is also possible to detect what Moore calls 'recurring elements in moral codes' (1978, Ch. 1) in the ways in which all societies have dealt with coercion and exchange in the division of labour and systems of social inequality. In his assessment of different social arrangements, Moore employs the concepts of reciprocity and mutual obligation as 'fact, ideology and ideal' (1978, Ch. 15), and uses them as the basis not only for analysis, but also for moral critique.

Several general methodological implications for comparative sociology flow from Moore's writings. Moore considers the usefulness and limitations of statistical analysis at a number of points in his work, and he is wary of the uncritical employment of quantitative techniques which fails to capture qualitative dimensions of social relations. He argues, for example, that 'In the analysis of qualitative changes from one type of social organization to another, let us say from feudalism to industrial capitalism, there may be an upper limit to the profitable use of statistical procedures' (1967, p. 519). Equally, however, Moore declares that he has 'no patience with the machine-breaking mentality that rejects figures out of hand' (1967, p. 510). This is demonstrated for example in his analysis of slavery and the civil war in the USA, which has much in common with other analyses in which quantitative data are combined with an appreciation of the moral issues involved, such as Marx's account in which 'the numerical proportion of slaves to free citizens' is seen as being of 'decisive importance' (1973, p. 348) to the political struggle, or Fogel's (1989) discussion of 'the moral problem of slavery' following his earlier painstaking statistical analysis of America's slave economy (Fogel and Engerman, 1974). Elsewhere, Moore draws on quantitative and qualitative perspectives to explore the ironies of situations in which peasant revolts may follow a period in which 'the economic and social position of a large sector had been improving for some time', while conversely, 'Economic deterioration by slow degrees can become accepted by its victims as part of the normal situation' (1967, p. 465, 474). In exploring such cases, Moore is not constrained by notions of typicality or representativeness, arguing rather that much can be learned from the study of 'extreme examples' (1978, p. xiv).

The comparative method employed by Moore is an essential part of his wider project in which he seeks to understand not only the range of types of society that there are, but also how it is that different possibilities emerge or are closed off. The case study of Germany in *Injustice* is concerned to explore 'the suppression of historical alternatives' (1978, Ch.11) as that society moved towards fascism, and it is an important message of *Social Origins* that certain patterns of industrialization, such as the bourgeois democratic route to the modern world, are no longer open. In considering the range of options facing a society, Moore is mindful of the need to steer a course between a conservative acceptance of whatever exists, as functionalism has a tendency to do, and entertaining utopian ideas about the future which are unrealistically optimistic. Comparative sociology has much to contribute to such debates because 'a comparative perspective can lead to asking very useful and sometimes new questions' (1967, p. x). A good example of how comparisons may produce insightful observations is Moore's sense of how Imperial China anticipated twentieth-century totalitarianism. According to Moore, Imperial China's 'whole combination of welfare policies, police surveillance, and popular indoctrination constitutes a revealing precursor of modern totalitarian practices' from which it is possible to conclude that 'the key features of the totalitarian complex existed in the premodern world' (1967, p. 206). Moore's (1962) demonstration that totalitarian elements were well-established in pre-industrial societies allowed him to argue against the suggested link between totalitarianism and industrialism, and contributed along the way to the revival of interest in the classical sociologists' work on 'oriental despotism' (Wittfogel, 1957). Comparative analysis of this sort requires the ability to distinguish 'between superficial and meaningful historical resemblances' (1967, p. 160). Moore suggests that this involves directing attention towards fundamental factors such as the different social bases of power. Combined with his 'strategy of constant scanning for comparisons over time and space' (Smith, 1983, p. 98), Moore has proved comparative analysis to be an enormously profitable method.

Moore's account in *Social Origins* of three routes to the modern industrial world along with a possible fourth route followed by India has had a significant effect on much subsequent analysis (Hall, 1986). There are, for example, echoes of Moore's analysis in Laite's identification of 'three main models of development: the capitalism of Europe and America, the statism of the Soviet Union and the agrarian socialism of China. A fourth way has been tried by countries such as Cuba and Tanzania, but they have run into difficulties and so adopted one of the former paths' (1984, p. 192). Of course, modifications and elaborations have had to be made in the light of further developments such as the transition from communism to what have been variously described as capitalist, post-communist and post-totalitarian societies in the former Soviet Union and Eastern Europe (Clarke *et al.*, 1993; Hamilton and Hirszowicz, 1993; Lewis, 1992), developments which will be examined in Chapter 5. This transformation, together with recent changes in liberal capitalist societies, developments in Germany and Japan since the defeat of fascism in 1945, and the rise of the newly industrializing countries, shows that 'modernity' is a dynamic phase of social development and that 'the modern world' is a more problematic concept than Moore's account of the different routes to it suggests. Moore's arguments have had to be further reassessed in the context of global movements towards democratization (Lewis, 1992), but it is interesting how much of his analysis remains valid. Szelenyi's account of changes just prior to the 1989 revolutions in Eastern Europe echoes Moore in its reference to a 'silent revolution from below' (1988, p. 214), while the 'authoritarian corporatism' (Deyo, 1989, p. 108) of the newly industrializing countries confirms Moore's views on the necessity for industrialization to be pushed through under regimes employing a high degree of political compulsion. The tensions between economic development and democracy highlighted by Moore have by no means disappeared.

It is clear that Moore's analysis needs to be updated in the light of several contemporary developments, not least those taking place outside the core of established industrial capitalist countries. The focus of *Social Origins* on large countries was justified by Moore in terms of the argument that 'smaller countries depend economically and politically on big and powerful ones' (1967, p. x), and that economic and political innovations tend to occur in big countries. This case does not square easily with the innovative role which has been played by smaller countries in several contexts. Recent debates on welfare-state regimes have highlighted the distinct character of Scandinavian welfare experiments, which are far from being derivative of those of larger countries, as Chapter 4 will show. Small countries such as Hungary can be considered to have been pioneers in the transition away from Stalinist state socialism, and this theme will be developed in Chapter 5. Similarly the newly industrializing countries have played an important role in the emergence of the modern global economy, a point which will be explored further in Chapter 7. Other parts of the global economy which have been frustrated in their efforts to industrialize raise more of a challenge to Veblen's term 'the advantages of backwardness', which Moore (1967, p. 414) quotes with approval. For those at the margins of the global economy, it is the disadvantages of late development which are most prominent, notwithstanding their possession of greater knowledge about what industrialization involves (Crow *et al.*, 1988).

Yet for all the modifications which have been put forward regarding Moore's model of the various routes to the modern world, it remains the case that he was responsible for developing some crucial sociological insights. By establishing that there is no necessary connection between capitalist industrialization and democracy, Moore highlighted the potential autonomy of political forms from economic processes and paved the way for the state to be 'brought back in' (Evans *et al.*, 1985) to the analysis of comparative economic development. Moore's argument put another way is that there are several forms which industrialization can take, and within that range there is more than one form of capitalism. The detail of Moore's distinction between repressive and market mechanisms of labour control may have been found to be 'too rigid' (Rueschemeyer *et al.*, 1992, p. 288), but the underlying point still stands, namely that there are dangers in referring in an undifferentiated way to 'capitalism'. It follows from this that just as the 'classic' model of capitalism has a problematic relationship to the empirical evidence of the historical record, so too do classic models of particular classes within capitalist societies. As Kumar notes, Moore's *Injustice* demonstrates that 'there was no such thing as a unified, homogeneous, industrial proletariat in Germany in 1914, let alone a revolutionary, class-conscious one' (1988, p. 141). The significance of these points and the wider relevance of Moore's historical sociology will become more fully apparent in the discussion of the debates concerning contemporary capitalism for which they form a backdrop and to which attention is now turned.

3

The Proliferation of Capitalisms: Organized Capitalism, Disorganized Capitalism and Beyond

The concern of sociologists to distinguish a number of different types of capitalism was noted earlier in Chapter 1. Moore's (1967) comparison between capitalist democracy and reactionary forms of capitalism directs attention towards the varying political frameworks within which capitalist industrialization has taken place. Other approaches highlight the importance of differences in the cultural context, as in Abercrombie *et al.*'s (1986) contrast between 'individualistic capitalism' (which is treated as a norm in the literature) and the 'non-individualistic capitalism' found in countries such as Japan. The conclusion to be drawn from such analyses is that neither democracy nor individualism should be considered a defining characteristic of capitalism. In recent years, the focus of attention has shifted more to the distinction between different phases of capitalism, and this shift in perspective is particularly marked in debates around the transition from 'organized' to 'disorganized' capitalism. The linkage of organized capitalism to 'Fordism' in the sphere of production and disorganized capitalism to 'post-Fordism' is central to this distinction, but connections to changes in the political and cultural spheres have also been made. Offe, for example, suggests that disorganized capitalism can be seen as a phase in which there is a failure to maintain welfare state capitalism's 'dynamic balance between social power and political authority' (1985, p. 6). Similarly, Lash and Urry employ the term 'disorganized capitalism' to denote not only altered economic and political arrangements but also the emergence of 'a cultural–ideological configuration of "postmodernism"' (1987, p. 7), in contrast to the modernism which characterized organized capitalism. For such writers, the 'disorganization' of capitalism has profound implications.

The development of several different models of capitalism is not in itself new. Weber, for example, distinguished between booty capitalism, pariah capitalism, traditional capitalism, political capitalism, imperialist capitalism, colonial capitalism, adventure capitalism and rational capitalism (Gerth and Mills, 1970, pp. 66–7; Parkin, 1982, p. 41), although it is his analysis of the latter type and its development in the modern West which has the most enduring sociological significance (Collins, 1986a, Ch. 2). Weber was particularly interested in modern Western capitalism because 'the Occident has developed capitalism both to a quantitative extent and... in types, forms and directions which have never existed elsewhere' (1930, p. 20), and only here was rational capitalism elevated 'into a system' (1981, p. 334). State regulation of capitalist enterprises became much more extensive in the half century following Weber's death in 1920, and this development, together with other changes in business organization, ownership and control, led to various reassessments of models of capitalism inherited from sociological classics such as Marx and Weber. Some of these reassessments suggested that it made more sense to speak of industrialism rather than capitalism, since the class inequalities and conflicts characteristic of nineteenth-century capitalism had been modified almost beyond recognition (Jessop, 1987; Scott, 1979, Ch.1). The end of the long boom of the 1950s and 1960s in turn forced further reassessment as a revitalized form of capitalism emerged. In Hall's account of the 'new times' in which we find ourselves, '"Post-industrialism", "Post-Fordism", "Post-modernism" are all different ways of trying to characterize or explain this dramatic, even brutal, resumption of the link between modernity and capitalism' (1989, p. 122). The changing nature of capitalism continues to be a hotly disputed subject, as it has been in every era since the inception of sociology (Kumar, 1995).

At the heart of debates about the nature of contemporary capitalism lie differing assessments of changes in workplace organization and the implications these have for the nature of work and the wider system of class relations. The capitalist enterprise in the era of disorganized capitalism is said by several commentators to be one in which rigid, hierarchical organization and assembly-line techniques appropriate to Fordist mass production have given way to more 'flexible' arrangements. According to Braham, 'Flexible specialization emphasises flexibility in a number of areas: in terms of a response to the market, in terms of an ability to produce economically in small batches, and in terms of the flexibility demanded of the workforce' (1992, p. 304). For workers, 'flexibility' means the requirement to be flexible in terms of their work practices and also their contracts of employment. These changes in the sphere of production have had a number of effects on the meaning of work in people's lives and the structure of class relations. Offe's (1985) discussion of disorganized capitalism suggests that 'work' may be losing its place as a central sociological variable, as working patterns become more heterogeneous and common bonds based on work are undermined at the same time as interests and social divisions relating to activities outside the work-place grow in importance. This scenario has been questioned on a number of counts, but the debate it has generated indicates the need for renewed scrutiny of sociological thinking about work and social class as former certainties about classes and their organizations are brought into question.

Trends towards restructured economic, social and political relations mean that contemporary capitalist societies are in many ways becoming more internally heterogeneous. Work in the expanding service sector has several characteristics which distinguish it from work in manufacturing, at the same time as both sectors are subject to pressures dividing 'core' from 'peripheral' workers (Warde, 1990). There is also a need to acknowledge that work has a gender dimension. Crompton notes that in the OECD countries since the Second World War, 'for a significant category of people – women – employment was becoming considerably *more* important' (1993, p. 84, emphasis in original), and in doing so she challenges Offe's generalization on the basis of men's experiences. A further force behind the growth of heterogeneity can be identified in the renegotiation of the relationship between the formal and informal economies, a change which writers such as Pahl (1984) argue has profound implications for class divisions through the process of social polarization, most ominously in the emergence of an 'underclass'. These various forces work themselves out differently in different countries, and national variations in the organization of production and in the distribution of income and wealth continue to be a prominent feature of contemporary capitalism, not least because of different political and welfare state arrangements. At the same time, it must be stressed that capitalism is very much an international system, and changes in capitalist production will have global consequences, including some which push in the direction of growing homogeneity. For example, Ritzer's account of 'McDonaldiza-tion' represents it as a process which has 'not only revolutionized the restaurant business, but also American society and, ultimately, the world' (1993, p. xi). Global processes transcend the frontiers of individual nation states, and recognition of the actions of what Sklair has called 'the transnational capitalist class' (1995, p. 68) is particularly important to an understanding of capitalism's global development and the limitations on the power of individual nation states to control it.

From organized capitalism to disorganized capitalism?

In the writings of the classical sociologists, capitalism is understood to have features which are quite distinct from those of slavery, feudalism and other socio-economic systems. Despite fundamental disagreements about several other aspects of modern capitalism (such as the role of Protestantism in its genesis, and its likely future), Marx and Weber both identified it as a system in which the owners of capital employ free wage labour in order to produce commodities for sale on competitive markets, and are driven by competitive pressures to innovate and accumulate further capital (Bottomore, 1985; Collins, 1986a; Davis and Scase, 1985; Giddens, 1985). Both also saw capitalist societies as characterized by class inequalities which had the potential to produce conflicts that could threaten to undermine the stability of those societies; put another way, capitalism's inherently dynamic character meant that social stability could never be assured. These classical writings seemed to many commentators increasingly outdated as the twentieth century wore on. Although there were important differences of opinion among these commentators about precisely what had changed and why, by the second half of the twentieth century arguments were being put forward which suggested that nineteenth-century capitalism had been profoundly modified, if not superseded altogether, requiring the development of new analytical models.

Prominent among writers seeking to revise accounts of contemporary capitalism were convergence theorists like Kerr and his colleagues (1973), who claimed that it was possible to identify growing similarities between industrial societies whatever the industrialization route they had followed. Certainly, the stark opposition between capitalism and communism appeared to them to be untenable as their researches showed that 'the East... was several things and not static; the West even more diverse. Instead of two worlds, there were several in the middle of this century of great transformation; and each of these several worlds was in transition' (1973, p. 36). The anticipation of the convergence of market capitalism and state socialism rested on the changing positions of managers and workers in both systems, together with shifts in the organization of enterprises and their relations with the state. Industrial societies were held to be tending towards more egalitarian, open and democratic arrangements which made the class divisions and conflicts of classical capitalism and the centrally planned structures of communist societies increasingly anachronistic. Techno-logical developments were regarded as sufficiently powerful to affect economic relations and in turn political relations, limiting the extent to which development could be shaped by ideology. In their debate with Marx's ghost, Kerr and his associates argue that 'the central problem of industrial relations around the world is not capital versus labour, but rather the structuring of the labour force – how it gets recruited, developed and maintained' (1973, pp. 280–1). As a result, bureau-cratic organization is a more prominent feature of industrial societies than is class conflict, even if the possibility of 'a temporary breakdown in consensus' (1973, p. 296) cannot be ruled out.

The key conclusion for comparative sociology reached by conver-gence theorists was that 'Industrial societies, with all their variations, are more like each other than they are like pre-industrial societies' (Kerr *et al.*, 1973, p. 280). Kerr (1983) later developed a more sophis-ticated version of this argument, but he continued to hold to the view that industrial societies have more in common with each other than characteristics which divide them. Other writers detected more fundamental changes underway, which they regarded as sufficiently important to justify the use of the term 'post-industrial'. Probably the most famous of these accounts is Bell's (1974) *The Coming of Post-Industrial Society*, which argued that developments were taking society beyond the industrial phase. Particularly significant in this respect were changes in the dominant economic sector (with services displacing manufacturing), in technology (with the need to process information becoming more important than the physical transforma-tion of nature) and in the stratification system (in which social positions increasingly hinge on skills acquired through education). Bell detects fundamental tensions between the principles underlying industrial and post-industrial societies, and while post-industrial society can be seen as 'a continuation of trends unfolding out of industrial society', it is nevertheless the case that 'for *analytical* purposes, one *can* divide societies into pre-industrial, industrial and post-industrial and see them in contrast along many different dimensions' (Bell, 1974, pp. 115, 116, emphases in original). Bell noted that this movement towards post-industrial society applied in principle to socialist as well as capitalist societies, although he suggested that in practice it had gone furthest in the USA.

Bell went on to develop his argument about the movement towards post-industrial society with specific reference to the implications of this shift for the future of capitalism. His scepticism about the idea 'that societies are organic or so integrated as to be analyzable as a single system' led to his sensitivity to 'the disjunction, in Western society, between the culture and the social structure' (1974, p. 114). In *The Cultural Contradictions of Capitalism* (1976), Bell elaborated on this theme, suggesting that it is in the cultural sphere that the greatest threat to capitalism originates. The traditional bourgeois values of 'thrift, frugality, self-control and impulse renunciation' (1976, p. 65) on which capitalism had been built were in Bell's view increasingly at odds with the ethos of a society in which sustained economic growth had given rise to mass consumption and a focus on the present rather than the future. The tension was particularly marked in the uneven reproduction of Weber's (1930) Protestant ethic since, in Bell's words, 'The "new capitalism"... continued to demand a Protestant ethic in the sphere of production – that is, in the realm of work – but to stimulate a demand for pleasure and play in the area of consumption. The disjunction was bound to widen' (1976, p. 75). The material 'abundance' which capitalism had successfully ushered in generated cultural shifts which, by undermining the traditional work ethic, threatened the 'moral foundation' (1976, pp. 78, 84) of capitalist societies and promised its replacement by the less rational ethos of post-modernism. Bell was less concerned with capitalism's efficiency than with its legitimacy, and his argument about the erosion of capitalism's 'moral grounding' (1976, p. 77) echoes Moore's analyses of the link between morality and social order.

The theories of industrial society and post-industrial society were both developed in order to make sense of developments which took societies beyond capitalism as it had been known by the classical sociologists. While neither involved uncritical acceptance of Dahrendorf's (1959) suggestion concerning the arrival of 'post-capitalist society', these theories nevertheless highlighted the need to address the obsolescence of inherited models. At the same time, writers in the Marxist tradition were attempting to come to terms with many of the same developments, even if they drew rather different conclusions. As Bell notes, his work shares common threads with that of Habermas relating to capitalism's legitimation and motivation crises, although he declares himself 'more pessimistic than Habermas about the long-run ability of capitalist society to maintain its vitality as a moral and reward system for its citizens' (1976, p. 250). Habermas' view is that advanced capitalism has 'surprising vigour' (1976, p. 17) and greater durability as a system than both Bell and orthodox Marxists supposed, for while capitalism's competitive and liberal characteristics may have been superseded by less competitive market structures and more state intervention, it remains appropriate to speak of capitalism, albeit in an 'organized or state-regulated' (1976, p. 33) form. Habermas suggests that the changes under discussion are best understood as a 'transition from liberal to organized capitalism' (1976, p. 33), a transition which varies in detail from country to country but which is identifiable at a general level.

Habermas' model of organized capitalism did not represent advanced capitalism as a stable system, however, but one in which there is always the potential for what his contemporary Offe called 'crises of crisis management' (1984, Ch. 1). Habermas identified a number of 'crisis tendencies' relating not only to economic processes, but also to the rationality and legitimation of organized capitalism and to the motivation of people within that system. He argued that while the possibility existed of averting crises in any one of these areas, doing so would increase the likelihood of crises in others. Thus economic crises may be averted through greater regulation of markets by the state, but only at the cost of exacerbating the system's difficulties relating to rationality, legitimacy and motivation, the general assumption being that 'even in state-regulated capitalism, social developments involve "contradictions" or crises' (1976, p. 1). As Held notes, Habermas' analysis leads to the conclusion that 'given its logic of crisis tendencies, organized capitalism cannot maintain its present form' (Held and Krieger, 1983, p. 496), although (as Held also observes) he is somewhat vague about the possible directions in which such societies might develop beyond specifying that they will be founded on different principles of organization in the economic, political and social spheres.

According to Keane, Habermas represents the transition from liberal to organized capitalism as a process which involves a 'drift toward an authoritarian, bureaucratic, state-administering capitalism' (1984, p. 95). Habermas' account has much in common with the work of Offe, as Keane and others have noted (Bauman, 1992; Held and Krieger, 1983; Pusey, 1987). Like Habermas, Offe emphasizes the susceptibility of contemporary capitalism to various crises, due to the contradictory pressures which are found within the system. Of particular importance in Offe's account are the contradictions between 'the legitimacy and efficiency of the capitalist state' (1984, p. 139). The vulnerability of capitalism to economic crises led to higher levels of state intervention over time in an effort to limit the social and political impact of unemployment and inequality, but such intervention tends to achieve greater legitimacy at the cost of losses in efficiency. Thus the state in advanced capitalism faces numerous dilemmas, such as that whereby 'the more the welfare state is made necessary by the shrinking employment opportunities provided by the economy, the less it is capable of playing that role because of the poor employment performance of the economy' (Hinrichs *et al.*, 1988, p. 221). State intervention in an attempt to reconcile the aspirations of citizens with the requirements of capitalist accumulation constantly highlights the contradiction between democracy and capitalism, which remain in dynamic tension.

Further consideration of Offe's theory of the welfare state's contradictions will be left until the next chapter, with attention for the moment directed towards his characterization of contemporary capitalism as 'disorganized'. Offe employs the term 'disorganized capitalism' in order to challenge the assumption that states can successfully achieve the balancing of competing demands made upon them. He and his collaborators argue that analysis should commence with the realm of work opportunities, since 'Any consideration of the present crisis and the future of the welfare state must begin with the conditions that prevail – and are likely to prevail in the foreseeable future – on the labour market' (Hinrichs *et al.*, 1988, p. 221). Among the developments which make the reproduction of welfare-state capitalism particularly problematic, Offe highlights the declining potential of labour markets to provide work, 'removing or excluding increasing numbers of potential workers from direct and full-time contact with the supposedly central power mechanism of capitalist society' (1985, p. 3). The move away from full employment is the most pressing development in contemporary capitalism, requiring renewed critical analysis of labour markets and of work more generally. Changes in the distribution and also the meaning of work have profound implications for class divisions and class consciousness as well as for politics more broadly, as traditional class-based organizations such as trade unions have to adapt to less favourable conditions and face increasing competition in the political arena from new social movements. Offe acknowledges that his use of the term 'disorganized capitalism' is heuristic, to be justified by its usefulness in going beyond other theories of contemporary society which 'amount only to *ad hoc* classifications which remain unintegrated into a dynamic theory of social change' (1985, p. 150). It has, however, been left to other writers, most notably Lash and Urry (1987, 1994), to develop a more systematic analysis of disorganized capitalism.

The claim that organized capitalism is being superseded by disorganized capitalism is one which challenges much conventional wisdom in sociology, as Lash and Urry recognize. The notion of a shift from liberal capitalism to organized capitalism from the end of the nineteenth century onwards is one which they accept, just as they acknowledge that during the twentieth century various trends towards centralization and state regulation can be seen to have deepened. What is distinctive about their argument is that a third era of capitalist development is identified as emerging, in which phase many of the features of organized capitalism are being transformed. Organized capitalism was characterized by 'the concentration of industry, increasing inter-articulation of banks, industry and the state, and cartel formation' at the 'top' of societies, and 'the development of national trade union bodies, working-class political parties, and the welfare state' at the 'bottom' (Lash and Urry, 1987, p. 4). Different countries underwent the shift from liberal to organized capitalism at different times, and the general rule that earlier industrializers are less organized than later industrializers is attributed to the fact that 'countries which are later industrializers need to begin at higher levels of concentration and centralization of capital to compete with those which have already been industrializing for some time' (1987, p. 4). There are echoes of Moore's (1967) analysis of forced industrialization in Lash and Urry's observation that 'German capitalism was organized early on at both the top and the bottom' (1987, p. 4), while in comparison American, Swedish, French and British capitalism became organized later and, in some respects at least, less comprehensively.

According to Lash and Urry, signs that capitalist societies could not indefinitely become ever more organized began to appear in the 1960s, since when several trends have indicated a shift to disorganized capitalism. Globalization of economic processes, liberalization of world trade and the decline of cartels have reduced the control which corporations can exercise over national markets. De-industrialization has led to the shrinkage of the traditional working class employed in manufacturing, while numbers of white-collar workers in the service sector have increased, a change which brings with it the development of a service class which has been 'an important and driving factor in capitalism's disorganization process' (1987, p. 11). There is also a challenge to class politics by new social movements. At the workplace, Taylorist organization based on hierarchies and notions of scientific management has come to be regarded as inflexible and in need of replacement by more flexible arrangements, including a move away from national level collective bargaining. Corporatist arrangements involving national labour organizations, business enterprises and the state combining in centralized economic planning have tended to break down, while the welfare state has come under attack for being excessively bureaucratic and inflexible. The growth of economic and political heterogeneity has been accompanied by 'an increase in cultural fragmentation and pluralism' (1987, p. 6) both nationally and globally. There is a further, global dimension to the relocation of production, as older urban industrial areas lose out both to more rural sites and emergent competitors in the 'third world'.

Lash and Urry's 'disorganization thesis', which suggests that capitalism is moving out of its organized phase, is complemented by their 'comparative thesis', which posits that 'the greater the extent to which a nation's capitalism has ever been organized the more slowly and hesitantly its capitalism, *ceteris paribus*, will disorganize' (1987, p. 7). Accordingly, they contend that the first signs of the end of organized capitalism emerged in the USA and Britain in the 1960s, coming later in France, Germany and Sweden where organized capitalism had been taken further. National differences affect the timing and speed of organized capitalism's decline but cannot prevent the general trend: 'disorganization is... a fairly systematic process of disaggregation and restructuration' (1987, p. 8). The comparisons which Lash and Urry make challenge the conclusion that the USA is somehow exceptional and following a path different from that of the presumed norm of corporatist organized capitalism, it being erroneous in their view to make 'general statements about contemporary capitalism drawing on data relating to large numbers of small countries'. In terms of number of people, the USA is much more the norm, since 'The size of the American population living under *non*-corporatist, low-welfare state disorganized capitalist relations is more than *three times* larger than the combined population of Austria, Switzerland, Denmark, New Zealand, Holland, Belgium, Finland, Norway and Australia' (1987, p. 10, emphases in original), countries commonly drawn upon to illustrate organized capitalism's supposed 'normality'. While the USA has gone further towards disorganized capitalism, other countries are also subject to the pressures which pushed it in that direction.

The implications of Lash and Urry's perspective are far-reaching, as is indicated by their statement that 'Disorganized capitalism disorganizes everything' (1994, p. 10). Changes in production, which becomes more fragmented and flexible than it was during the phase of organized capitalism, combined with changes in politics and in culture, add up to a profound social transformation. For Lash and Urry, disorganized capitalism's 'transformed political economy is both "post-Fordist", in that it succeeded the era of mass production and mass consumption, and postmodern' (1994, p. 2). The term 'disorganized' is preferred to 'reorganized' as a label for contemporary capitalist societies on the grounds that there is no co-ordination or synchronization of economic, political or cultural processes, which become increasingly uncontrolled, in contrast to the way in which control was attempted in organized capitalism. Indeed, Lash and Urry claim that 'individual societies are subject to systematic de-synchronization, and in a way so is the globe as a whole' (1994, p. 10). The suggestion that disorganized capitalism ushers in new relations of time and space invites serious re-thinking of how comparative sociology is practised, since social processes are more fluid and indeterminate than conventionally understood, while the growth in flows of people, objects and ideas across national boundaries reveals the limitations of the idea of autonomous 'societies'. This said, Lash and Urry wish to retain a place for 'cross-societal' analysis 'in order to show that there are major differences between apparently similar advanced capitalist societies' (1994, p. 321). The history of individual societies modifies the extent to which they conform to general categories such as 'organized capitalism' or 'disorganized capitalism', although the presence of 'major differences in the form of accumulation and in the pattern of services as between Germany, Japan, certain Scandinavian countries, and the UK and USA' (1994, p. 321) does not in their view invalidate the idea of a broad trend towards disorganized capitalism.

The changing nature of work

Lash and Urry's thesis concerning the transition from organized to disorganized capitalism has a bearing on several crucial sociological debates concerning the changing nature of work and class in contemporary societies, the implications which these changes have for social cohesion and social divisions, and the shifting role of the state. In these debates, much hinges on the interpretation of how far things have changed in recent decades, which in turn requires analysis of the ways in which things were in the past, and here it is important to note that the extent to which previous economic, social and political arrangements conformed to the model of organized capitalism is a matter of dispute. A second area of contention relates to competing accounts of what is responsible for bringing about the changes under discussion, with explanations varying in the degree to which they emphasize different processes such as technological innovation, class conflict, cultural change and globalization. Thirdly, disagreements exist about the implications of these changes for the future direction of social change and the part which states and other political forces can play in shaping this. Lash and Urry's view that disorganized capitalism has led to 'the declining effectivity and legitimacy of nation-states' (1994, p. 323), which are thereby progressively less able to control processes which cross their boundaries, makes even more crucial the issue of whether organized opposition to disorganized capitalism is possible (Byrne, 1989), as well as raising once again the vexed question of the relationship between capitalism and democracy (Kumar, 1988).

The thesis that the world of work in capitalist societies is undergoing a shift from Fordism to post-Fordism has several variants (Amin, 1994; Wood, 1989), although certain themes are recurrent within the broad perspective. The essential contrast involves a number of changes, away from the Fordism of organized capitalism with its 'homogeneity, standardisation and... economies and organisations of scale' (Hall and Jacques, 1989, p. 11) to a much more diverse, fragmented and differentiated situation. The idea of post-Fordism suggests that what is emerging is 'an altogether different kind of economy; one which is organized around flexible forms of production, in both the technologies used and in the kinds of work expected' (Allen, 1992b, p. 170). The transition is taken to herald the displacement of mass production and consumption as the employment of flexible production techniques becomes increasingly widespread, due in no small part to the growing heterogeneity of markets. Overall, post-Fordism has been taken to pose a challenge to 'the centrality of large industrial complexes, blue-collar work, full employment, centralized bureaucracies of management, mass markets for cheap standardized goods, the welfare state, mass political parties and the centrality of the nation state as a unit of organization' (Amin, 1994, p. 2), but it is on the sphere of production that most attention has been focused. In particular, the flexibility which is taken to be the hallmark of post-Fordism has been examined in terms of its implications for workplace organization and workers' experiences of work, and in turn to wider patterns of capital accumulation.

Assessment of the argument that a transition from Fordism to post-Fordism is occurring requires careful specification of what these terms mean, but this is not always forthcoming. Savage *et al.* have commented that 'Fordism is a delightfully vague concept', while 'The concept of Post-Fordism... covers a multiplicity of aspects of social life' (1992, pp. 59–60) extending far beyond the workplace. Savage and his colleagues are sceptical of some of the wider claims made in relation to post-Fordism, but accept that it does serve a useful purpose in pointing to 'the changing relationship between organisations and capital accumulation', where firms have responded to the inflexibility of Fordist organizational hierarchies by developing 'a series of alternative ways of producing and distributing profitably' (1992, p. 61). Other writers also acknowledge that there have been developments in the world of work which 'represent some pretty fundamental moves away from the original Fordist conception with its emphasis on a clear specification of individualized jobs and separation of supervisory and managerial roles from operational duties' (Wood, 1989, p. 26). These various shifts can be understood as the growth in flexibility in four distinct senses relating to 'changes in technology, products, jobs and employment contracts' (Warde, 1990, p. 87). New technologies mean that mass production is no longer essential for output to be cheap, and they assist producers in meeting the requirements of more specialized markets for differentiated products. The greater versatility of producers in how and what they produce requires greater flexibility on the part of workers in terms of what they do and/or the terms and conditions under which they do it. As Warde notes, 'functional flexibility' is associated with the 'multi-skilling' of workers who can be 'moved around from job to job within the factory', while 'numerical flexibility' describes the situation where 'firms employ on a permanent and full-time basis only those workers who can be fully occupied for 40 hours per week' (1990, p. 87), with other workers engaged on less secure temporary, part-time, casual or sub-contracting bases.

The central dispute concerning post-Fordism is not whether such changes have occurred but how they should be interpreted. No-one suggests that all work now conforms to the model of flexible production, but proponents of the idea of post-Fordism do see the growth of flexibility in industrial production as heralding a more general tendency. Thus Hall and Jacques argue that while 'Fordism is still alive and well in many places... Post-Fordism is at the leading edge of change' (1989, p. 12). There are several elements involved in this interpretation, including the idea that it is in the manufacturing sector that the decisive changes are taking place. Undoubtedly, the restructuring of the manufacturing sector is important, but it should not be forgotten that manufacturing industry 'now employs a relatively small proportion of the labour force' (Warde, 1990, p. 90), while approximately two-thirds of workers in countries such as the UK are in service sector employment (Jenkins, 1992). The suggestion that changes in manufacturing represent the shape of things to come for workers in other sectors overlooks the fact that 'outside the manufacturing sector there have always been plenty of jobs that are seasonal or temporary – for instance in the tourist or catering trades', while more generally 'casual and temporary work was very much the norm in Victorian times and probably until the mid-twentieth century' (Warde, 1990, p. 90). Furthermore, there remains considerable diversity within the manufac-turing sector, and here as elsewhere there are few if any 'powerful homogenizing forces to push work organizations and market strategies down one channel' (Wood, 1989, p. 26). Just as the hegemony of Fordism over production in the middle of the twentieth century can be exaggerated (Allen, 1992a), so too can news of its demise.

In some ways, the argument about the transition from Fordism to post-Fordism echoes Bell's analysis of the shift from industrial to post-industrial society. As Allen notes, 'Both post-industrial and post-Fordist accounts stress the role of knowledge and innovation in the organiza-tion of production, and the rise of "lead" industries based upon breakthroughs in microelectronic and information technologies' (1992b, p. 201). There are, however, several differences between the two approaches, not least in their explanations of the causes and consequences of the move away from organized industrial production. Bell interpreted the emergence of post-industrial society as a reflection of the growing importance of information-based activities, technolog-ical advances having eased the contest with nature which characterized pre-industrial production and the struggle against the fabricated nature of machine-dominated industrial societies. For Bell, 'A post-industrial society, because it centers on services – human services, professional and technical services – is a *game between persons*... In the salient experi-ence of work, men [*sic*] live more and more outside nature, and less and less with machinery and things' (1976, pp. 147–8, emphasis in original). Bell's optimism about the liberating potential of new technologies has been challenged for its concentration on the position of professional élites (Bell having claimed that in post-industrial society 'The central person is the professional' [1974, p. 127]) and its neglect of the routine, relatively unskilled, poorly rewarded and insecure work which is also characteristic of the service sector, and which is in addition performed predominantly by women (Allen, 1992b; Kumar,

1988; McDowell, 1992; Payne, 1987; Rose, 1985; Warde, 1990). This sober view of modern service work is more likely to be highlighted in post-Fordist accounts, emphasizing as they do that post-industrial societies are still very much shaped by capitalist forces.

In contrast to Bell's representation of the development of post-industrial society as the outcome of a secular sectoral shift, post-Fordist perspectives stress the continued influence of capitalism. The restructuring of contemporary work patterns along post-Fordist lines is explained in terms of the crisis of Fordist mass production. Harvey dates the crisis of Fordism from the 1960s, by which time 'the West European and Japanese recoveries were complete, their internal market saturated, and the drive to create export markets for their surplus output had to begin' (1989, p. 141). In Harvey's view, the shift from Fordism to what he calls 'flexible accumulation' was driven by 'the inability of Fordism and Keynesianism to contain the inherent contradictions of capitalism' (1989, pp. 141–2). The declining profitability of capitalist enterprises at this time reflected the system's rigidity, notably 'the rigidity of long-term and large-scale fixed capital investments in mass-production systems that precluded much flexibility of design and presumed stable growth in invariant consumer markets' (1989, p. 142), but also rigidity in the labour market and in the state's economic and social policies. In Harvey's account, the demand for greater flexibility came from employers who were coming under growing pressure because of intensified competition in what were increasingly global markets, and who in response 'have taken advantage of weakened union power and the pools of surplus (unemployed or underemployed) labourers to push for much more flexible work regimes and labour contracts' (1989, p. 150). From this perspective in which employers' power over employees is reasserted, Bell's suggestion that property has been replaced by knowledge as the most important basis of power and dynamism in society looks decidedly premature.

The model of social change employed by writers like Harvey is a more complex one than Bell's. For Harvey, 'How the Fordist system was put into place is, in fact, a long and complicated story, stretching over nearly half a century. It depended on myriad individual, corporate, institutional and state decisions, many of them unwitting political choices or knee-jerk responses to the crisis tendencies of capitalism' (1989, p. 127). His account of the breakdown of Fordism is similarly multi-faceted, and within the bounds of the argument that 'flexible accumulation is still a form of capitalism' (1989, p. 179), and thus subject to certain limits, he is able to incorporate political and cultural as well as economic forces into his explanation. Sensitivity to contrasting roles played by the state in mediating class conflicts also figures in explaining the varying degrees to which Fordism was established in different countries, as in Jessop's (1992) contrast between Britain's 'flawed Fordism' and Germany's 'export-oriented Fordism'. Similar points could be made about differences in the degree to which 'flexible specialization' or 'Japanization' has displaced Fordism (Lane, 1988; Thompson and McHugh, 1990). The contrasting role of the state is also central to Lash and Urry's (1987) account of the different paths to and from the corporatism of organized capitalism in countries such as Britain and Germany, while their more recent writing on what they call 'reflexive accumulation' stresses 'the ways in which economic life is itself becoming cultural and aestheticized' (1994, p. 109) and thus moves further away from analyses which attach primary importance to narrowly economic explanations.

Lash and Urry's incorporation of global political and post-modern cultural as well as flexible economic processes in their analysis of the transition to disorganized capitalism leads them to a view of the future in which work is increasingly distinct from Fordist and modernist patterns. Other writers have perceived less of a fundamental shift and more elements of continuity. Allen, for example, notes the possibility of seeing the growth of new technologies and flexibility as 'a *continuation* of the modern economic era rather than a move beyond it', and counterposes the argument that 'post-Fordism represents a qualitatively new economic direction, a *step beyond* Fordism' with the ideas of others for whom 'Neo-Fordism represents an *adjustment* to the problems of Fordism' (1992b, pp. 201, 193, emphases in original). Reviewing the same literature, Amin concludes that 'what comes after Fordism may well be an open matter' (1994, p. 6), particularly when global responses to the crisis of Fordism are considered. The 'de-industrialization' of the advanced capitalist economies has to be understood in the context of the relocation of much industrial production to other parts of the world, a subject which will be examined in greater detail in Chapter 7. For the moment, it is sufficient to note that globalization has not brought with it a uniform movement away from Fordist work patterns, since industrial and service production both vary significantly in different parts of the global economy. In the context of 'the off-loading of crisis tendencies from core regions to the periphery' (Ray, 1993, p. 101), the implications for the third world of the movement beyond Fordism remain unclear (Wield *et al.*, 1992), just as they do for the former state socialist world in which Taylorist ideas of scientific management were enthusiastically embraced (Corrigan *et al.*, 1978).

Even in the advanced capitalist countries the idea of a dramatic break with Fordism has been contested. For example, Ritzer claims that the 'McDonaldism' which he sees as 'growing at an astounding pace in contemporary society' is 'a phenomenon which has many things in common with Fordism' (1993, p. 155). Lyon's analysis of workplace surveillance concedes that 'post-Fordist practice plainly differs from the old Taylorism', but it also notes a strong thread of continuity, because while 'New technologies permit a relaxing of centralized, bureaucratic management supervision and monitoring... they simultaneously make possible a new intensity of surveillance, penetrating much more deeply into the daily routines of workers' (1994, pp. 135, 128). With a somewhat different focus, McDowell argues that 'for most women their increasing integration into the wage economy of post-Fordist Britain has reinforced rather than challenged existing structures of inequality in the labour market' (1992, p. 188). Accounts such as these do not deny the presence of rapid change in recent decades, but they do at the same time point to strong continuities in many other features of work organization and employment. The contrasting emphases placed by different writers on these themes of continuity and change in the nature of work have an important bearing on wider debates about contemporary capitalism. Offe (1985), for example, argues that in disorganized capitalism the sphere of work and production has lost much of its former power to determine other aspects of social life, and with this the class-based patterns characteristic of organized capitalism have been subject to serious modification. Others are unconvinced by Offe's speculation that work is 'becoming subjectively peripheral' (1985, p. 148) and that class consciousness is consequently undermined, sensing that while recent changes in the labour market and beyond have complicated class relations, they have not superseded them (Edgell and Duke, 1991; Eldridge *et al.*, 1991; Marshall *et al.*, 1988; Westergaard, 1995).

Social class and social polarization

No shortage exists of competing perspectives on the issue of how relevant the concept of social class is to the analysis of contemporary Western societies, as various overviews of current debates show (Crompton, 1993; Edgell, 1993). The shifting popularity of different theories can be linked, as Marshall and his colleagues (1988) have suggested, to changes in prevailing economic circumstances, with the optimistic accounts contained in Bell's post-industrial society model being displaced by theories of proletarianization as the long period of post-War prosperity gave way in the 1970s and 1980s to growing economic stresses. Marshall *et al.* note that the data from their investigation into class structure and class consciousness in modern Britain 'vindicate neither perspective' (1988, p. 271). The prediction that class divisions are progressively disappearing as the growth of service sector work produces a more open and mobile society is no more supported by the data than is the Marxist idea that work is subject to 'deskilling', with workers in all sectors experiencing downward mobility. The situation is more complicated than either scenario suggests. Marshall and his collaborators highlight in particular the incompatibility of significant upward mobility into the service class and shrinkage of traditional manual working-class occupations 'with Marxist theories about the rigidity of class structures in advanced capitalism', while they note that the persistence of 'collective identities and collective action of a class-based kind' (1988, pp. 271, 273) stands in equal contrast to liberal theories.

While Marshall *et al.* are sceptical concerning predictions of a 'transition to a post-industrial society in which the structure of class inequalities, together with class-based political action, have given way to the purely status politics of the open society' (1988, p. 274), they are also wary of implying that nothing in the field of capitalist class relations has changed. Significant in this respect are perceived changes which include 'the decline of traditional proletarian occupations and communities; the expansion of working-class "affluence"; the growth of service sector and white-collar employment; the professionalization of certain nonmanual occupations and routinization or deskilling of others; and the increasing participation of women in paid employment' (1988, p. 269). Marshall and his colleagues are mindful of the tendency of some commentators to exaggerate the extent and implications of these changes, but their account of contemporary Britain as 'a capitalist *class* society' (1988, p. 11, emphasis in original) recognizes the importance of treating class relations as part of developing processes rather than static structures. Rejecting the view that these processes are economically determined, Marshall *et al.* conclude that 'whatever happens will not be the result of some underlying logic or dialectic in the development of industrial capitalist societies' (1988, p. 274). The future course of class relations will be influenced to an important degree by political strategies and moral notions of social justice as well as by economic forces, there being no inevitability about processes leading to the disappearance or alternatively the polarization of social classes.

The salience of non-economic factors for the shape of class structures is also suggested by other participants in the cross-national project of which Marshall *et al.*'s research was a part. Wright, for example, notes that advanced capitalist countries can vary greatly despite having similar levels of technological development and average standards of living, with the USA and Sweden constituting 'almost polar cases'. What stands out is that the USA 'has among the highest levels of real income inequality (that is, after taxes and transfers) of any developed capitalist society, while Sweden has the lowest', a contrast which has more than a passing connection with the fact that 'Sweden has the highest proportion of its civilian labour force directly employed by the state (over 45 percent), while the USA has the lowest (under 20 percent)' (1989, p. 33). The contrast between the strength of social democracy in Sweden and its weakness in the USA indicates the importance of politics in shaping class relationships, and Wright draws attention to the way in which the distribution of income is subject to much more extensive modification by the welfare state in Sweden than it is in the USA. Stated more generally, there are significant variations between the class structures of different capitalist societies, and the simple model of a process of polarization between working and capitalist classes overlooks all of the political and cultural as well as economic factors which produce diverse class situations and capacities.

The conclusion that contemporary societies are not inevitably subject to social polarization is one widely shared, but for writers such as Therborn the growth of inequality remains 'an inherent potentiality of capitalism' (1986, p. 32) and a likely course of events in the absence of the political will to challenge mass unemployment. Therborn sees as a distinct possibility 'the *Brazilianization of advanced capitalism*', producing a society in which 'the permanently and the marginally unemployed' find the gap between themselves and those in stable employment widening constantly, while both groups fall further behind the 'increasing wealth and incomes of capitalists and top business managers' (1986, pp. 32–3, emphasis in original). The theme of the progressive marginalization of those at the bottom of Therborn's 'two-thirds, one-third society' has parallels with other studies of social polarization in which radical conclusions are drawn about the changing class structure. Pahl (1984, 1988), for example, regards the division between an affluent, work-rich 'middle mass' of the population and an increasingly impoverished 'underclass' starved of employment opportunities and dependent on the state for its main source of income as a line of cleavage which has become more important than the formerly prominent division between the working and middle classes. Conventional analyses suffer from an 'over-emphasis on male workers and formal employment' (1984, p. 86), and a very different picture emerges when women workers and informal work are included in research perspectives. Such a change of focus highlights the development of 'a new form of polarisation' (Halsey, 1988, p. 16) which has profound economic, social and geographical implications (Townsend, 1993; Townsend *et al.*, 1987). Hutton's appraisal of contemporary Britain as a society in which 'Only around 40 per cent of the work-force enjoy tenured full-time employment or secure self-employment... another 30 per cent are insecurely self-employed, involuntarily part-time, or casual workers; while the bottom 30 per cent, the marginalised, are idle or working for poverty wages' (1996, p. 14) very much fits into this emerging tradition of analysis.

A crucial part of the background to the current trend towards growing inequality in Western capitalist societies lies in their restructured labour markets. What Therborn refers to as 'the high noon of industrial society' (1995, p. 65) was reached in much of Europe in the 1960s and 1970s, as is indicated by figures charting when the proportion of the workforce in industrial employment peaked. The subsequent 'rapid dismantling of industrial society' and its replacement by an emerging 'service society' (1995, pp. 65, 72) has seen a sharp contraction in the size of the industrial working class and the growth of service sector employment, particularly among women, and to a significant degree in the public sector fuelled by the expansion of welfare states. The 'feminization of the labour force' (Jenson *et al.*, 1988) has not produced gender equality at work, however, and according to Therborn may even have reinforced occupational segregation. Bakker's conclusion that 'Women's concentration in low-wage occupations is the primary factor contributing to the wage gap between women and men' (1988, p. 40) ties in with McDowell's suspicion that 'women are the new model workers of the post-Fordist regime' (1992, p. 182), for whom 'flexibility' means acceptance of part-time, temporary and poorly remunerated work. According to Scase, social polarization has its roots in 'the polarization of labour markets' where 'the fragmentation of the secondary sector according to age, gender and ethnic groupings' (1989, p. 8) spells disadvantage for young people, women and ethnic minorities. People with disabilities, older people and migrants are further groups vulnerable to 'poor work' (Brown and Scase, 1991) or exclusion from the labour market, while in contrast the position of employers, managers and professionals has strengthened.

The full significance of these changes remains uncertain. Esping-Andersen's analysis of 'post-industrial class structures' argues that 'advanced capitalist societies are regulated by institutions that hardly existed in the era of industrialization: the welfare state, collective bargaining systems, mass education and the modern corporation' (1993b, p. 8). The bases of class formation have been thrown into a state of flux by the decline of the Fordist industrial order, the growth of the service sector and the rise of institutions which 'were more or less unknown to Durkheim, Weber and Marx' (1993a, p. 2). In particular, Esping-Andersen claims that 'the welfare state has revolutionized labor market behavior' through the provision of welfare benefits and as 'the employer of up to a third of the entire labor force' (1993b, pp. 18, 20), recruited predominantly from among women. These developments have had the effect of challenging the model of the male breadwinner around which post-War welfare programmes were constructed, but no convergence exists among the post-industrial societies which are emerging. Esping-Andersen's thesis is that such societies are witnessing the transformation of Fordism's unskilled manual proletariat into either 'a large service proletariat' of relatively unskilled and poorly paid service workers or 'a large outsider surplus population' who become 'a welfare state client class' (1993b, pp. 28, 19) through being denied access to employment opportunities. Cross-national comparisons confirm divergence between countries, the extreme cases being the North American system of limited welfare provision and labour market intervention and Norway and Sweden's extensive 'welfare state and industrial relations institutions that are explicitly designed to influence the employment structure' (Esping-Andersen *et al.*, 1993, p. 35). From this point of view, the welfare state and governmental economic regulation are key institutional determinants of employment change and of the future of post-industrial societies more generally.

Esping-Andersen's proposition that de-industrialization need not lead to social polarization depends on governments having a higher degree of influence over economic and social affairs than theorists of disorganized capitalism regard as possible. In this debate, much hinges on precisely how polarization is defined and measured, as Esping-Andersen and his collaborators (1993) recognize in focusing their attention on trends in jobs rather than incomes, but essentially the same argument can be put about the process of 'de-commodification' which Esping-Andersen (1990) identifies as a crucial aspect of the development of modern welfare states. The restriction of the effects of market forces by the extension of citizenship rights has been taken further in Scandinavia than it has in Anglo-Saxon countries, and raises once again the classic sociological question of the relationship between the state and the economy. Albert's (1993) claim that there are now essentially two types of capitalism, distinguished by whether capitalism is disciplined by the state or displaces it, follows Esping-Andersen in seeing European and North American models as alternatives between which a political choice needs to be made. How we have reached this point in the relationship between modern capitalism and the state now needs to be examined.

4

Modern Capitalism and the State: the Contradictions of State Welfare and Corporatism

The contours of modern capitalist societies vary considerably. The preponderance of capitalist enterprises in the sphere of production may be the single most important influence on the shape of the social structures of these societies, but it is not determining in the strict sense. Chief among the forces which act to modify the effects of market relations on social life is the state. In all industrial capitalist societies during the twentieth century, the state has played a growing role in effecting a redistribution of resources among its citizens through the expansion of welfare provision, although recent decades have seen some reversal of this trend in response to the widely discussed 'crisis' of the welfare state. State bodies also play a role in modifying the impact of capitalism through market regulation, the legal and political frameworks within which market forces operate being subject to considerable variation. At its most extensive within capitalist societies, this regulation takes the form of corporatism, with state bodies engaging in far-reaching planning activities in the economic and social arenas. The broad move away from corporatist arrangements during the final quarter of the twentieth century has been interpreted by some commentators as a reflection of a more general reduction of the state's activities as the boundaries of public and private responsibilities are re-drawn. Others perceive fewer indications of Crook *et al.*'s 'shrinking state' (1992, Ch. 3) and point rather to evidence that the restructuring of state activities has fashioned more sophisticated

73

mechanisms of surveillance and social control. Such developments pose fundamental questions about the current relationship between state and society.

Among the starkest of the questions raised in current reassessments of the role of governments is that of whether we are moving beyond the welfare state (Pierson, 1991). It has become increasingly apparent that no necessary link exists between capitalism and the welfare state, and Esping-Andersen's (1990) identification of 'three worlds of welfare capitalism' is one particularly influential attempt from a comparative perspective to make sense of the diversity which characterizes the relationship. Esping-Andersen's critique of earlier analyses for their insensitivity to the diversity of forms which welfare-state regimes can take has in turn been followed by criticisms of Esping-Andersen's work for its neglect of the gendered nature of citizenship (Sainsbury, 1994), and the contested character of citizenship rights is central to current debates (Culpitt, 1992; Riley, 1992; Turner, 1986; Twine, 1994). The belief that the progressive extension of citizenship rights leads to the steady reduction of social inequalities and the growth of social cohesion has lost much of its power to convince in the face of mounting evidence of social polarization and fragmentation. Changes in the world of work are not the only cause of social polarization and fragmentation (Mingione, 1991, Ch. 7), but the connection is sufficiently powerful to generate debate about whether a movement towards a 'post-Fordist welfare state' (Burrows and Loader, 1994; Gould, 1993) can be discerned.

Arguments about the movement away from Fordism and organized capitalism which were discussed in the previous chapter also tie in closely with debates about the demise of corporatism. Lash and Urry's general conclusion is that 'as capitalism disorganizes, corporatism wanes' (1987, p. 280). The rise of corporatism can been understood as an attempt by governments to manage economic affairs and distributional conflicts within mature industrial capitalist societies, but from the 1970s onwards corporatist arrangements in countries such as Britain failed to prevent the re-emergence and subsequent persistence of mass unemployment, and this worked to undermine the political consensus on which (to greater or lesser degrees in different countries) corporatism rested. Full-blown corporatism was never the only future towards which capitalist societies were moving, not least because of their contrasting cultural and political traditions (Dore, 1987; Goldthorpe, 1984, 1987; Lash and Urry, 1987; Skocpol, 1985), but its decline has further emphasized 'the incredible diversity of state forms amongst those nations which make up the advanced capitalist world'

(McGrew, 1992b, p. 67). The thesis that corporatism represents the form of state best suited to modern capitalism is no more justified than the view which takes the social democratic welfare state as a model towards which others are gravitating. Both arguments are flawed by their reliance on the functionalist assumption that state and society necessarily fit together. Having said this, corporatist structures do become increasingly vulnerable in the context of the growing heterogeneity and fragmentation of societies (Mingione, 1991), in particular their class structures (Bauman, 1982; Roberts _et al._, 1977). The declining power of traditional working-class organizations such as trade unions has not made capitalist societies any easier to manage, and the inability of corporatist politics to accommodate and incorporate new social movements which are not class-based has further weakened corporatism's hold.

Some attempts have been made to account for these developments by highlighting the contradictions which are inherent to the modern bureaucratic welfare state and corporatism (Bauman, 1982; Keane, 1984; Offe, 1985). Contradictions do not in themselves explain social changes, however, as Kumar recognizes in his observation that 'societies can live with their "contradictions", if not comfortably at least tolerably, for long periods' (1988, p. 102). A similar conclusion can be drawn about the tensions which exist between the various legitimations developed to support the social and economic arrangements of advanced capitalism. Habermas' (1976) 'legitimation crisis' has not materialized, at least not in the way anticipated, and the implications of this deserve exploration. One possible line of argument stresses that the decline of corporatism has affected the power of organized capital and organized labour very differently. Indeed, it has been suggested that while relations between the state and the capitalist and working classes are clearly in a process of transition, 'the destruction of tripartite corporatism does not mean that instrumental connections between capital and the state do not persist. They may even be strengthened' (Byrne, 1989, p. 20). While the access to political power of the organized working class has been attenuated, various studies point to 'the persisting concentration of economic, organizational and political power within an "upper" class which comprises only a small minority of the population' (Crompton, 1993, pp. 191–2), a capitalist class for whom control over the state is a crucial resource (Bottomore and Brym, 1989; Scott, 1991). Legitimations of the expansion of state activities in terms of the pursuit of greater equality have become progressively harder to sustain as class and other inequalities have persisted and deepened, while pressure for change from below has weakened. At the same time as faith in the ability of state institutions to reduce inequality has declined, the part played by state agencies in securing social order and social control has become a more prominent feature of discourses on the role of the modern state.

The contradictions of the welfare state and citizenship

Marshall's writings on citizenship have long been an obligatory starting point for discussions of the connection between the welfare state and capitalism. Published originally in 1950 at a time when the foundations for the modern welfare state and corporatist consensus were being laid, Marshall's analysis focused on the equality embodied in citizenship and the inequality entailed by social class in order to explore the question of their compatibility. Marshall's argument that 'our society today assumes that the two are still compatible, so much so that citizenship has itself become, in certain respects, the architect of legitimate social inequality' (1992, p. 7) was necessarily somewhat tentative, since he was aware of the complex and shifting nature of their relationship. His belief that 'the modern drive towards social equality is... the latest phase of an evolution of citizenship which has been in continuous progress for some 250 years' (1992, p. 7) led to his celebrated distinction between the civil, political and social elements of citizenship which he employed to trace the development of the rights and duties of a citizen of a managed capitalist society. Over the course of three centuries, a transformation had been effected whereby the rights of the citizen had been extended from civil rights (such as freedom of speech) to political rights (for example the right to vote) and then in the twentieth century to social rights, which he described as 'the whole range from the right to a modicum of economic welfare and security to the right to share to the full in the social heritage and to live the life of a civilised being according to the standards prevailing in the society' (1992, p. 8). Marshall's optimism is very much in keeping with the spirit of the time, which saw governments putting into effect welfare measures designed to eradicate the five giant social evils of want, disease, ignorance, squalor and idleness identified by Beveridge (1942). It is important to bear in mind, however, that Marshall's anticipation of an on-going trend towards a more integrated society rested on the assumption that public policy would continue to maintain full employment and would prevent widening disparities in the distribution of income and wealth.

Marshall's overview of the development of the modern welfare state has been subjected to much critical reassessment over the half-century since it was written (Bottomore, 1992; Giddens, 1982, Ch. 12; Lister, 1990; Riley, 1992; Turner, 1986). Three particular issues stand out. The first of these relates to the question of whether it is possible to identify an evolutionary logic in the development of welfare states, and whether they are 'reversible'. Much of this debate has been conducted around the concept of 'de-commodification', which highlights the potential that exists for welfare provision to be removed from the sphere of market relationships. Commentators who are sceptical of this thesis are also doubtful of the suggestion that, once established, welfare states are irreversible. The related point of cross-national variations in welfare states is the second issue on which recent debates have focused. Analysis of how and why welfare-state regimes vary between different countries to the extent that they do has led to several attempts to classify welfare-state types, the idea of a generic welfare state having been discarded for the same reasons that saw the idea of a single type of capitalist society abandoned. The third issue around which discussions have revolved concerns the relative importance of different dimensions of inequality, of which social class is only one. Feminist critiques of welfare-state arrangements give a different perspective on claims made about the movement towards greater equality, and analyses of the positions of minority ethnic groups, people with disabilities and disadvantaged age groups (such as the elderly) also cast doubt on how far towards universal citizenship modern capitalist societies have progressed (Ginsburg, 1992).

The account of the progressive development of citizenship put forward by Marshall has an apparently close parallel in Offe's analysis of the expansion of the modern state. According to Offe, it is possible at an abstract level to identify an 'evolutionary sequence of the functions of legitimate authority' (1985, p. 4). In this schematic sequence, the state first needs to secure peace (both internally and externally) and then institutes 'passive' citizenship rights (such as *habeas corpus*), which serve to defend the individual from the state. This is in turn followed by the establishment of equality of rights, notably democratic entitlements to participate in political processes such as elections, a development which embodies the notion of 'active' citizenship. In the twentieth century, democratization has provided the impetus for the expansion of the state's role in managing and distributing resources in the pursuit of social justice, culminating in 'the Keynesian welfare state and its designs for social, economic and industrial policies' (1985, p. 5). Offe's approach is more than a simple re-statement of Marshall's argument, however, not least because of reasons relating to the very different theoretical bases from which the two writers proceed. The broadly Marxist starting point adopted by Offe is indicated by the way in which his analysis is couched in terms of processes of legitimation and of commodification and de-commodification, together with his focus on the contradictions of the welfare state. In addition, Offe has the benefit of hindsight in relation to the ways in which welfare-state programmes have fared in practice in the period since mid-century.

Offe's analysis carries many of the evolutionary overtones of Marshall's work. The thesis that 'the welfare state has become an irreversible achievement', 'an irreversible structure' (1984, p. 287, 152), rests in part on the argument that modern capitalist societies need welfare states in order to function. In Offe's view, 'In the absence of large-scale state-subsidized housing, public education and health services as well as extensive compulsory social security schemes, the working of an industrial economy would be simply inconceivable' (1984, p. 153). This situation can be understood as the outcome of long-term processes, treating the development of welfare institutions as a response to the shortcomings of unregulated labour markets which have been apparent from the outset. For Offe, '"welfare" institutions are a precondition of the commodification of labour power' (1984, p. 263), a point which is made in criticism of the view attributed to Marshall that welfare arrangements develop only during the later stages of capitalist societies; earlier periods of capitalism also needed some mechanisms for dealing with the inability of market arrangements to provide adequate support to workers and their families. A bigger role was previously played in the provision of welfare by 'private, religious and philanthropic organizations', but the supersession of many of these organizations by state bodies operating more rational, universal and legitimate welfare programmes cannot overcome the fact that the 'relationship between "welfare" and capitalism is contradictory' (1984, p. 263). Indeed, the development of the welfare state highlights the contradictions inherent in the relationship by politicizing the provision of welfare.

The evolution of welfare states can be understood as an attempt to resolve the social problems and conflicts which characterized liberal capitalism. Offe's view that 'The welfare state has served as the major peace formula of advanced capitalist democracies for the period following the Second World War' (1984, p. 147) embodies this line of thinking, although he argues that the development of the welfare state has in turn generated new contradictions which show the fragility of the class compromise involved. From the New Right, critics of the welfare state see welfare entitlements as a cost which reduces investment incentives for employers, while at the same time undermining the work ethic among members of the working class, resulting in a loss of economic dynamism and competitiveness. Conversely, from the political left, other critics of the welfare state see it as having not gone far enough in effecting a redistribution of resources in favour of the working class, and they criticize it for dealing only with the consequences and not the causes of market failures, for the repressive, moralistic and bureaucratic form in which it operates, and for the veneer of legitimacy which it gives to the *status quo*. The inherent tension between market pressures associated with the accumulation of capital and political pressures for social justice has not been resolved by the development of the welfare state. In Offe's view, 'capitalism cannot coexist *with*, neither can it exist *without*, the welfare state' (1984, p. 153, emphases in original). The contradiction between efficiency and legitimacy remains at the heart of welfare state capitalism, and the 'potential inconsistency of functions which have been assigned to the modern state' (1985, p. 5) reflects this incompatibility of objectives.

Another way of expressing this contradiction is as a struggle between processes of commodification and de-commodification. In the Marxist tradition of analysis, capitalism is understood to involve the re-working of social relationships around market principles, and the development of market relationships between employers and employees is the ultimate expression of such commodification. At the same time, various groups struggle to limit and reverse the expansion of the sphere in which market forces determine outcomes, and welfare-state interventions in the fields of housing, education, health and social security signal their achievements to the extent that provision of these aspects of welfare has been made an entitlement rather than a reflection of ability to pay. Offe recognizes that the range of forces behind the expansion of the welfare state has varied enormously from country to country, and includes 'Social democratic reformism, Christian socialism, enlightened conservative political and economic elites, and large industrial unions' (1984, p. 148). It is also important to note that the adoption of de-commodification as a common objective by these diverse groups occurred in particular historical contexts which were favourable to political consensus: 'The accomplishments which were won under conditions of war and in post-War periods were regularly maintained, and added to them were the innovations that could be introduced in periods of prosperity and growth' (1984, p. 148). Therborn (1995, p. 93) shows that the welfare states of Western Europe expanded significantly against the backdrop of the post-War economic boom, with key strategic decisions to expand social entitlements being taken around 1960. The economic and political climate has changed dramatically following the end of the long post-War boom, however, and the move away from commitment to state welfare programmes of de-commodification makes problematic Offe's case for seeing the welfare state as irreversible.

Korpi (1989) has noted that much of the debate about the relationship between the welfare state and capitalism has been conducted by reference to abstract theories and that surprisingly few hypotheses have been tested out against available data. He points out that the trade-off between economic efficiency and social equality is presumed rather than empirically established, and suggests some reasons why welfare-state programmes may be considered more economically efficient than free market alternatives. Active labour market policies are a case in point, since 'To provide those presently unemployed with jobs or occupational training would... not necessarily require a long-term increase in tax levels' (1989, p. 304). Indeed, public expenditure on unemployment and its effects is in many ways wasteful, and growth of such spending as a response to rising levels of unemployment can disguise the fact that in the period since the mid 1970s 'the foundation of the welfare state has been eroded' (1989, p. 298). Thus while 'social expenditures have continued to grow in most Western nations', social expenditure as a proportion of the gross domestic product 'is only a partial indicator of the condition of the welfare state, and an indicator which in addition can be a seriously misleading one' (1989, p. 297). The strain imposed on social expenditure budgets by the return of mass unemployment is a principal reason why 'the conclusion about the irreversibility of the welfare state is probably too hasty' (1989, p. 297). Growth in social expenditure does not necessarily signify the development or even the maintenance of social rights and social citizenship, and may even be compatible with their gradual erosion.

Korpi's reservations about the value for comparative analysis of social expenditure levels are shared by Esping-Andersen, who proposes an alternative approach in which countries are grouped according to how far they have taken the process of de-commodification. By Esping-Andersen's definition, a de-commodifying welfare state entails 'that citizens can freely, and without potential loss of job, income, or general welfare, opt out of work when they consider it necessary' (1990, p. 23). The volume of social expenditure varies considerably between welfare states, but this does not indicate with any accuracy the extent to which they have managed to free their citizens from dependence on the market. Esping-Andersen starts from the premise that 'Variations in the de-commodifying potential of social policies should be empirically identifiable across time and nations', and goes on to argue that this potential can not 'be captured by social expenditure levels, but requires analysis of the rules and standards that pertain to actual welfare programs' (1990, p. 47). His focus on eligibility for and entitlement to benefits, the levels at which benefits are set, and the range of benefits available allows him to construct 'de-commodification scores' for the eighteen countries in his study according to their provision of pensions, sickness and unemployment benefits. On the basis of these scores, Esping-Andersen identifies three clusters of welfare-state regimes which are qualitatively as well as quantitatively distinct.

The variability of welfare states in capitalist societies is reflected in Esping-Andersen's distinction between 'liberal' welfare-state regimes in which assistance is typically means-tested and minimal, conservative 'corporatist' regimes which have been generally less restrictive in granting social rights, and 'social-democratic' regimes in which there is a greater commitment to universalism in the provision of welfare. While some countries such as the UK have moved between clusters over time, Esping-Andersen highlights the importance of continuities by pointing out that countries such as the USA and Canada have been in the low de-commodification group of liberal welfare states since the 1930s, while France and Germany have consistently had conservative corporatist welfare states. The smaller states of Scandinavia have been the pioneers of the social-democratic regimes in which de-commodification has been taken furthest. In the light of these variations, Esping-Andersen concludes that 'The hope of finding one single powerful causal force must be abandoned', the diversity of welfare-state arrangements in contemporary capitalism reflecting a range of factors, notably 'the nature of class mobilization (especially the working class); class-political coalition structures; and the historical legacy of regime institutionalization' (1990, p. 29). Thus countries are more or less likely to develop a particular welfare-state regime according to factors such as the power of working-class organizations, political and cultural traditions (in which religious traditions figure prominently), and social policy traditions going back decades, if not centuries. The embeddedness of these traditions also leads Esping-Andersen to anticipate the emergence of 'three post-industrial employment trajectories' (1990, Ch. 8). While all contemporary capitalist societies are experiencing certain common trends, such as the decline of industrial jobs and the growth of women's employment, Sweden, Germany and the USA are not converging. As representatives of socialist, conservative and liberal regime types respectively, these three countries demonstrate the significance of 'welfare-state-regime effects' (1990, p. 222) on wider patterns of social development.

The typology of capitalist welfare states put forward by Esping-Andersen has been the subject of much debate, and several alternative perspectives have been suggested (Gould, 1993; Pierson, 1991; Sainsbury, 1994; Williams, 1994). Gould, for example, has questioned the validity of treating Japan as having a corporatist welfare-state regime in the light of his finding that Japanese welfare provisions are less comprehensive than those of Britain (which Esping-Andersen placed in the liberal welfare state cluster). His view that Sweden is undergoing a process of 'recommodification' involving 'use of unemployment as a policy device, the privatisation of public services and reductions in welfare benefits' (1993, p. 233) leads him to the further conclusion that, in the future, welfare state diversity will diminish as different capitalist welfare systems converge. Gould's case for anticipating a 'new convergence' towards 'welfare pluralism' places great importance on the power of economic forces to shape welfare arrangements, treating it as 'the consequence of the dynamics of post-Fordist capitalism' (1993, p. 10). This is a direct challenge to the view held by Esping-Andersen and others that political forces can be crucial to the way in which welfare states develop. Esping-Andersen's account of welfare-state diversity notes that 'welfare-state construction has depended on political coalition-building' (1990, p. 30), and his historical analysis emphasizes the role played by working-class organizations in this process.

Indeed, Esping-Andersen may have underestimated the potential for welfare-state diversity which exists by focusing too narrowly on the impact of working-class political action. De Swann's history of the development of social security provisions in various European countries and the USA sees the emergence of modern welfare arrangements as the outcome of a complex 'four-sided figuration' involving 'the small property owners, the industrial entrepreneurs, the industrial workers, and the regime in power' (1988, p. 167). The particular balance of power among these forces varied from country to country, and altered over time, not least because of the changing fortunes in the international sphere to which different countries were subject. Similar reservations about the relative neglect of classes other than workers in the literature on the development of welfare states led Baldwin to argue that 'an analysis is required of the role played by the middle classes, with their varying and internally divergent fortunes, prospects and therefore interests' (1990, p. 293). Mindful of the need to be 'cautious in drawing extravagant comparisons between places and times far removed', Baldwin nevertheless argues that in both Britain and Scandinavia pressure from below for the introduction of extensive welfare provisions would have been unsuccessful had the programmes not also been 'equally a victory for the middle classes' (1990, p. 292). For these and other countries considered by Baldwin, 'it is not until one examines the middle between the have-alls and the have-nothings that solidaristic social policy and its vacillating fortunes can be explained' (1990, p. 296). His point that the disadvantaged have changed over time from being primarily the industrial working class to now include also 'ethnic minorities, the handicapped, single mothers and other – from a traditional blue-collar point of view – marginal groups' (1990, p. 295) offers a further reason why the diversity of welfare-state types is likely to continue.

Esping-Andersen's concentration on the role of the working class has also been criticized for its neglect of non-class social divisions such as those relating to gender, race and disability (Ginsburg, 1992; Sainsbury, 1994; Williams, 1994). The measurement of decommodification employed by Esping-Andersen is intended to capture 'the degree of market independence for an average worker' (1990, p. 50), a notion which several commentators regard as problematic given the persistent inequalities which are known to exist in the labour market. Speaking of Britain, Williams notes that the '"universalism" of many of the post-War services and benefits was based on the norm of the white, British, heterosexual, able-bodied Fordist man, and often excluded women and black people upon whose paid and unpaid labour it depended' (1994, p. 61). Closer inspection of the assumptions about gender relations embodied in social policies reveals significant variation between welfare states which operate with a male breadwinner/housewife model and others which emphasize women's roles as mothers and carers and/or workers and citizens (Leira, 1992; Sainsbury, 1994). The general trend in recent decades may have been away from the male breadwinner model, but it has not been towards any one alternative, and much of the thinking about the purposes and objectives underlying policies remains muddled and contradictory. This is true not only of policies relating to gender divisions, but of welfare policies more broadly, developed as many of them have been in a piecemeal, incremental fashion. A good example of this point comes from the USA, where Skocpol's (1992, 1995) recent work on the history of social policy shows how early welfare programmes emerged in response to the needs of Civil War veterans and then focused on mothers, rather than on workers who occupied centre stage in European welfare states.

Detailed accounts of the history of welfare provision, such as those produced by Skocpol, show that, counter to anticipations of convergence, what is striking about capitalist welfare states is the persistence of diversity among them. Several other typologies besides Esping-Andersen's identification of three worlds of welfare capitalism have been developed (Alber, 1988; Cochrane and Clarke, 1993; Therborn, 1995; Turner, 1990), each highlighting different aspects of their complex structures and their 'contradictory impact on class, "race" and gender divisions' (Ginsburg, 1992, p. 28). The resultant range of typologies reflects differences in the countries included in the analyses, the historical time frames employed, and the theoretical perspectives adopted. Both Dominelli (1991) and Therborn (1995) note that much can be learned through broadening the countries considered, to include socialist and ex-socialist states (such as China and the countries of Eastern Europe), and a similar point applies to welfare policies in the 'third world' (Mayo, 1994), subjects which will be returned to in later chapters. In the analysis of advanced capitalist societies on which attention is focused for the moment, much hinges on how profound the current restructuring of welfare arrangements is taken to be. Turner is among several writers who regard globalization as having seriously limited the power of nation states to control what goes on within their own borders, leading him to the conclusion that Marshall's theory of citizenship 'is no longer relevant to a period of disorganized capitalism' (1990, p. 195). Turner also draws on Moore's (1967) writings (examined in Chapter 2) to highlight the peculiarities rather than the typicality of the British route to the modern world, and follows Giddens (1982) in criticizing Marshall for underplaying the unevenness and the contradictory character of the development of citizenship. These are valid criticisms, but it remains the case that Marshall's work has stood Weber's test of time far more effectively than have many more recent theories, of which theories of capitalism's relationship to corporatism are a prime example.

The rise and fall of corporatism

The idea that a connection exists between organized capitalism and corporatism (or, in some accounts, 'neo-corporatism') carries with it the suggestion that disorganized capitalism will be associated with the demise of corporatism, and this perspective is an important one in the analysis of the current restructuring of welfare capitalism. Corporatism is treated by Lash and Urry as 'One of the central characteristics of organized capitalism in at least some societies', and while it became a more prominent feature in Europe than it ever was in the USA, everywhere it is in retreat: 'Whatever corporatist arrangements that had developed began one after the other to collapse or enter into crisis in the 1970s (Britain, West Germany) and the 1980s (France, Sweden)' (1987, pp. 232–3). Central to this crisis has been the return of mass unemployment to societies in which a political commitment to full employment had been established, but wider economic, social and political changes have also contributed to the growing stresses to which corporatism has been subject. The shift away from corporatism has been unexpectedly rapid. It was not long ago that Newman could declare that 'Corporatism as a late capitalist form of accommodation seems firmly ensconced' (1981, p. 249), while for Mishra corporatism appeared 'well suited to harmonise within a national framework – a market economy, a liberal democracy, full employment and a system of social welfare aimed at ensuring a decent minimum standard of living for all' (1984, p. 120). Others have been more wary of such generalizations, mindful of the diversity of forms which corporatism can take and the important differences in national traditions which limit the effectiveness of corporatist institutions (Dore, 1987; Goldthorpe, 1984, 1987; Johnson, 1987), but the speed of the move away from corporatism and 'the expanding state' (McEachern, 1990) has by and large taken commentators by surprise.

The corporatist arrangements which developed in many countries during the phase of organized capitalism were made possible by the faith in the efficacy of government intervention and centralized direction which characterized that period. Keynesian policies of demand management were taken to be central to the maintenance of full employment, and the expansion of the public sector through the nationalization of key industries and the growth of the welfare state also reflected confidence in the ability of governments to secure outcomes superior to those produced by market forces. Governmental involvement in planning in a 'mixed economy' went hand-in-hand with 'corporatist democracy' and with what has been called 'a corporatist approach to welfare' (Johnson, 1987, p. 185), and some observers even saw the growth of such arrangements as evidence of a peaceful transition from capitalism to socialism (Stephens, 1979). More cautious interpretations of these developments perceived a modification of the economic, political and social structures of capitalist societies rather than their transcendence (Goldthorpe,

1984; Westergaard, 1995). Either way, it is clear that changing relations between classes (and in particular between the organized representatives of the capitalist and working classes) prompted rising levels of involvement in economic and social affairs by governments in an effort to regulate patterns of social development which appeared to threaten conflict.

The main attraction of corporatism lay in its emphasis on the advantages of co-operation over conflict in organized capitalist societies and the potential for collective benefits which accompanies co-operation between the various elements of the social body (Winkler, 1977). In particular, corporatist thinking stressed the need to incorporate working-class movements into national decision-making processes, reflecting their augmented prominence and power. Scase is typical of several authors whose account of the rise of corporatism stresses 'the growth of organized labour and its increasing economic and political influence', while treating corporatism's subsequent decline as 'directly associated with the weakened influence of labour movements' (1992, pp. 70–1). The increased involvement of working-class organizations such as trade unions in the political process promised a number of benefits to their members in terms of conditions of employment, standards of living and wider welfare provision, but corporatist efforts 'to bring together in an institutionalized way state agencies, bodies representing employers and others representing the interests of workers' (McCrone *et al.*, 1989, p. 44) enjoyed varying degrees of success in different countries. The best example of what 'welfare corporatism' can achieve is Sweden, where policies have been followed on the basis of 'a contract between the citizenry and the welfare state to ensure that welfare and employment needs are adequately catered for in exchange for industrial peace and reasonable freedom of manoeuvre for capital' (Ginsburg, 1992, p. 9). Extensive welfare provision and market regulation have significantly 'improved the material and cultural conditions of the Swedish working class' (Scase, 1992, p. 75). The modification of the impact of class inequalities on everyday life in areas such as health supports the claim that Sweden has managed to steer a path of social development between (and significantly different from) free market capitalism and state socialism.

If Sweden's experience of almost continuous social democratic government since the 1930s shows the potential of welfare corporatism to reduce social inequalities, it also illustrates the limits to which programmes of reform within capitalist societies are subject. As Scase notes, 'Sweden is characterized by a class structure common to that found within other capitalist countries. Patterns of economic reward and opportunity are not fundamentally unlike those of other countries' (1992, p. 74). Even with its 'degree of collaboration between organized labour, capital and the state which has not existed in other welfare states' (Ginsburg, 1992, p. 64), the inequality of power between employers and employees remains a potent influence on 'who gets what' (Westergaard, 1995). It is important to recognize that representation does not necessarily bring power, given what Offe has called 'the class bias of corporatism' (1985, p. 256). Corporatism in Sweden may have been favoured by the fact that it is a small and relatively socially homogeneous society with a centralized labour movement (Grant, 1985; Lash and Urry, 1987; Scase, 1992), but here as elsewhere 'labour has stayed effectively the junior partner in corporatist set-ups' (Westergaard, 1995, p. 53). Winkler's description of corporatism as 'an economic system of private ownership and state control' (1977, p. 48) points to the central tension with which it has to contend, and because this tension is unresolved, and perhaps irresolv-able, 'corporatism may be regarded as an unstable phase in the development of the capitalist mode of production' (Davis and Scase, 1985, p. 145). Even in Sweden, with its strong labour movement bolstered by very high levels of union density in the labour force, what stands out about the society is how resistant to change its class structure has been (Tåhlin, 1993).

If corporatist arrangements have tended to reproduce rather than eradicate the broad structure of class inequalities, they have also been subject to criticism for their failure to secure representation for all groups in capitalist societies. In countries such as Britain, corpor-atism's class compromise 'rested upon the organized power of the male, full-time, permanently employed working class' (Crompton, 1993, p. 105). Such individuals have become less and less typical of the workforce as a whole as the proportions of female, part-time, temporary, non-unionized, home-based and self-employed workers have risen, and the general trend towards labour market fragmenta-tion has made thinking in terms of an average, typical worker increas-ingly anachronistic. In addition, corporatism's institutionalization of co-operation between organized employers and employees raises the danger that 'Ethnic minorities, unskilled workers, the elderly, youth, and the disabled could... be marginalized or excluded from the incorpo-ration process and their needs ignored' (Mishra, 1990, p. 57). The possibility exists, of course, that corporatist arrangements may be developed to incorporate organizations which represent these and other groups which are not class-based, but the costs of being drawn into new commitments has on the whole made corporatist bodies wary of forging close links with new social movements (Scott, 1990). Attempts to maintain the legitimacy of the state by incorporating all citizens have become more problematic as capitalist societies have become more complex and heterogeneous, at the same time as the capacity of corporatist states to achieve their objectives has been circumscribed by the forces of globalization.

With hindsight it is possible to appreciate the extent to which corporatist theories exaggerated the state's power to direct economic and social affairs. Even in Sweden, state institutions continued 'to be fraught with contradictions because of the attempts to accommodate the irreconcilable needs of capital and labour' (Scase, 1989, p. 13), and the instability of the class compromise on which corporatism rested was illustrated by the growth of investment abroad rather than at home by Swedish corporations (Davis and Scase, 1985, p. 145). It is through such developments, Giddens suggests, that 'globalization attacks not only the economic basis of the welfare state but the commitment of its citizenry to the equation of wealth with national wealth' (1994, p. 140). The shift from organized capitalism has undermined the capacity of governments to exercise effective control over economic affairs within national borders. This has serious implications for the provision of welfare, since 'The welfare state was an integrated national state in which "corporatism" enhanced – but also presumed – national solidarity' (1994, p. 140). Pressure on the welfare state to extend the realm of social citizenship through the expansion of national welfare provisions sits uneasily alongside the trend towards greater international interconnectedness which limits the power of governments to follow independent economic strategies. Global population movements have also contributed to the need to re-think the welfare–corporatist model, highlighting its tendency to rely on a narrow, monolithic conception of citizenship which is at odds with the growing diversity and complexity of capitalist societies (De Swann, 1994a).

The parallels between the decline of corporatism and the shift from organized to disorganized capitalism are striking, and there are undoubtedly links between the two trends, not least of which is the broad move away from large-scale, bureaucratic organization. Yet it is important to bear in mind that the ideology of corporatism in modern capitalist societies stressed its flexibility and its pragmatic character (Winkler, 1977), distinguishing it from centralized, authoritarian regimes. Corporatist theorists recognized that 'in the long run, more may be achieved by co-operation than through direct state action which may, ultimately, start to undermine the state's most important possession – its ability to exercise legitimate power' (Grant, 1985, p. 8). The justification of corporatist arrangements in terms of their capacity to achieve outcomes preferable to those of unregulated, free market situations makes such arrangements vulnerable to criticism in times of poor economic performance by corporatist states. It is precisely this context in which the New Right's critique of corporatism and case for 'rolling back the frontiers of the state' have been most effective. There is, however, an irony in the fact that in the wake of Britain's corporatist structures being dismantled in the period after 1979, 'the power of the state has, in many respects, been *extended* rather than diminished' (McCrone *et al.*, 1989, pp. 57–8, emphasis in original). A similar point can be made about the move away from the standardized and paternalistic provision of welfare corporatism towards welfare pluralism, since withdrawal from direct public provision of services such as housing has 'not necessarily meant a saving to the public purse' (Pierson, 1991, p. 167). Neither does the growth of civil society automatically entail loss of overall control by the state, which often plays a key role in guaranteeing 'community' institutions (Offe, 1993). Established forms of state activity and their underlying legitimations have been challenged by the move away from corporatism, but the state remains a powerful force in contemporary capitalist societies.

From legitimation crisis to the shrinking state

Predictions of a progressive expansion of state activity in capitalist societies have been confounded by the general retreat from corporatism. Theses like Habermas', that state involvement in economic and social affairs tended to grow (albeit in a contradictory fashion) in response to various crises to which advanced capitalism is subject, including the need to develop new legitimations of social inequalities, require reassessment. The persistence of economic difficulties and of class and other inequalities despite corporatist economic management and the extension of the welfare state played an important part in discrediting some of the grander expectations of state bodies and illustrated what Offe (1993) calls 'limited state capacity'. Crook and his colleagues have detected, in recent developments, indications that 'both the functions of the state as a tool of social and economic regulation and reconstruction, and the scope of state power and responsibility, have started to diminish' (1992, p. 79). How far this process goes in different countries will depend on how far it is allowed to go by political forces.

While it true that globalization has reduced the leeway which states have to organize their economic and social affairs, it remains the case that 'nationalizations and privatizations are both also issues of power' (Therborn, 1995, p. 125). At its starkest, the political choice facing the electorates of contemporary capitalist societies is that between 'the Rhine model' of capitalism with its social market economy and the 'neo-American' model in which capitalism progressively displaces the state (Albei 1993), although Hutton suggests that this distinction needs to have a third type added to it, that of the 'East Asian capitalism' (1996, p. 268), pioneered in Japan. He also suggests that Britain may be considered to have developed its own distinct type of modern capitalism. Either way, the extent of state activity is a distinguishing feature not only of capitalism and state socialism, but also of different types of modern capitalism, and Albert would not contest Hutton's argument that institutional and cultural differences stand in the way of the convergence of capitalist societies 'towards an Anglo-American norm' (1996, p. 257).

In his influential account of the shift from liberal to organized capitalism, Habermas attaches great significance to the growth of the state. The 'supplementation and partial replacement of the market mechanism by state intervention' (1976, p. 33) relieves some of the social tensions generated by capitalism, but the growth of state involvement does not overcome the system's vulnerability to crises. Habermas identifies four possible crisis tendencies to which organized capitalism is subject. Economic, rationality, legitimacy and motivation crises relate respectively to crises of production and profitability, irrationalities in the system of decision-making and control, difficulties in the maintenance of mass loyalty, and the fragility of cultural values and moral commitments. Habermas recognizes that attempts by the state to deal with any one of these crises may have unintended consequences which exacerbate difficulties relating to another. For example, as Offe (1985) notes in his analysis of the contradictions of the welfare state, the extension of entitlement to welfare benefits may be seen to contribute to the legitimation of the social order by modifying market-based inequalities at the same time as it undermines incentives to work and the work ethic. Habermas suggests that the long-run tendency is for the state to be drawn further into previously private areas of life as traditional legitimations prove progressively less convincing, and pressure builds for arrangements which are more rational and democratic (Abercrombie *et al.*, 1984; Held and Krieger, 1983; Keane, 1984).

By highlighting the pressures which push governments towards expansion of their activities, Habermas' work offers a plausible account of the development of capitalist societies in the direction of corporatism, but its success in doing this only makes the reversal of the trend towards more extensive government more puzzling. Part of the explanation for this may be found in the loss of faith in reason and modernity which are central elements of Habermas' analysis. As Layder has noted, 'Habermas believes that there are unfulfilled potentials in modern society... he is very much of an optimist about modernity and its future as regards the elimination of the grosser forms of inequality and domination, the securing of an enhanced quality of life and the safeguarding of the natural environment' (1994, p. 187). The grounds for such optimism have been brought into question by the failure of governments to achieve expected solutions to economic and social problems. In the period of organized capitalism, it was increasingly the case that 'the legitimation of state power depended on the ability to spread the benefits of Fordism over all and to find ways to deliver adequate health care, housing and educational services on a massive scale but in a humane and caring way' (Harvey, 1989, p. 139). Discontent at the inadequate quantity and quality of welfare was aimed primarily at the state and its managers and experts, who found themselves squeezed between rising demands driven by social polarization and curtailment of available resources due to economic recession. Habermas may have been right to anticipate contradictory pressures arising out of economic and legitimation crises, but his theory did not predict the hostility of political responses to the state which have developed.

Crook *et al.*'s attempt to explain the move away from corporatism towards a more limited state identifies a number of different processes at work. Movement in the direction of 'the shrinking state' is most obvious in programmes of 'privatization, marketization and deregulation', which constitute corporatism's 'most radical challenge' (1992, p. 99). The sale of state-owned corporations, the commercialization of state-provided welfare and the withdrawal from the regulation of markets (including labour markets) reflect widespread loss of legitimacy by the corporatist state and its association with bureaucratic inefficiency and restrictive control by officials. Processes of decentralization of some state functions and globalization of others, together with the growth of the 'citizen politics' of new social movements, give further indications of the reduced role of national governments compared with what was undertaken at the height of corporatism. The reversal of state expansion is understandable in Crook *et al.*'s view because capitalist societies have become 'more pluralistic, fragmented and polycentric' (1992, p. 98) and in the process centralized regulation and uniform citizenship have become less appropriate and less workable. Changes in the class structures of capitalist societies have disrupted corporatist arrangements, as the organized working class has declined in strength. At the same time, some commentators have detected the emergence of an 'underclass' of people excluded from the labour market and the wider society, and dependent on welfare benefits. In some quarters, the situation of 'welfare dependency' is perceived as a product of the welfare state, a notion linked to the revival of the old distinction between 'deserving' and 'undeserving' groups of poor people (Dean and Taylor-Gooby, 1992; Morris, 1994). Amongst other things, welfare-state restructuring involves restricting state commitments while the boundaries of individual responsibility are extended.

By and large, the restructuring of the welfare state has not reduced aggregate levels of social expenditure in capitalist societies, but it has altered the balance of objectives. In a political context very different from the 'genuine sense of national community' (Morris, 1994, p. 46) which formed the backdrop to Marshall's writings on the extension of citizenship, progressive erosion of state welfare commitments has gone hand-in-hand with a renewed emphasis on the responsibility of the state for social control. In Cohen's view, 'the true meaning of the minimum state is the minimum *welfare* state' (1985, p. 133, emphasis in original), and he points out that this is quite consistent with increased intervention in the field of law and order. Thus economic crises have 'resulted less in an overall cut in social expenditure... than a redistribution from the soft to the hard edge of the system' (1985, p. 133), and while some privatization measures have diminished the direct role of the state, other developments have continued to expand the public sphere at the expense of the private. The rise of new forms of surveillance might be given as an example here, although, as Lyon points out in his discussion of Marshall's analysis of citizenship, 'modern surveillance is simultaneously a means of social control *and* of guaranteeing rights of social participation' (1994, p. 33, emphasis in original). As a result, it is possible to look at the co-ordination of people's activities by bureaucratic state organizations from two very different perspectives.

The role of the state in capitalist societies has undergone dramatic change over time and also varies significantly between countries. Albert's (1993) identification of 'the three ages of capitalism' distinguishes between the phase of 'capitalism against the state' which dates from 1791, 'capitalism disciplined by the state' dating from 1891, and 'capitalism instead of the state', a phase dating from around 1991. These three phases correspond roughly to the distinction between liberal, organized and disorganized capitalism, but Albert's purpose is not to suggest an inexorable process leading to the state's displacement, since his case is that a choice exists between the neo-American model of capitalism, in which social and economic relations are shaped principally by free markets and individualism, and the Rhine model of capitalism, in which the impact of market forces is modified by collective institutions. Others too have noted the link between the degree of social polarization and the extent of government intervention in markets, and there is extensive evidence to support Esping-Andersen's argument that 'contemporary social stratification is heavily shaped by institutions, the welfare state in particular' (1993a, p. 1). Cross-national variations in the proportions of national workforces employed by the state provide an excellent illustration of this point (Therborn, 1995).

Many of the themes of this chapter also apply to the changing role of the state in state socialist and former state socialist societies. Programmes of welfare provision far more ambitious than anything envisaged by Beveridge and Marshall have had to contend with a number of the same contradictions to which capitalist welfare states have been subject. Economic management in state socialist societies was in many ways corporatism writ large (Crook *et al.*, 1992; Ray, 1993) and the process of *perestroika* has many characteristics in common with the shift from Fordism to post-Fordism in contemporary capitalism. In both cases, the state's multi-faceted involvement in economic restructuring and social reorganization has suggested that it may be more fruitful to think of the state as 'disunited' (Gray, 1989) than to regard it as a monolithic entity. There is, for example, no straightforward link between the state's role in de-militarization and its other functions (Shaw, 1991). The observation that political and economic élites have demonstrated a remarkable hold on state power despite radical upheavals is, as with other aspects of the comparison between capitalist and state socialist societies, subject to the qualification that important national variations between states must be borne in mind. Similarities in patterns of change undergone by capitalist and state socialist societies are in many ways to be expected, given the fact that they are two types of industrial society, and both subject to the increasing pervasiveness of globalization processes. However, it would be wrong to suggest that political revolutions in the former Soviet Union and elsewhere in the state socialist world have been sufficient to allow a straightforward transition from socialism to capitalism. The very different histories of these countries and the legacies of their distinct patterns of industrialization continue to set them apart in the eyes of comparative sociologists.

5

The Rise and Transcendence of State Socialism: Stalinism, De-Stalinization and Beyond

From the point of view of the theorists of mid-century who divided the countries of the globe into three parts, several characteristics set state socialist societies apart as a distinct 'second world'. In contrast to industrial capitalism's primarily privately owned system of production, state socialism involved collective ownership and centralized planning and control. The separation of economic and political spheres of capitalist democracies is contrasted with the fusion of economics and politics in the state socialist system, in which all spheres of life are potentially open to being politicized and subordinated to the goals laid down in state socialist ideology as interpreted by the political leadership (Davis and Scase, 1985). In consequence, individuals and the institutions of civil society have little independence in what have been called (controversially, as Giddens [1985] and Rupnik [1988] note) 'totalitarian states'. The alternative route to industrial society and the modern world offered by state socialism was not a polar opposite of the capitalist democracies, however, and it took some of the features of capitalist industrialization to the extreme. The scale of state socialist industrial plants often dwarfed that of their capitalist counterparts for example, the prime illustration of this being the giant steel-making works at Magnitogorsk where production grew to parallel the output of entire countries such as Britain (Kotkin, 1992). In other areas, too, state socialism exhibited a fixation on a '"steel-per-head" philosophy' (Bauman, 1992, p. 171) as these societies went further in putting into practice modernity's faith in rationality in the pursuit of technological solutions to economic and social problems. In Bauman's view, 'communism was thoroughly modern in its passionate conviction that a good society can only be a carefully designed, rationally managed and thoroughly industrialized society... Communism was modernity in its most determined mood and most decisive posture; modernity streamlined' (1992, pp. 166–7). As a result, the crises of economic and political restructuring facing state socialist societies have been of considerably greater magnitude than those arising in industrial capitalist societies.

It was noted in Chapter 2 that the 'revolutions from below' which ushered in communist rule in the Soviet Union and elsewhere led to a programme of forced industrialization from above. Industrialization was a key element in Stalin's programme of transforming the Soviet Union from an economically backward, primarily agrarian society (where peasants made up over 80 per cent of the population) into a modern industrial one which had 'caught up' with the capitalist West. Prior to the 1917 revolutions, Russia had undergone a degree of 'state-guided industrialization' (Skocpol, 1979, p. 90), but this paled in comparison to what followed. The attainment of annual rates of growth of industrial output of 15 per cent or more during Stalin's first Five Year Plan was astonishing by any standards, and it was achieved within an economic and political framework very different from that in which earlier industrializers had worked. As Davis and Scase observe, 'The ambitious policies of the first Five Year Plan (1928–33) could only be achieved by coercion' (1985, p. 79), and the coercive character of the Stalinist regime was expressed most brutally in the forced collectivization of agriculture, which had millions of victims (Nove, 1989). Stalinism did not operate solely through repressive measures, however, since the concentration of economic and political power through nationalization of property, centralized planning and consolidated control over the various arms of the state was sustained in part by claims to legitimation as an alternative social order to Western capitalism.

Some historians take the view that Stalinism's dirigiste methods were counterproductive (Moore, 1967), but whether or not this is the case, it has become increasingly clear with the passage of time that the Stalinist system was unsustainable. Having 'developed into a full-fledged dictatorship that for more than a decade waged against society a social, economic, cultural and political revolution from above' (Bialer, 1983, p. 418), a number of factors combined to exacerbate the contradictions of Stalinism and generate pressure for de-Stalinization. The global situation changed dramatically following the Second World War, as what had previously been 'socialism in one country' spread to several states in Eastern Europe, China and other parts of the world.

International pressures also took the form of military competition with advanced capitalist nations, and the drain of resources into state socialism's military–industrial complex heightened the economic tensions which characterized Stalinist regimes. Attempts to de-Stalinize state socialist systems have taken various forms and proceeded at different paces in different countries, but in all of them conflicts between economic and political forces have made programmes of dismantling highly centralized societies a complex and delicate process. From the mid-1970s onwards the view gained ground that the inherited model of development had 'in a sense achieved its object and outlived its usefulness' (Kilminster, 1992, p. 248). The political revolutions which brought the end of communist rule in Eastern European satellite states in 1989 and the Soviet Union in 1991 signalled the failure of attempts there to reform state socialism from within, although China has so far managed to combine economic reform with continued political control by the Communist Party (G. White, 1993).

Societies which have followed and subsequently abandoned the alternative route to the modern world offered by state socialism present acute difficulties for comparative sociologists. Recourse to the category 'post-communist societies' is justifiable in the light of the manifold legacies from the period of state socialism which continue to shape social and economic life, but it leaves unresolved the question of how far these societies have become or are moving towards something else. Sklair (1995) employs the term 'the New Second World' on the grounds that political changes in terms of who controls the state have not necessarily altered the position occupied by these societies in the global system. Internal economic realities also change at a pace different from that of political institutions, and authors such as Clarke *et al.* (1993) have rightly pointed out the error of equating privatization with the re-establishment of capitalism. Similarly, the legacy of Stalinist suffocation of civil society means that post-revolutionary developments are far more complex than a simple transition to pluralist democracy akin to that found in Western capitalist societies (Lewis, 1993; Ray, 1993). Neither can it be assumed that the social movements which played a key role in challenging state socialism will necessarily play an equivalent role in influencing the direction taken by the new societies emerging to replace it. Ferge's (1993) provisional assessment of winners and losers after the collapse of state socialism seems to confirm Bauman's prediction that 'the social forces which led to the downfall of the communist power... are not those that will eventually benefit from the construction of the new system' (1992,

p. 157). Social development in the wake of state socialism is very much movement into uncharted territory.

Stalinism and the legacies of forced industrialization

The system of state socialism which was established in the Soviet Union after 1917, and which was later copied more or less closely in other countries in Eastern Europe and elsewhere, reached its apogee shortly before the death of Stalin in 1953 (Fejtö, 1974). The achievements of the Stalinist system in the Soviet Union by this time were considerable. The transformation of an agrarian into an industrial society, a process which in countries like Britain had proceeded comparatively gradually, was in the Soviet Union compressed into a brief historical period. The difficulties of this process had been compounded by the massive losses sustained during the Second World War and the drain on resources of post-War reconstruction. Under Stalin's leadership, the Soviet Union had become a world power in economic and military terms, and the education and material welfare of its population had increased dramatically as industrialization and urbanization proceeded. Set against this, the costs of these achievements were considerable too, primarily in terms of the millions of victims of Stalinism's ruthless employment of political repression and terror, but also in terms of the irrationalities and wastefulness of the overcentralized economic system (Kilminster, 1992; Nove, 1989). In coming to terms with Stalinism, Hall suggests, 'it must always be remembered that despite all the barbarities involved, and the creation of long-lasting economic inefficiencies, Stalinist centralisation did *succeed* in turning the Soviet Union into a member of the world polity capable of contending as a superpower with America' (1986, p. 196, emphasis in original). The social and economic development of state socialist societies by no means came to a halt with the death of Stalin, but from this point onwards the overarching system of centralized control became subject to increasingly urgent reassessment and pressure for reform, thus beginning the long process of liberalization and de-Stalinization.

A key support of the Stalinist system was the personality cult built up around the leader, and this made it inevitable that a crisis of succession would follow his death. It is significant that Khrushchev, the Soviet leader who eventually emerged to succeed Stalin, denounced many of the excesses of his predecessor's period in terms of the cult of personality which Stalin had orchestrated in order to sustain his preeminent position. This account, as Nove points out, 'was not a very convincing picture' (1989, p. 137) in that it presented explanations in terms of the evil of an individual rather than the economic, political and social circumstances which threw him forward. Several writers have noted the continuities between the regime set up by Lenin and the Bolsheviks after 1917 and the Stalinist system, in terms of both the overriding importance attached to the goal of industrialization and the consideration of the means employed to attain this goal (Cohen, 1986; Corrigan *et al.*, 1978; Nove, 1989; Wood, 1990). In short, 'The ugly side of the Stalinist era had institutional roots' (Moore, 1967, p. 507). Khrushchev's own experience of the difficulties of relaxing the system's grip on society also indicated that Stalin's presence was not essential for the operation of a Stalinist system, and he captured a crucial dilemma of de-Stalinization when he talked of being 'afraid the thaw might unleash a flood, which we wouldn't be able to control and which could drown us' (quoted in Cohen, 1986, p. 111). Stalin's successors in the Soviet Union and the leaders of the state socialist societies established after the Second World War were only too aware that the system embodied a brutal logic as well as involving features which were uniquely the products of Stalin's personality.

The Stalinist system contained many self-reproducing elements, not least of which was the concentration of power and privilege in the hands of élite groups of party officials, bureaucrats and technical experts, and this 'party-state bureaucracy' (Hamilton and Hirszowicz, 1993, p. 231) ensured that Stalinism survived the death of its founder. Debates about the nature of Stalinism have included discussions of whether such groups constitute a new ruling class running a form of state capitalism (Callinicos, 1991; Davis and Scase, 1985; Lane, 1985b), but while some similarities exist between capitalist and state socialist patterns of industrialization and development, it is ultimately the differences which stand out as more important. The substitution of competitive market forces by centralized state planning and the absence of capitalist firms employing wage labour organized into independent trade unions mean that command economies have a different rationality and operate according to a logic different from those of capitalist economies (Clarke *et al.*, 1993). In the political sphere, too, Stalinism operated with distinct arrangements between party and state which set the 'people's democracies' apart from their Western counterparts, as did the ideology of state socialism on which these arrangements were founded and the expression of this ideology in socialist rituals (Davis and Scase, 1985; Lane, 1981; Lane, 1985a). Of course, similarities of outcome can be identified in terms of the persistence of social stratification and the subordination of social development to the requirements of the accumulation process, but two important principles of comparative sociology are that (as De Swann has expressed it in another context) 'similarity does not mean that like effects were begotten by like causes, or that differences are unimportant' (1988, p. 153). In any event, it is possible to exaggerate the degree to which state socialist societies were converging with capitalist ones (Goldthorpe, 1971; Rakovski, 1983), due in no small part to the legacies of their very different past.

One of the most powerful legacies of forced industrialization was that the élites at the top of state socialist societies were locked into the pursuit of ever-greater material welfare, which meant that much pressure for change was generated from within the system. Ideological emphasis on the efficiency of command economies appeared to be justified by the success of forced industrialization, but the social transformation which this brought meant that new problems had to be faced. In the period following Stalin's death, three specific economic problems needed to be addressed: 'the lagging agriculture, the underdeveloped consumer industries, and the lack of flexibility inherent in the Stalinist planning model' (Hettne, 1995, p. 233). Agricultural productivity had not seen the same dramatic increases as industrial production, reflecting the way in which, to quote Worsley, 'the peasants had been sacrificed by Stalin to build industry' (1984, p. 70), but despite subsequent reforms, agriculture continued to be 'a major source of weakness in the Soviet economy' (Lane, 1990, p. 45). Here, as elsewhere in the economies of state socialist societies in the period after 1953, various schemes of decentralization and the controlled introduction of market mechanisms such as private ownership and price incentives brought a degree of greater flexibility but could not reverse the long-term fall in economic growth rates. Even though standards of living rose, output fell short of planned targets, and the failure to fulfil 'the aspirations engendered by an overoptimistic leadership... led to popular disgruntlement' (Lane, 1989, p. 174). Furthermore, the sense that 'the classic communist strategies, far from overtaking the prosperity of the capitalist centre, were unlikely to provide even for the necessities of their own citizens' (Sklair, 1995, p. 248) was reinforced by the growing impact of global economic influences on state socialist societies from the 1970s onwards.

The fusion of economic and political spheres in state socialism made the state open to potentially limitless criticism. In such highly centralized societies, 'Aiming at the regulation of all aspects of social and economic activity, the state assumes willy-nilly explicit responsibility for each and every failing and suffering. All grievances are authoritatively interpreted as malfunctionings of the state and automatically politicized' (Bauman, 1992, p. 159). Strategies of reform were adopted by the leaderships of several state socialist societies, most notably in Hungary and Czechoslovakia, prompted in part by the 'hope that a more affluent country would allow the party to retain legitimacy by means of growth rather than through ideological indoctrination' (Hall, 1986, p. 199). Military intervention by the Soviet Union prevented some of these reform programmes from being pursued, and it was not until the mid-1980s that this threat was lifted. By this time, the Soviet Union's leadership under Gorbachev had also adopted a programme of reform involving '*uskorenie*' (acceleration), '*perestroika*' (restructuring), and '*glasnost*' (openness), but while the origins of the state socialist system lay in imposition from above, it became increasingly apparent that 'the Soviet system could not be reformed from above' (Clarke *et al.*, 1993, p. 47). It was one thing for the leadership to recognize the need for reform of a system suffering from structural problems which had produced a period of economic stagnation and ossification (Kennedy, 1993; Littlejohn, 1984), and growing social problems such as rapidly rising mortality rates (Doyal and Gough, 1991; Kennedy, 1993), but attempts to change this system whilst maintaining political control merely exposed what Callinicos (1991) has termed 'the contradictions of authoritarian reform'. The reforms of the Gorbachev period did not represent a fundamental break with the past; rather they were the culmination of the long and uneven process of de-Stalinization sponsored by party leaders which had been underway for more than three decades (Lane, 1990).

Arguably, the most profound legacy of forced industrialization lay in the overestimation of what centralized planning and control could achieve once the transition to industrial society had been effected. In the changed economic, social and political context, direction from above was increasingly problematic. As Callinicos has expressed it, 'The USSR's authoritarian modernization had run up against its limits. The organizational forms which had made possible rapid industrialization after 1928 now inhibited further development... industrialization had created an urbanized and educated population no longer willing to put up with the inefficiencies and inequities of the Stalinist system' (1991, p. 48). Against this background, efforts to liberalize economic arrangements and democratize the political system could appear to be attempting too little, too late, and prompted by a concern to rein in forces which were beyond state control. In Clarke *et al.*'s view, 'The programme of the "transition to a market economy" was not so much a coherent programme of reform from above, as a recognition that the system was falling apart in response to pressures from below. In this sense the rhetoric of transition constantly lagged behind the reality of disintegration' (1993, pp. 47–8). In the sphere of production, the functioning of the bureaucratic command economy had to be complemented by the operation of unofficial arrangements and an extensive 'second economy' of varying degrees of illegality (Lane, 1985b; Spybey, 1992). A gap between theory and practice was also apparent in the extent to which those in command of the state were able to exercise centralized political control. Kotkin (1992) argues that the Soviet political system was far-reaching but clumsy, and required the co-operation of key groups in the new social structure which Stalinist industrialization had created. Groups such as engineers, scientists and other members of the 'intelligentsia' were less susceptible than peasants had been to manipulation by coercion, and they could achieve for themselves a considerable degree of autonomy (Lane, 1989). Burawoy (1985) suggests that a long-term tendency existed also for shop-floor workers in state socialist societies to gain greater autonomy as extensive development gave way to intensive development, a change which brought with it labour shortages and the need for factory managers to secure the co-operation of their workforces.

The limitations of the power of the state were even more apparent in the Eastern European countries which had become state socialist after 1945. Here, the fact that state socialism was widely resented for having been imposed placed limits on how closely the Stalinist model had been followed in different countries, and factors specific to particular nations also contributed to the diversity of Eastern European state socialist regimes (Davis and Scase, 1985, Ch. 6). Poland, for example, never collectivized its agriculture, and more generally, Hall has observed, its 'Communist party *did* rather little. It served as a capstone to a society that had changed little since the nineteenth century' (1986, p. 202, emphasis in original). The strength of the independent trade union Solidarity, the imposition of martial law in 1981 and the serious international indebtedness of Poland reflected the general weakness of the state there (Lewis, 1983). In contrast, economic reform was pioneered in Hungary, where Soviet-type arrangements 'proved increasingly unable to function efficiently' and the growing power of the informal second economy in agriculture and other sectors constituted a 'silent revolution from below' (Szelenyi, 1988, pp. 213–4; see also Burawoy, 1985). Hungary's path brought it a favourably prosperous position in Eastern Europe, but with this came new challenges to the state in terms of demands for wider participation in decision-making (Ferge, 1979, 1989). The experiences of Poland and Hungary illustrate that whether or not the economic strategies adopted were successful in bringing sustained growth in living standards, the relationship between state and people in Soviet-type societies was an uneasy one.

In spite of widespread recognition of crisis tendencies in state socialism, the revolutions of 1989–91 which ended communist rule in Eastern Europe came to many observers as a surprise. The identification of state socialism's contradictions (Callinicos, 1991; Clarke *et al.*, 1993; Kennedy, 1989; Lane, 1990) allowed predictions to be made about the unsustainability of the system in the long term, but the speed of the collapse when it came was nevertheless bewildering, not least because periods of reform and liberalization prior to the 1980s had all been contained. Explanations of the end of state socialism in Eastern Europe remain somewhat tentative, and it is Therborn's view that 'What brought down Eastern European Communism will have to await more historians' time before an answer is clear' (1995, p. 294). Part of this answer is likely to be that the legitimacy of these regimes was subject to erosion (Lewis, 1983; Ray, 1993) as they failed to live up to their promise in terms of delivering not only greater material welfare, but also freedoms. Thus, as Lewis observes, 'Those Europeans who had lived through most of the post-World War II period under communist rule had had enough of centrally-organized political activity, the dominance of the party over social life and the ubiquity of the leadership's propaganda and political slogans' (1992, p. 43). By the end of the 1980s, according to Scase, 'The repressive, totalitarian nature of these countries and their socio-economic structures produced forms of society in which the majority of citizens concluded that the costs greatly outweighed the benefits' (1992, p. 83). In such a climate of disillusionment, attempts to introduce reform from above revealed the limits of the inherited system of centralized state power as the societies over which state socialist élites presided began to fragment and disintegrate.

The disintegration of state socialist societies

The long and complicated history of de-Stalinization in the Soviet Union and the rest of Eastern Europe is a testimony to both the strength and the weakness of the state in state socialist societies. Accounts of precisely why the system ultimately collapsed differ in terms of the varying emphases which they give to particular factors, but all attach great importance to the state's role. There are parallels between state socialist regimes and what Hall has called 'capstone states', which have 'strong blocking but weak enabling powers' and are 'incapable of generating a large sum of social energy' (1986, p. 35). The speed and scale of forced industrialization required a marked concentration of power in the hands of the Stalinist system's élite, and the extensiveness of the bureaucratic political and economic structures which operated the centralized command structure created a sizeable stratum whose material interests and loyalties lay with this system. Opposition to change also existed among those who appreciated the benefits of extensive state provision and regulation, and Bauman suggests that support for the operation of the 'patronage state' (1992, p. 163) came not only from those who were most privileged in the system but also from others who were conscious that planning reduced many of the risks to which they would otherwise be subject. Routine white-collar workers may be understood as having 'constituted the backbone of the bureaucratic regimes' of state socialist societies, being 'malleable, obedient and utterly dependent on their pay-masters' (Hamilton and Hirszowicz, 1993, p. 231) and supportive of an expanded role for the state, even though they were relatively poorly remunerated. Pakulski argues that in Poland 'The lower ranks of the apparata' were characterized by compliance which 'rested on pragmatic grounds – institutional involvement, expectations of rewards, fear of sanctions and fatalistic helplessness' (1990, p. 58), and that in this respect they were typical of much of the broader public.

Ranged against these conservative forces there emerged a number of groups within state socialist societies pushing for reform. Intellectuals, students, workers and peasants have all at various times figured as opponents of the rigidities of state socialism, but each group on its own was unable to generate sufficient force to bring about fundamental change. Thus, for example, intellectuals were too isolated from the mass of the population and too prone to incorporation into the bureaucratic system to pose a sustained threat to the stability of state socialist regimes (Konrad and Szelenyi, 1979). Students did eventually play 'a major part in the tender revolution' (Sayer, 1991, p. ix) of countries like Czechoslovakia, but they have been isolated and suppressed in other places and at other times. By contrast, peasants were far more numerous and have been surprisingly effective in resisting state-sponsored programmes of proletarianization, but their maintenance of a degree of autonomy did not undermine the state socialist system, and may even have contributed to its more efficient operation (Szelenyi, 1988). The hierarchical structure of state socialism militated against co-operation between the various groups seeking change, and it was only when elements of the political leadership also acknowledged the need for reform were the supporting pillars of the Stalinist system irretrievably modified, unintentionally opening up the possibility of a far more thoroughgoing change than had been anticipated. Internal pressures for reform played a part in bringing about this shift among the leadership, but the distinguishing feature of the Gorbachev era of 1985–91 was the threat posed to state socialism by internal opposition in combination with dynamic global forces which undermined the system's reproduction.

Kennedy has identified three interrelated dimensions of the growing difficulties which were to prove terminal for the state socialist system in the USSR. In his account, 'A crisis in the *political legitimacy* of the Soviet system interacted with a crisis in *economic production and social provision*, and both were exacerbated by a crisis in *ethnic and cultural relationships*. The result was an unsurmountable mix of challenges' (1993, pp. 230–1, emphases in original). In the economic sphere, the need for reform was most obvious in the agricultural sector, which had from the outset thwarted the ambitions of socialist planners. According to Kennedy, agriculture was 'the most critical area of weakness in the economy during the entire history of the Soviet Union' (1989, p. 633), and similar statements could be made about other state socialist societies. Stalinist collectivization of agriculture did not achieve the increases in output expected by planners, and the industrialization of agricultural production brought poor returns. The reorganization of production on larger and larger scales (what Shanin refers to as 'gigantomania') went hand-in-hand with the idea that problems were open to technological solutions in the shape of 'more chemicals, more energy, more iron and steel' (Shanin, 1990, p. 190). In reality, small-scale, family-based production was the source of a quarter of the Soviet Union's crop output from only 4 per cent of the country's arable land (Kennedy, 1989), and in other parts of Eastern Europe, such as Hungary, the non-collectivized sector was even more important (Szelenyi, 1988). Szelenyi's account of the growth of 'highly specialized, primarily market-oriented, family agricultural enterprises' (1988, pp. 12–13) in the context of economic liberalization highlights the dilemma of socialist planners. Mindful of 'how difficult it is to impose social change from above' (1988, p. 22), planners needed to tap the initiative and resourcefulness of the rural population but were equally aware that the relaxation of central controls promised to bring with it not only increased production but also widening inequalities in the countryside as a resurgent class of entrepreneurs developed. Rural Hungary's 'silent revolution from below' did not usher in a particularly rational alternative to collective production, since the new entrepreneurs frequently responded to the uncertainties of their situation by attempting 'to rip off the system – and their customers – as often and as quickly as possible' (1988, p. 213), behaviour which Szelenyi notes bears some resemblance to the operation of the informal economy in capitalist societies.

The position of rural populations in state socialist societies bears out the importance of Kennedy's linkage between crises of political legitimacy and economic production and social provision, since the people of the countryside were conscious of being the poor relations of urban dwellers. Collective farm workers were the lowest paid in the Soviet system, while rural welfare services were generally less good than those provided in urban areas. This situation had its origin in the period of forced industrialization, when 'Stalin's desire to industrialise rapidly stratified the working class through a division of labour which turned industrial workers into a "labour aristocracy" while relegating other workers to an inferior status' (Dominelli, 1991, p. 98). Programmes to overhaul collective agricultural production were resisted by the bureaucrats and managers who ran the system, and they were further impeded by fear that 'increases in the prices paid for agricultural produce would imply significant rises in the peasantry's share of national income – to the detriment of the resentful urban population' (Kennedy, 1989, p. 635). The preferential treatment of urban industrial workers was an important element in securing their loyalty to the system, and the essentially pragmatic nature of their attachment to the system posed a threat to its legitimacy when it failed to meet their aspirations (Lane, 1985b). Legitimation based on 'an instrumental exchange of loyalty for social security' (Ray, 1993, p. 114) was vulnerable when the systems of production of consumer goods and welfare services failed to deliver expected improvements in standards of living, and planning came to be widely associated with inefficiency and shortages (Lane, 1990).

Developments in the industrial sector paralleled those in agriculture in several ways. In both cases, decentralization of the command economy promised to reduce some of the grosser inefficiencies, but fundamental problems of control over the production process remained. The policy of maintaining full employment produced labour shortages which, along with planning constraints, limited the extent to which managers could exercise control over industrial production.

Workers in factories such as the Hungarian steel mill studied by Burawoy and Lukács (1989) enjoyed a surprising degree of autonomy in the production process and 'a limited form of workers' control' (Burawoy, 1988), but economic liberalization did not do away with the dilemmas of the 'shortage economy'. Burawoy's general conclusion is that the problem of shortages in state socialist economies led to 'the promotion of domestic production, petty commodity production and small private enterprises operating through *markets*' (1985, p. 162, emphasis in original). The 'socialist entrepreneurs' described by Szelenyi (1988) were by no means restricted to agricultural production, and the informal or 'parallel' economy of state socialist societies may have been responsible for generating about a fifth of the total output (Pahl, 1989). The expansion of this informal economy brought with it difficulties. Ray has noted how 'the more the socialist economy relied on an informal and semi-legal sector to satisfy consumer demand, the less legitimacy the system had, since moonlighting and illegalities became institutionalized' (1993, p. 117). In addition, the growth of informal economic activity tended to generate a widening gap 'between work-rich, multiple-earning individuals and households and those with low and limited sources of income' (Pahl, 1989, p. 103), a process of social polarization comparable to that found in modern capitalist societies.

The development of the informal economy deepened divisions which already existed between workers, the Stalinist system having been a rigidly hierarchical one (even if the range of inequalities was narrower than that in capitalist societies). Gender divisions were prominent among these lines of cleavage (Charles, 1993). Women's high levels of participation in paid work did not prevent them from being 'the low income earners in Soviet society' (Dominelli, 1991, p. 91), nor from being subordinate to male supervisors in the workplace (Burawoy, 1988). The concentration of poverty among women indicates that gender was 'a significant feature of Soviet inegalitarianism' (Dominelli, 1991, p. 104), an unsurprising finding when it is recognized that in the Soviet Union and elsewhere in Eastern Europe 'the provision and financing of social programmes was closely linked to the structure of the command economy and most welfare payments were linked directly to employment status' (Makkai, 1994, p. 190). Along with gender inequalities, state socialist societies were also marked by deep divisions along ethnic lines. According to Dominelli, Stalin's concentration of industrialization in the western parts of the Soviet Union, together with 'enforced Russification made racism an integral feature of Soviet development' (1991, p. 99). Of all the difficulties facing the Soviet leadership, Kennedy has called 'the reemergence of the nationalities problem... perhaps the most serious and intractable of all' (1993, pp. 235–7). The multi-ethnic character of the Soviet Union made it vulnerable to the centrifugal forces of resurgent nationalism and religious affiliations which Stalinism had suppressed but not eradicated. Nationalism also played an important part in the growth of pressure for change in the other state socialist societies of Eastern Europe, where there was a strong sense of resentment at the imposition of the Soviet model in the context of military occupation following 1945 (Hettne, 1995).

At the same time as internal economic and social forces were working to undermine the viability of centralized control over state socialist societies, a further challenge to their integrity came from external sources. The political priority given by Soviet leaders to global military competition meant that the armed forces there 'siphoned off vast stocks of trained manpower, scientists, machinery and capital investment which could have been devoted to the civilian economy' (Kennedy, 1989, p. 644). The strong position of the military establishment in state socialist societies made it a significant obstacle to *perestroika* (Lane, 1990) but, as observers (Collins, 1986a, Ch. 8; Kennedy, 1993) have pointed out, continuation of the arms race risked military overextension, which in the modern global context threatened to lead to political disintegration. Global economic pressures also increased in the final years of Eastern European state socialism as it became apparent that growing involvement in the world economy did not offer a panacea for the problems generated by Stalinist programmes of inward-oriented industrialization. Involvement in world trade had expanded markedly in the 1970s but, as Clarke and his collaborators note, 'Recourse to the world market as the means of relieving the pressures within the domestic system was necessarily only a temporary expedient' (1993, p. 35). The mushrooming international debts run up by state socialist societies further convinced their political leaderships of the need for systematic restructuring (Ray, 1993), mindful though they were of the risks of social disintegration which this course entailed.

The state's gradual disengagement from overextended military commitments and centralized planning revealed the limited development of an autonomous civil society under state socialism. The stability of the Stalinist system in part rested on military strength, the arms race having 'helped to maintain conformity and obedience at home, since an evident outside threat was, as always, the most powerful social cement known to humankind' (McNeill, 1983, p. 382). The stability of the system relied also on the credibility of claims about the superiority of socialism compared with capitalism, but such claims ran counter to 'the daily evidence of shoddy consumer goods, terrible housing, and mediocre health care' (Kennedy, 1993, p. 235), and the gap between ideology and reality worked to undermine the legitimacy of the political system and to generate pressure for democratization. The programmes of *perestroika, glasnost* and *uskorenie* introduced under Gorbachev may be seen as a response to the legitimation crisis faced by the old order, but they revealed the weakness of 'a plural and independent civil society separate from the state' (Ray, 1993, p. xi) upon which the success of democratization turns. State socialist systems had generally been characterized by 'the *absence* of a division between civil society and the state' (Keane, 1988, p. 4, emphasis in original), and the steps taken towards establishing an independent civil society risked opening up numerous conflicts. As Lane observes, under Stalinism 'manifest social struggle was contained by a unitary ideology, by political manipulation, and, when all else failed, by force. In breaking this ideological and political mold [*sic*], Gorbachev... undermined the ideological and political basis on which rule [had] been legitimated since 1917' (1990, p. 107). The growing heterogeneity of state socialist societies as they matured made containment of social diversity within a uniform framework problematic although, as previous episodes of de-Stalinization had revealed, the alternative strategy of thoroughgoing reform also carried high risks.

The replacement of centralized control by greater pluralism in the political sphere and liberalization in the economic sphere hastened the disintegrative processes at work in state socialist societies. Greater openness allowed extensive criticism of state socialism as a system 'marked by chronic planning failures, technical stagnation, waste and scarcity, and a staggering overdevelopment of an unproductive apparatus of bureaucratic organization and control' (Keane, 1988, p. 4). *Glasnost* and *perestroika* were thus a 'desperate experiment' (Kumar, 1995, p. 164) conducted by Gorbachev and other leaders as they attempted to dismantle the more regimented aspects of state socialism without unleashing revolutionary forces. The speed with which communist regimes collapsed in the Eastern European satellite states in 1989 and in the Soviet Union in 1991 indicates the difficulties of controlling the process of democratization (Lewis, 1992) and suggests that a 'parallel society' made up of diverse informal social movements had developed alongside the informal economy which ran parallel to the official one (Ray, 1993). Therborn distinguishes between three distinct ways in which Eastern European state socialist societies were ended, 'by dissolution, by negotiation and by surrender' (1995, p. 326). In the Soviet Union and also in Yugoslavia, dissolution of the system was initiated from above, while in Hungary and Poland more established traditions of opposition allowed more of a negotiated ending worked out between Communist leaders and 'an increasingly complex civil society' (1995, p. 326), and in Romania and Czechoslovakia (and to a lesser extent Albania, Bulgaria and East Germany), mass displays of discontent by urban crowds forced the former rulers from power without negotiations. In none of these cases, Therborn argues, were 'demands for democracy, capitalism or even more consumption' (1995, p. 329) the principal goals of the revolutionary movements, despite the temptation of later observers to reinterpret them in this light.

Democratization and capitalism in post-communist societies

The identification of several routes out of state socialism warns against the simplistic idea that former state socialist societies have a uniform path of development ahead of them. Uneven development within and between state socialist societies had been a characteristic of Stalinist industrialization, while programmes imposed from above which attempted to make populations more homogeneous ran counter to traditions of regional and national diversity rooted deep in the pre-communist past (Szelenyi, 1988). In this respect, it makes more sense to speak of 'state socialisms' than 'state socialism' (Hall, 1986). Therborn's identification of distinct patterns of revolutionary change which marked the end of state socialist regimes in Eastern Europe coincides broadly with Lewis' grouping of countries there into three types following the collapse of communist rule. Hungary, Poland and Czechoslovakia were all able to draw on long-standing opposition movements, and these countries 'have made a decisive break with their communist past, taken concerted steps towards the establishment of a democratic political system, [and] embarked on privatization and the construction of a market economy' (1993, p. 291). Lewis notes that the transition from state socialism has 'not progressed without serious problems and setbacks' in these countries, but he points out that such difficulties need to be set against the 'greater problems in confronting the tasks of democratic transition and economic transformation' (1993, pp. 291–2) experienced in the Balkan countries of Albania, Bulgaria, Romania and Yugoslavia, where lower levels of economic development and a greater fragility of civil society heighten the tensions inherent in these processes. The countries of the former Soviet Union constitute a third type in which 'the more fundamental problems of state formation and territorial realignment' (1993, p. 309) remain to be resolved before democratization can come to the fore on the political agenda. Of particular importance for these states is the legacy of the highly militarized nature of Soviet society (Shaw, 1991).

The varying degrees to which previously monolithic political systems have been replaced by more democratic ones reflects the influence of several factors. Against the background of 'the economic failure of the command economy... and the disappointed hopes of Eastern consumerism', disenchantment with the formal political system under state socialism led to 'the crystallization of new ideas of democracy rooted in the experience of everyday life' (Lewis, 1992, p. 33). The Solidarity movement which emerged to challenge the state socialist regime in Poland in its final decade illustrates well the strengths and weaknesses of this alternative form of politics which grew up in Eastern Europe. Described by Konrad as 'Eastern Europe's most significant democratic movement' (1992, p. 56), Solidarity was a popular movement arising out of the struggle to establish an independent trade union which rapidly gained mass appeal, reflected in its membership of over ten million, which dwarfed the membership of the Communist Party (Lewis, 1983; Sułek, 1992). As an opposition movement, Solidarity set out 'to establish a civil society alongside a totalitarian state', but not 'to form a political party nor to "capture" state power. It sought neither the restoration of capitalism nor the withering away of the state' (Keane, 1988, p. 5). In this respect, it was similar to other social movements in Eastern Europe which 'did not have as a purpose the transformation of "the system"' (Szabó, 1992, p. 175). In the context of the declining legitimacy of state socialism in Poland, however, Solidarity could not easily remain 'just a pragmatic, sociopolitical movement, organized to achieve specific goals', because in opposing the established bureaucratic power structure it came also to have 'the aspect of a moral crusade' (Pelczynski, 1988, pp. 371–2). Given that a state socialist society was 'a *total order*' (Bauman, 1992, p. 178, emphasis in original), opposition to particular aspects of it was always likely to provide 'a focus for the aspirations of society and its resentment against the agencies of the state' (Lewis, 1993, p. 295) on a much broader front.

Solidarity proved to be a more effective force for bringing about change than it was for governing. Like other opposition movements in

Eastern Europe, Solidarity 'served to integrate those who shared the widespread disillusion with and antipathy against communist authority' (Lewis, 1993, p. 295). Yet the unity of the movement, which was founded on shared opposition to the communist authorities, proved impossible to maintain following the collapse of state socialism. The dissolution of Solidarity and similar movements was in part a result of unrealistic expectations of what post-communist society might deliver in terms of standards of living and political liberalization; in Bauman's words, Solidarity 'triggered off ambitions that elsewhere looked more like idle utopias' (1992, p. 161). There is a bitter irony, as Bauman notes, in the role played by industrial workers in speeding the demise of Poland's state socialist regime, since these were 'the workers of the largest industrial enterprises, those most obsolete dinosaurs of the failed communist industrialization, least capable of entering the dream of Europe and marked for extinction' (1992, p. 162). By 1992 in Poland, and even more markedly in Hungary and elsewhere, those who thought that they had been better off under communism significantly outnumbered those who felt the reverse, while in Russia capitalism's popularity quickly waned and Stalin's popularity underwent a dramatic revival (Hamilton and Hirszowicz, 1993; Therborn, 1995).

Broadly speaking, the transition from state socialism constituted a 'trade-off between increasing freedom and decreasing equality' (Ferge, 1993, p. 281), with winners and losers being unevenly distributed. The state's withdrawal from previous welfare commitments has a greater negative effect on women than it does on men (Funk and Mueller, 1993; Makkai, 1994; Phillips, 1993; Sklair, 1995), and Ferge's general conclusion regarding the costs of the transition is that 'The bulk of them falls on those who are the least prepared to bear them' (1993, p. 285). Social polarization is a widely recognized feature of capitalism, as has been noted in previous chapters, and its re-emergence despite the social objectives of the forces which overthrew communist governments may be taken as evidence of their limited power to control global economic forces (Sklair, 1995). As Ray describes it, 'the closer oppositional movements came to power-sharing or a negotiated transition, the more earlier visions of social re-organization were revised to accommodate market ideologies' (1993, p. 119). In addition, it is a reflection of the ability of advantaged groups in the state socialist system to maintain privileged economic and political positions in post-communist societies (Ferge, 1993; Ray, 1993). The long-running argument about the link between capitalism and democracy which so concerned writers such as Moore (1967) has been given a particular twist by the developments in Eastern Europe, although how accurate it is to describe these emerging societies as 'capitalist' remains a matter of debate.

The development of capitalism and the development of democracy are both long-term processes, and just as the civil society necessary for the effective functioning of multi-party democracy could not be created overnight, nor was it possible to effect an immediate transition from the state socialist economic system. Command economies operated according to a rationality different from that of capitalist market economies, and while de-Stalinization may have brought a degree of decentralization and liberalization to the organization of production in state socialist societies in more recent years, important differences remained (Burawoy, 1985; Clarke *et al.*, 1993). Kennedy (1989) has noted how enterprises in state socialism were shielded from the full force of market competition by the fact that they could not go bankrupt, as a consequence of which they were under less pressure to achieve efficiency in production. According to Burawoy, 'The capitalist firm makes investment decisions on the basis of profitability, leading to cycles of over-production, surplus capacity and reluctance to undertake new investments. Under state socialism, soft budget constraints and pressures to expand lead to an insatiable investment hunger. *Over*-investment predominates' (1985, p. 161, emphasis in original). Privatization of the ownership of state socialist enterprises in post-communist societies did not herald wholesale economic change, however, since many of the new entrepreneurs were formerly state enterprise managers and bureaucrats (Clarke *et al.*, 1993; Ray, 1993; Sklair, 1995). In addition, privatization has generally not introduced competitive markets akin to those of Western capitalism, which Clarke *et al.* (1993) argue gives workers a powerful position from which to influence the course of development of post-communist societies.

Contrasting scenarios have been put forward concerning the future of former state socialist societies in Eastern Europe. As Ferge has pointed out, 'the rejection of state socialism by a huge majority did not automatically imply the espousal of capitalism in its purest form'. She argues that many people sought a 'third way' which synthesized the preferred features of the two systems, 'combining the advantages of a market economy and a pluralist parliamentary democracy with the more acceptable features of "state socialism" such as full employment, job security, universal public services and the containment of inequalities' (1993, p. 271). Such a scenario envisages movement in the direction of the type of corporatist welfare state capitalism developed most extensively in Sweden (Scase, 1992). Other writers have been struck by the dramatic fall in many groups' living standards to which opening up Eastern Europe to the forces of global capitalist competition led in several countries of the region; in Poland, for example, living standards fell by 30 per cent within two years of the 1989 revolution (Deacon, 1994). In the light of this, it is possible to draw the very different conclusion that what Sklair (1995) calls 'the new second world' is acquiring more of the characteristics of the underdeveloped 'third world' than it is becoming closer to the 'first world' of advanced industrial capitalist nations. Positioned geographically and economically between the periphery and the core of the global capitalist system, Eastern Europe is vulnerable to a process of 'caribbeanization' (De Swann, 1994b, p. 106) as it grows in importance as a source of capital and of raw materials for world markets and also acts as a supplier of migrant labour. Bryant and Mokrzycki conclude that it may be necessary 'to find new terms for new phenomena rather than try to fit everything into familiar Western moulds' (1994, p. 4), since events in Eastern Europe are not unfolding according to any simple model of a transition to capitalism.

Discussion of the future of countries which have industrialized under the auspices of state socialist regimes would not be complete without some mention of China, where economic development remains compatible with communist politics, although here too there has been significant movement away from centralized control. In China, the conventional socialist model 'has had to be revised fundamentally as it failed to ensure industrialization and development' (Kilminster, 1992, p. 248). Starting out on the modernization process later and with a smaller industrial base compared with that on which Stalin built, it proved 'extremely difficult for the Chinese to carry through a similar process of industrialization to that which had occurred in the USSR... Industrialization based upon the break-up of rural society was not a feasible project in China' (Wield *et al.*, 1992, p. 307). Compared with Stalin's programme of forced industrialization, there was in China under Mao's leadership a greater emphasis on co-operation with rather than compulsion of the peasantry, although, as Moore (1967) points out, the rural population continued to be treated as a source of economic surplus to feed the modernization process. Moore also notes that the structure of peasant communities inherited from the imperial past in Russia and China 'were about as different as could be imagined' (1967, p. 469), and this too helps to explain the diversity of state socialist development strategies.

In the light of these differences, we need to be cautious about accepting Moore's analysis of Russia and China as both following the same route to the modern world (discussed in Chapter 2). It is instructive to note, however, that recent decades have seen China go through several changes akin to the process of de-Stalinization undergone in Eastern Europe. Selective economic decentralization as part of an industrialization programme was adopted as a response to fears that centralized planning and control were leading to stagnation (Kilminster, 1992). China has also become increasingly integrated into the global system as its economy has rapidly expanded (Sklair, 1995, Ch. 7). According to Kennedy, 'since 1978 China's foreign trade has risen by an average of 13.5 percent a year and equals almost one-third of national income' (1993, p. 176). One difference is that the Communist Party maintains a tighter grip on power in China than was the case with *perestroika* in Eastern Europe, but Gordon White (1993) has argued that this situation is likely to be progressively undermined, not least because of the growth of civil society which economic development has sponsored. How far China will be able to sustain an alternative course to the path of capitalist development remains an open question, although there is an important sense in which the choice between capitalist and socialist development strategies has become outmoded. As White recognizes, 'the crisis of the developmental state' (1993, p. 4) has become prevalent throughout the developing world, reflecting the widespread loss of confidence about the meaning and purpose of development, which is a central theme of the next chapter.

6

The Rise and Fall of the Third World: Development, Disillusion and Divergence

Previous chapters have suggested that the diversity of industrial capitalist societies is lost to view when they are collectively classified as the 'first world'. Similarly, while former state socialist societies may have been more uniform than their capitalist industrial counterparts, the idea of their constituting a 'second world' also masked important differences between them, differences which tended to widen over time. Countries placed into the 'third world' category are more heterogeneous still, and the very concept of a 'third world' has been the subject of an extensive and on-going debate since the term was coined in the early 1950s. From the outset, the 'third world' was made up of 'a diverse set of countries, extremely varied in their cultural heritages, with very different historical experiences and marked differences in the patterns of their economies, whatever their common history of subjection to colonialism and their common underdevelopment both as colonies and as independent states' (Worsley, 1984, p. 306). The definition of the third world as those nations which were not industrialized bestowed upon it the character of 'a negative unity' (Worsley, 1984, p. 306), given coherence only by member countries' shared deficiencies in terms of development indicators. This unity was always likely to break down as the societies which comprised the third world became more diverse, and Harris (1987) has argued that the emergence of the newly industrializing countries heralded 'the end of the third world'. Countries which have fared less well in terms of material development have been identified as a 'fourth world' on the margins of the global system, and the crystallizing hierarchy among the countries of the South is reflected in 'the growing awareness that the Third World is disappearing' (Hettne, 1995, p. 265), even if it is not clear what scenario is unfolding in its stead.

For a period, it was possible to sustain the fiction that the third world was held together by the shared experience of late development and a common future of following in the footsteps of the industrialized nations. Mid-twentieth-century optimism about the progressive spread of modernity across the globe found its expression in modernization theory, with its identification of stages of development and its suggestion that the arrival of what Rostow called 'the age of high mass consumption' (1960, p. 3) was only a matter of time. Such linear theories of development came under increasing criticism, notably in Frank's damning indictment of modernization theory as 'empirically invalid, theoretically inadequate and politically ineffective' (Harrison, 1988, p. 78). Explanations of the gap between rich and poor countries which were framed in terms of the latter's 'late start' to the industrialization process proved more and more difficult to adhere to in the face of evidence of 'a continuing widening of the gap in income levels between developed and developing countries in the years since the end of the Second World War' (Adams, 1993, p. 8). The presence in parts of the third world of slower rates of economic growth than those of the industrialized nations, together with persistent underdevelopment in many other third world countries, led to the demise of modernization theory. In its place emerged analyses which stressed the vulnerability of non-industrialized nations to dependency on the industrialized world, and the need to understand the unequal nature of the relations between the core and peripheral areas of the global economic system.

The passage of time made it increasingly apparent that, at the level of societies, global processes were producing what Caldwell (1977a) called 'the wealth of some nations' but the impoverishment of others. Growing disillusionment with the project of development reflected the realization that Western capitalist societies' levels of affluence would be unattainable on a global scale, and also that development processes entail numerous hidden social costs. These costs have tended to fall most heavily on the least powerful members of third world societies, and critiques advanced from the points of view of peasants, women and the environment have helped to make development a hotly contested concept (Escobar, 1995). The voices of these and other 'victims of development' (Seabrook, 1993) have played a significant part in highlighting the need to re-think social development in order better to confront the situation of the world's poorest people (Booth, 1994). The elusiveness of agreement about definitions of development is connected to growing diversity of ideas about the future of third world societies (Crush, 1995), and to explorations of what may lie ahead through debates conducted around concepts such as 'sustainable development' (Smith, 1992), 'another development' (Hettne, 1995) 'alternative development' (Amin, 1990a), 'anti-development' (Corbridge, 1995) and 'post-development' (Latouche, 1993). Rethinking the meaning of development has challenged the conventional focus on variations between different countries' levels of development by drawing attention to the diversity of experiences within individual societies and by opening up the question of what are the most appropriate bases of comparison.

Criticisms of reliance on quantitative measures of development have been touched on already in Chapter 1. However illuminating they may be in other respects, statistical analyses of income levels do not convey the complexities of the social relationships in which people are engaged. In this context, it is interesting to note that Latouche (1993) in his exploration of African material and Scott (1994) and Roberts (1995) in their work on Latin America independently draw similar conclusions about the need to re-think the distinction between the formal and informal sectors of production and the importance of recognizing the potential which exists for social solidarity among marginalized groups divided along gender, class and other lines. Analyses of community solidarity in a range of third world settings cast serious doubts on the ideas of the classical sociologists about the tendency of industrialization and urbanization to undermine community ties, and it is instructive that this conclusion has been reached by a variety of methodological routes, including Scott's (1994) combination of qualitative and quantitative techniques. Yet while these and many other pieces of research may suggest that informal social networks operate to modify the effects of polarized distributions of income within many third world countries, there is little evidence of comparable processes of redistribution between these countries. Whatever their limitations, figures show that in the period since 1945 'it is the growing disparities in income levels... that have been the significant feature in the experience of the developing countries group' (Adams, 1993, p. 13). At one end of this process of polarization among third world nations are those newly industrializing countries which have, in the language of modernization theory, 'taken off' and are in the process of 'graduating' to the status of a developed society (Toye, 1995). At the other extreme are those countries caught in the trap of international indebtedness and experiencing 'development in reverse' (Hewitt, 1992, p. 231). If there is still a unity among these increasingly diverse societies of the third world, it is not to be found in the realm of development statistics.

The modernization project and its critics

The contested nature of development is immediately apparent from the range of perspectives contained in the sociological literature on the third world. The proliferation of competing paradigms in this field confirms the view that the sociology of development constitutes several 'battlefields of knowledge' (Long and Long, 1992). This is particularly true following the breakdown of the simplified opposition between modernization and dependency theories, a widely disseminated dichotomy which never adequately captured the full range of issues involved in explaining development processes (Hettne, 1995). One of the most important spurs to re-thinking development has been the recognition that existing theories failed 'to reflect the diversity and complexity of the real world of development' (Booth, 1994, p. 4). Despite their other differences, modernization and dependency perspectives both tended to focus on levels of economic development and to operate with conceptions of the third world as relatively homogeneous. Dependency theorists had played a major part in challenging modernization theory by pointing to evidence of persistent and growing underdevelopment which went against the expectation of universal progress, but in turn such theorists' ideas became anachronistic in the context of 'increasingly dramatic divergencies in development experience between the different subdivisions of the developing world' (Booth, 1994, p. 7). It would be inappropriate to rehearse the detail of arguments which have now been superseded, not least because several accounts of the changing nature of development theory exist already (V. George, 1988; Harrison, 198º; Hettne, 1995; Hulme and Turner, 1990; Kiely, 1995; Sklair, 1995; Spybey, 1992), but it is important to sketch the ways in which current perspectives arose as reactions to the perceived inadequacies of earlier generations of research.

As was noted in Chapter 1, modernization theory contained within it several elements of the functionalist approach to the study of society. Modernization theorists tended to rely on notions of societies as integrated systems and on the idea of evolutionary processes of development. Thus Rostow's (1960) celebrated model which identified five stages of economic growth (passing from traditional society through the preconditions for take-off into self-sustaining growth, the take-off itself, the drive to maturity and then arrival at the age of high mass consumption) presents a unilinear model of development in which countries follow the same path, albeit at different times. In the process, societies necessarily undergo fundamental changes to their system of values as traditions are discarded in favour of modernity's emphasis on 'achievement' (McClelland, 1967) and as economic and political institutions become progressively specialized to meet the requirements of an urbanized, industrialized social order. The roots of these ideas can be found in classical European sociology's construction of the traditional/modern dichotomy, and the impression that modernization is 'synonymous with Westernisation' (Hulme and Turner, 1990, p. 35) was always a likely outcome, even if the understanding of development in modernization theory was more narrowly economistic than classical sociological conceptions of social change had been.

Such an approach places a conceptual strait-jacket on comparative sociologists, reducing their role to the location of societies along a single dimension (the tradition–modernity spectrum) and restricting explanations of the varying locations of societies on this spectrum to those which give prominence to factors internal to these societies, in particular local cultures. Vic George has claimed that, in addition to operating with an excessively rigid and Eurocentric conception of development processes, modernization theory is flawed because it 'uses values and concepts which are vague and almost impossible to define precisely for any scientific measurement' (1988, p. 11). The crude equation of the agrarian sector with tradition and the industrial sector with modernity which underpinned the notion of a 'dual economy' in third world societies appears to bear out this charge, as more recent interpretations of the 'marginal' or 'informal' sector (to be discussed below) show. A further difficulty relates to the conclusion drawn from modernization theory that third world populations 'are poor because they do not possess and hence are not motivated by entrepreneurial values' (V. George, 1988, pp. 10–11), that is, its tendency to blame the victims of poverty for their situation. With the benefit of hindsight, it is unsurprising to note that 'Third World realities failed to match First World expectations' (Hulme and Turner, 1990, p. 33), and that as a result modernization theory with its naive optimism about the prospects for development ran into serious difficulties. Preston has described modernization theory, with its mechanical conception of developmental stages, as marking 'the positivist high tide' (1982, Ch. 4) in the sociology of development, and notes how by the mid-1960s growing criticisms were leading to the disintegration of the modernization paradigm.

No brief account can do justice to the range of ideas within the modernization paradigm, which it is important to recognize altered its emphasis over time (Harrison, 1988). Hettne (1995) suggests that Gerschenkron's work of the early 1960s on comparative industrialization in Europe marks a significant shift within the broad modernization paradigm through its focus on the influence of the international context in which development occurred. Gerschenkron's view that 'the industrial history of Europe appears not as a series of mere repetitions of the "first" industrialization but as an orderly system of graduated deviations from that industrialization' (1962, p. 44) is clearly an advance on earlier accounts which neglected this dimension, but it was left to later writers to draw out the full significance of external influences on development processes. Moore's writings examined in Chapter 2 also contained some telling criticisms of modernization thinking by elaborating on how later industrialization differed from earlier patterns, not least because of differences in the political regimes under which it took place. It was, however, the adoption of a yet more radical perspective which shifted attention away from the modernization paradigm to the unequal relations between the countries of the industrialized and third worlds. As Webster observes, the fact that modernization theory 'entirely ignores the impact of colonialism and imperialism on Third World countries... is a staggering omission' (1990, p. 61). From the point of view of dependency theorists, modernization theory's concentration on internal processes of change prevented acknowledgement of the more important external processes which produced and reproduced underdevelopment.

Like modernization theory, dependency theory has a number of variants, but the central thrust of its protagonists is that third world peoples have for several centuries been subject to exploitative economic relationships with the countries which became the advanced industrial metropolises. Writers like Frank see the development of the metropolitan countries as being inextricably linked with the underdevelopment of satellite states, both during periods of colonialism and subsequently. Unequal power relations underpin the systematic transfer of surplus resources along the 'chain of dependency' from satellites to metropolises, reproducing and intensifying the dependency of the former on the latter. By such reasoning, Frank arrived at the conclusion that 'Economic development and underdevelopment are the opposite faces of the same coin' (1967, p. 9). New approaches to the study of underdevelopment were necessitated by the argument that development and underdevelopment are relational, which rendered it inappropriate to view them 'as the products of supposedly different economic structures or systems, or of supposed differences in stages of economic growth achieved within the same system' (1967, p. 9). Comparisons between societies had to be framed in terms of their respective positions within the world capitalist system, which allowed for relatively little variation among satellite countries except for those which sought to secure autonomous industrialization as an alternative to dependent capitalist development.

The fact that Frank's writings were grounded in evidence relating to the history of Latin America supported his scepticism about the benefits brought to the third world by contact with metropolitan countries. Frank argues, for example, that 'underdevelopment in Chile is the necessary product of four centuries of capitalist development' (1967, p. 3). Indeed, he suggests that the longer the period over which economic ties with metropolises have existed, the greater the risk is of underdevelopment becoming consolidated, in the extreme producing a state of 'ultra-underdevelopment', an argument directly contradicting 'the generally held thesis that the source of a region's underdevelopment is its isolation and pre-capitalist institutions' (1969, p. 13). First as colonies and then from the nineteenth century onwards as politically independent states, Latin American societies found their production geared towards exports to meet the interests of the metropolitan countries, at the same time stifling prospects for autonomous industrialization. Frank portrays third world societies as locked into a system of international trade in which the underdeveloped parts of Asia, Africa and Latin America consistently export more merchandise than they import, providing an excess which has 'made a fundamental contribution to the accumulation of capital, technological progress and economic development of the now developed countries' (1978, p. 172). He also draws on reworked international trade statistics in support of his argument that over time such exchanges are likely to accentuate rather than modify the geographical unevenness of development.

The idea that the economic development of the industrialized world is systematically linked to the underdevelopment of the third world revolutionized thinking about development, and it continues to provide an influential perspective in debates about globalization which will be examined in Chapter 7, most obviously in Wallerstein's (1979, 1991) work on the capitalist world economy. The critique of modernization theory from the dependency perspective established the inappropriateness of thinking in terms of stages of development which apply to all countries. It also highlighted the inadequacy of equating urbanization and industrialization with the development of modern capitalism by showing that capitalist influences had extended to rural areas of the third world for several centuries, thus challenging the description of the agrarian sector as 'traditional' and 'pre-capitalist' (Harrison, 1988). Worsley's observation that colonial rule led to countries such as India being 'agriculturalized' (1984, p. 16) could be drawn on in support of this case, although Worsley goes on to make the point that political as well as economic forces lay behind such processes. Worsley is by no means alone in criticizing dependency theory's focus on economic relations leading to the neglect of the scope which exists for states to influence patterns of development (Spybey, 1992), and in this respect Wallerstein's work can be considered more sophisticated than Frank's (Waters, 1995). Typical of Frank's perspective is the claim that 'The domestic economic, political and social structure of Chile always was and still remains determined first and foremost by the fact and specific nature of its participation in the world capitalist system' (1967, p. 29), and the economic determinism of this perspective appears to offer little hope for third world development. Frank's statement that 'no country, once underdeveloped, ever managed to develop by Rostow's stages' (1969, p. 47) led to the conclusion that, in place of modernization theory's unilinear model of development, he is offering a bilinear model of development for some countries and dependent underdevelopment for others (Foster-Carter, 1985).

The recognition that dependency theory suffered from many of the same shortcomings as modernization theory produced something of an impasse in the sociology of development. Both approaches were excessively abstract and general, both embodied functionalist assumptions, and both treated economic factors as having a determining role in development processes (Barnett, 1988; Booth, 1994; Kiely, 1995; Leys, 1975; Long, 1992). Dependency theorists' denial of the legitimacy of extrapolating from the experience of the first world of capitalist industrial nations offered the basis for a powerful critique of modernization theory, but it left unexplained why development was unfolding in several parts of the third world. This point was made particularly forcefully by Warren (1980), who argued that, contrary to the claims of dependency theory, there exists ample evidence of development in the third world, including evidence of the spread of industrialization and of rising levels of output. Such development was a prominent feature of the group of third world societies in parts of Asia and Latin America which came to be known as the newly industrializing countries, although as Hettne (1995) and Hoogvelt

(1992) note, development here took place under the auspices of authoritarian and repressive governments. The experiences of the newly industrializing countries bear out the view that 'In all modern examples of rapid industrialization, the state has played a central role' (Crow, 1988, p. 339). The newly industrializing countries can be seen as confirmation of Moore's argument (examined in Chapter 2) about the extensive involvement of the state in late development, in the process vindicating approaches which treat the political dimension of development as much more than the reflection of economic forces. In other countries too, underdevelopment was not straightforwardly reproduced, as for example Leys' (1975) study of Kenya showed by highlighting the unstable and contradictory nature of post-colonial societies. Put more generally, there are significant variations in patterns of development within the third world, and these can be attributed at least in part to variations in state structures and the development strategies which are adopted (Booth, 1994). As Bernstein (1982) points out, appreciation of these variations has exposed the oversimple nature of dependency theory's suggestion that a stark choice exists between independent development and dependent stagnation.

The critique of the modernization paradigm has been taken further still in recent years. Dependency theorists raised important doubts about the comfortable assumption that development was taking place in the third world, and highlighted the unevenness and exploitation which tended to characterize the process. The point made by Frank and others that within third world societies different classes experience development and underdevelopment in very different ways challenged the functionalist premise that societies develop as a collectivity under the guidance of an impartial state. Subsequently, other lines of cleavage besides those of social class have become more prominent in the assessment of who benefits and who loses from development processes, most notably in the great expansion of writing on the uneven impact of development on women and men (Pearson, 1992a, 1992b). According to Booth, the 'discovery' of the diversity of class and gender relations in third world contexts has opened up the possibility of 'systematic comparisons between different locations and countries' (1994, p. 10), including comparisons of contrasting development policies and the institutional contexts in which they are formulated. Furthermore, the research agenda has broadened to embrace not only questions of how widely the rewards and costs of development are spread, but also issues relating to the desirability and the very meaning of 'development'. Wallerstein (1994) makes the telling remark that the apparent unanimity about development being a good thing masks fundamental differences of opinion about what 'development' actually is and about how it embodies progress. As an increasing number of writers have broken with the former broad consensus about the desirability of development, it has become clear that there will have to be further consideration of fundamental questions of definition if the problem of the term meaning 'everything and nothing' (Munck, 1994, p. 22) is to be resolved.

Contesting the meaning of 'development'

Use of the word 'development' has become thoroughly pervasive in the modern world, whilst at the same time an agreed definition of the concept has remained elusive. A useful starting point is Bernstein's observation that 'development' can be taken to mean 'significantly increasing the productive capacities of societies, establishing new and better (more productive) ways of doing things and making things so as to make more wealth available' (1988, p. 67). Bernstein goes on from this to emphasize that development is not synonymous with economic growth, and he notes that the incorporation of qualitative as well as quantitative change in the definition helps to explain why 'development is invariably a normative as well as an analytical concept' (1988, p. 67). A typical illustration of this point is Jones' view that 'Development is more than growth; it should be social development: progress should also be made towards social justice and an improvement in the quality of life' (1990, p. 2), echoing the theme of the Brandt Commission that 'if there is no attention to the quality of growth and social change one cannot speak of development' (Independent Commission on International Development Issues, 1980, p. 48). According to Preston (1982, 1985) the history of development studies since the Second World War has been the story of changes to how 'development' is conceived, broadening and deepening the initially rather narrow technical and economistic understanding of the term. Against this background, Wallerstein (1994) proposes that it is necessary to address a number of questions concerning what development is, who has been involved in this process, where the demand for development has come from, what conditions allow for development and what the political implications of development are. The attempt to answer these questions reveals for Wallerstein the central tension which exists between development understood as growth, as 'more', and development, understood as 'more equal' (1994, p. 19). In contrast to the former, the latter offers the prospect of a transformation towards a different type of society and world-system characterized by greater egalitarianism, treating equality as 'an objective in its own right' (Seers, 1995, p. 5) and as an integral element of development.

Recognition that more resources do not necessarily mean more equally distributed resources played an important part in undermining the case for modernization theory. In addition to the gulf between the developed and underdeveloped regions to which Frank and other dependency writers drew attention, it became increasingly apparent that, in practice, development frequently entailed social differentiation within national boundaries. Of particular concern in this context was the tendency for the fruits of development to be concentrated dispro-portionately in the hands of the richer classes of third world societies, while poorer sections of the population gained fewer if any of the benefits and may even have suffered impoverishment in absolute terms while the country as a whole prospered. As Hoogvelt (1982) notes, the marginalization of large groups of peasants and poor urban dwellers is masked when figures for output per head are considered, since these are averages for the whole societies. She cites the case of Brazil, where significant gains for the top 10 per cent of the population had to be set against the impoverished position of the bottom half, before going on to caution that 'there is no firm empirical basis for the view that higher rates of growth *inevitably* generate greater inequality' (Hoogvelt, 1982, p. 40, emphasis in original). Vic George's conclusion, also drawn from the analysis of statistical data on income distribution, follows suit in stressing that 'What determines the pattern and degree of income inequality in a country is not its level of economic growth but the type of industrial, agrarian and other relevant government policies that are being pursued' (1988, p. 74). Rising output per head of population does not necessarily indicate rising living standards for all groups in the population, and it is as a result an unreliable measure of 'development' in the more extensive sense of the term.

Awareness of the shortcomings of narrow economic indicators of development formed the backdrop for the attempt to construct more sophisticated measures of social progress than those employed in classifications of countries based on income. Grouping countries as 'low-income', 'middle-income' and 'higher-income' economies is, as Sklair notes, misleading in several ways, not least because average gross national product per head measures 'obscure the fact that often differences within countries are just as important as differences between them' (1995, p. 16). A pioneer among alternative approaches to quantification of 'development' is Morris' 'Physical Quality of Life

Index' which sought 'to measure how well societies satisfy certain specific life-serving social characteristics' (1979, p. 4). Morris' work showed that richer countries do not necessarily have higher levels of welfare defined in terms of life expectancy, infant mortality and adult literacy, the three elements which went into his composite physical quality of life index. While it was generally the case that 'poor countries... tend to have low PQLI's' (1979, p. 60), the deviations from this were sufficiently significant to demonstrate that rising incomes do not translate automatically into the satisfaction of needs. Morris' work has been subject to extensive criticism for the narrowness of the conception of welfare on which the PQLI was constructed (justified by Morris in terms of the limited range of data which are available for all countries) and the confusion of quality of life with quantity of life, but the general thrust of the argument that income statistics and welfare levels do not correlate particularly closely has been sustained by the more sophisticated measures subsequently devised (Barnett, 1988; Hulme and Turner, 1990; Sklair, 1995; Todaro, 1989).

The formulation of measures of the quality of life makes possible a broader range of comparisons both among the countries of the underdeveloped world and between them and the rest of the global system. Data from such measures allow the conclusion to be drawn that societies differ significantly not only in the absolute amount of resources available to them, but also in the way in which those resources are distributed among the population, although Morris (1979) himself was careful to avoid the suggestion that a higher overall quality of life could be achieved simply by a more equal distribution of a society's income. Broadening the range of criteria upon which comparisons are based may have been undertaken in part to meet the criticism that income-based measures are inappropriate indicators of social relations in non-industrialized countries, but the problem of the applicability of methodological tools outside the cultural contexts in which they were formulated applies also to the identification of other variables such as literacy, as markers of 'development'. For writers like Sen (1995), statistics relating to income per head, literacy and life expectancy have to be analyzed in the context of wider debates about competing conceptions of freedom and their connections to political alternatives in public policy. The detection of Western biases in the ranking of human needs has contributed to a situation in which 'the movement for social indicators and human development appears to have run into the sand' (Doyal and Gough, 1991, p. 153). More generally, a reassessment of how best to conceptualize 'development' is one of the effects of the growing strength of what Hettne calls 'the voice of the other' (1995, Ch. 2) which has emerged to confront Eurocentric perspectives in debates on development strategies.

Development theory has in recent years challenged the legacy of ideas rooted in classical European social science, in terms of both the applicability in third world contexts of central concepts such as social class and the neglect of other social divisions such as those relating to gender. Thus Scott argues that, if it is to be a useful tool of analysis in the study of development processes, the concept of social class needs to be modified, since 'class analysis has been too narrowly focused on work-based categories' (1994, p. 1) and is insufficiently sensitive to interconnections with other systems of inequality as they operate in third world contexts. Researchers in countries throughout the third world have noted how the patterns of stratification to be observed in cities there are very different from those which were characteristic of earlier industrialization paths (Lloyd, 1982; Roberts, 1995), a point which is exemplified in the enormous diversity of informal sector occupations by which urban dwellers make a living. The view that industrialization had an inherent logic to it which would bring the development of an organized, urban, industrial working class has been confounded by the presence in third world countries of large numbers of non-proletarian groups securing an existence at the fringes of the conventional, waged labour market and the 'formal' sector of the economy. The reality of many third world cities is of a significant part of their population being composed of marginal workers employed in small-scale enterprises not effectively regulated by the state. Numbered among these are workers in sweat-shops, home workers, self-employed artisans, street vendors, personal service workers, casual wage-labourers, refuse collectors and beggars, who share the common situation of being 'poorly paid for long hours of work, often in impermanent, hard-labour, dirty and dangerous occupations which do not make them eligible for whatever meagre social security benefits exist' (Worsley, 1984, p. 195). In addition, marginality is reinforced by physical segregation in slums and shanty towns and by social exclusion through lack of formal education and denial of other citizenship rights to welfare and political expression which were acquired by the European industrial working class during the industrialization process.

Comparison of the patterns of industrialization and urbanization in the third world with those of the classical European model is not a straightforward matter. In particular, it needs to be noted that capitalist industrialization in Europe during the nineteenth century had itself generated large numbers of economically marginal urban dwellers, many of them migrants displaced from the countryside, who were perceived to be outside mainstream society and, as a result, politically dangerous (Lloyd, 1982; Worsley, 1984). Only later did this 'outcast' section of society come to be incorporated (more or less effectively) as citizens through their enfranchisement and the expansion of welfare-state provision, and even then citizenship ties were frequently combined with older kinship, ethnic and religious affiliations rather than displacing them. Yet even if it is recognized that the classical industrialization pattern created an organized working class only as it underwent the transition from liberal to organized capitalism, there remain doubts about how far the urban poor of third world societies are becoming proletarianized, as predicted by Marx and other classical sociologists. Lloyd notes that it is true of skilled industrial workers as well as others that they have not 'ruptured their rural links, abjured their aspirations to self-employment, or withdrawn from ethnic and community associations' (1982, p. 118). More generally, he argues that while a substantial minority, and in some cases even the majority, of urban dwellers may be described as 'marginal', it is important to specify what 'marginalization' means in this context. He is sceptical of the usefulness of defining marginality in terms of 'those with no function in the capitalist system' (1982, p. 121), posing the question of why involvement in capitalist production should be taken as a norm. Lloyd's plea for an alternative categorization more sensitive to the operation of the informal sector alongside the formal, large-scale capitalist and state-regulated sector bears a strong resemblance to the cases made by writers such as Pahl and Szelenyi (considered in Chapters 3 and 5 respectively) for recognition of the importance of the informal economy in industrialized societies and its extensive interconnections with rather than marginality to the formal economy.

The continued vitality of informal economic activity on a scale far beyond that anticipated in conventional theories of development may be accounted for in a number of ways. Lloyd stresses the impact of involvement in the informal sector on political consciousness and behaviour, collective action of the classic proletarian type being inhibited by participation in 'modes of production in which personal betterment is seen in terms of individual achievement and in which relationships of patronage are seen as the means of such achievement' (1979, p. 221). Lloyd's approach also emphasizes the background of migration to the towns from the countryside on a scale beyond that which the formal economy could adjust to, making it inevitable that 'Most will have to be absorbed into the informal sector' (1979, p. 218).

The divergence from classical European patterns of the commercialization of agrarian production found in many third world countries also
helps to explain the greater significance of the informal sector there.
As Goodman and Redclift note, there is no uniform transformation of
the rural population 'from peasant to proletarian', and they describe
how parts of Latin America have seen 'the emergence of a free rural
labour force', while other areas have witnessed 'the survival and
reproduction of the mass of impoverished household commodity
producers' (1981, p. 216). The persistence of small-scale peasant
production in the countryside is connected to the urban informal
economy, through the maintenance of extensive social networks
which continue to link individuals following migration. In Scott's
study of Peru, 'many urban workers were first-generation migrants
who had maintained their links with the countryside and continued to
support kinship networks and principles of reciprocity which enabled
them to integrate rapidly into the urban economy' (1994, p. 221).
Scott found that people's work histories and their networks of social
support and solidarity frequently crossed the boundaries between rural
and urban communities and formal and informal economies, and that
as a result workers in the informal sector were less marginalized than
many observers supposed. Scott (1986) argues that this is particularly
true of women workers, whom many other writers have argued were
subject to a process of 'female marginalization'.

A further element in the explanation of the continued significance
of informal economic activity is the role of the state and the development policies its agencies pursue. Roberts argues that in Latin
America during the period from the 1940s to the 1970s, when
development strategies founded on the idea of import-substitution
industrialization predominated, the informal sector declined in the
face of the expansion of state intervention and regulation. In the
1980s by contrast, 'the informal sector, defined as the sum of self-
employment, unremunerated family employment and employment in
enterprises of less than five workers... grew substantially both in
numbers and as a proportion of the urban labour force' (1995,
p. 123). Roberts links this growth to the greater economic uncertainties which have accompanied the shift towards free trade and export-
oriented industrialization in development policies. Other interpretations of the relationship between the state and the informal
economy draw more radical conclusions and see in informal
economic activity an alternative path of social change which is quite
distinct from conventional progressive conceptions of development.
According to Llosa, 'The informal economy is the people's creative

and spontaneous response to the state's incapacity to satisfy the basic needs of the impoverished masses' (1995, p. 289), while for Latouche (1993) the existence of the informal sector indicates not only the inability of the state to promote development which brings benefits to the poor, but also raises more fundamental doubts about the desirability of attempting to become 'modern'.

Development policies and development objectives

The practical experience of 'development' during the second half of the twentieth century has been complex and contradictory. In some parts of the third world, economic and social transformations have proceeded at an incredible pace, while in others what stands out is the failure of development policies to achieve the promise of modernization, and the high costs of this failure. As an illustration of the divergent fortunes of what he refers to as 'winners and losers in the developing world', Kennedy directs attention to the statistics which show that 'in the 1960s, South Korea had a per capita GNP exactly the same as Ghana's ($230) whereas today it is ten to twelve times more prosperous' (1993, p. 193). On the face of it, these two countries occupied a similar starting point in the 1960s, since 'Both possessed a predominantly agrarian economy and both had endured a half century or more of colonial rule', and upon gaining political independence 'each faced innumerable handicaps in trying to "catch up" with the West' (1993, p. 193). In the space of three decades, South Korea has demonstrated the transformative potential of export-oriented industrialization, while Ghana and other West African states are located among the poorest countries of the world, bedevilled by 'chronic poverty, malnutrition, poor health, and underdevelopment' (1993, p. 193). As Kennedy notes, such divergent trajectories make the notion of a homogeneous 'third world' redundant, and place centre stage the issue of what role different development strategies have played in bringing about this situation.

Competing theoretical perspectives on development have led to the adoption of markedly different viewpoints about the most appropriate strategies to pursue. In modernization theory, as Gurnah and Scott observe, '"Progress" is equated with capitalist economic progress' (1992, p. 134), and the principal objective of development policy is to promote modern economic, political and social institutions at the expense of traditional ones. Dependency theorists drew opposite conclusions about the connection between integration into the

capitalist world economy and development, favouring more autonomous development strategies on the basis of the argument that
involvement in global capitalist relations promoted not the development but the underdevelopment of third world countries. Yet attempts
to secure national development independently of integration into
global capitalism proved no more viable when practised as socialism in
one country than they had as nationalist programmes of import-
substitution industrialization, highlighting the contemporary reality
in which 'there are no countries which are completely autonomous
and self-reliant' (Hettne, 1995, p. 105). The greater success of newly
industrializing countries such as South Korea in following the strategy
of export-oriented industrialization offers further support to theories of
global interdependence, although such countries are in many ways
exceptional within the third world overall, and some writers have
expressed serious doubts about the sustainability of this strategy in the
longer term (Bello, 1995). All general theories of development and
underdevelopment have foundered on the extreme heterogeneity of
'third world' societies, and the realization that 'no universal cures can
be valid for the category as such' (Hettne, 1995, pp. 129–30) has
reasserted the importance of the comparative dimension in the study
of 'development'.

The promotion of industrialization lies at the heart of many
development strategies. Industrialization has frequently been associated with economic expansion, rising standards of living and political
independence (Jenkins, 1992), not least because this seemed to be the
central lesson of earlier patterns of development, both capitalist and
state socialist. It is therefore no surprise that the sociology of development has seen so much attention devoted to the dramatic expansion of
industrial output and employment in the newly industrializing
countries. The most celebrated cases are South Korea, Taiwan, Hong
Kong and Singapore, and while several other countries, such as Brazil
and Mexico, have been discussed in this context (Ingalls and Martin,
1988), it is the four Asian 'tiger' or 'dragon' economies which are held
up as examples of successful export-oriented industrialization (Harris,
1987; Kennedy, 1993). Statistics relating to the South Korean
economic 'miracle' show manufacturing growing at over 18 per cent a
year in the later 1950s, and at an average of 20 per cent a year in the
following two decades (Edwards, 1992). This spectacularly rapid rate
of growth in manufacturing output was driven primarily by the
expansion of exports, which grew at close to 40 per cent a year during
the 1960s and 1970s, while gross national product increased at some
9 per cent annually, and attainment of these economic objectives

contributed to rising standards of living, life expectancy and literacy rates (Edwards, 1992; Kennedy, 1993). On the basis of such achievements, claims have been made that the newly industrializing countries represent a model of development which offers other third world countries a route out of poverty and dependence, although these claims, to say the least, are contentious (Hettne, 1995).

The attachment of priority to the objective of industrialization in development strategies has been questioned on a number of counts despite the successes of the Asian tiger economies. Among the costs of export-oriented industrialization are the long hours of work required of workers for comparatively low rates of pay, women workers being particularly vulnerable to such exploitation. Commentators have also noted the environmental costs of rapid industrialization and the need to resort to authoritarian political practices in order to push through profound socio-economic transformations, including the reorganization of the agricultural sector in order to allow the concentration of investment in industrial production (Amsden, 1985; Bello, 1995; Edwards, 1992; Wield and Rhodes, 1988). Disagreements exist about how sustainable these bases of development are within the newly industrializing countries (Edwards, 1992; Jenkins, 1994), but even those writers who anticipate continued industrial growth in these economies are wary of the suggestion that this pattern of development is easily replicated elsewhere in the third world. As Jenkins notes, 'It clearly does not follow that if some peripheral countries can develop then any must be able to do so' (1994, p. 83). The assumption that such a model of industrialization could be repeated elsewhere is ahistorical and unsociological, as Kiely (1995, p. 97) has pointed out. Hettne is more cautious still in reaching his conclusion about the cases of Taiwan and South Korea, that 'The reasons for their successful transformation are more or less unique', citing factors peculiarly to their advantage such as 'their Confucian work ethic, their radical land reforms... their geopolitical importance... their closeness to the Japanese giant... and the world-economy context for their take-off' (1995, pp. 127–8), a list to which might be added their relatively small size. For Hettne, the absence elsewhere in the third world of these distinct characteristics makes the comparative study of development strategies all the more urgent.

The centrality of industrialization to development strategies can be traced back to the way in which 'development' was conceptualized in the period following the Second World War, when faith in the power of modern technology and large-scale economic organization to transform social relations was accepted far more uncritically than it is today. Escobar (1995) has charted how the second half of the twentieth century has seen this developmentalist discourse gradually unravel in the face of the failure of development programmes to solve the problems of underdevelopment and impoverishment in the third world. Early critics of modernization theory from the dependency perspective emphasized the presence of obstacles to industrialization rather than fundamentally challenging its centrality to development, but in doing so they highlighted the need to examine previously unquestioned assumptions in development thinking. Subsequently, attention focused more directly on some of the paradoxes of development processes, such as the puzzling situation in which 'Although agricultural output per capita grew in most countries, this increase was not translated into increased food availability for most people' (Escobar, 1995, p. 104). Further examples of development's failure to bring benefits to all groups of the population came with the identification of urban bias (Lipton, 1977) and gender bias (Boserup, 1970; Rogers, 1981) in the way in which development worked in practice, and added to the pressure on policy-makers to intervene more effectively to ensure that development programmes achieved a wider range of objectives than simply growth through industrialization.

Industrialization may promise a host of benefits over the long term, but in the interim period active policy interventions will be necessary to meet immediate needs. Sen has argued that while countries such as South Korea have eliminated widespread undernourishment as a result of their successful modernization strategy, other much poorer economies such as Sri Lanka and China 'have been able to deal effectively with endemic hunger without having to wait for their general opulence to reach levels comparable with the more successful newly industrializing countries' (1995, p. 82). This has been achieved through public provisioning in the context of policy-makers' treatment of food as a matter of entitlement which requires planning rather than being something to be left to the operation of market forces, although Sen recognizes that not all intervention strategies have been successful in combatting hunger. Awareness of the importance of increasing food supply as part of broader development strategies led to the adoption of new seed varieties and new technologies in agriculture in several parts of the third world. This so-called 'Green Revolution' was promoted particularly enthusiastically by the Indian government in the 1960s, but its quantitative success in raising output did not bring universal benefits to rural populations (Bernstein, 1992; Byres and Crow, 1988; Wilson, 1992). The concentration among richer farmers of the gains from the Green Revolution meant that it was not a costless exercise, since it caused an 'increase in social inequality, elimination of poor farmers as well as of small-scale peasant farmers and dependence on imports of machinery... and other sophisticated products' (Latouche, 1993, p. 170). Peasants experienced the Green Revolution as 'a losing class struggle against capitalist agricultural development and its human agents' (Scott, 1985, p. 42). For Latouche, the Green Revolution and its broader impact exemplify 'the fuzziness of policy objectives' (1993, p. 171) in many development strategies, reflecting the failure to think through the wider social implications of technological innovation and economic change.

The issue of gender inequalities provides a further example of the way in which development strategies may in practice produce unintended or unanticipated outcomes. Pearson's examination of the development record found 'substantial evidence that women have consistently lost out in the process' (1992a, p. 291), including statistical evidence relating to work and employment, income, property and political representation. Examining the effects of the Green Revolution in terms of impact of gender relations, Pearson directs attention towards 'the increases in women's workloads and to the fact that women often fail to receive an equitable share in the extra income earned, even though their labour is often central to achieving higher levels of productivity' (1992a, p. 306). Women's contribution to development was for a long time eclipsed by narrow conceptions of what constitutes productive activity, and the broadening of the policy agenda through the adoption of 'Women in Development' policies represents an acknowledgement of this, although it is doubtful whether such programmes can in themselves override the structural bases of gender inequalities (Charles, 1993; Pearson, 1992a; Scott, 1984). In contrast to rural development programmes, which have tended to marginalize women's formal contribution, export-oriented industrialization strategies have generally given greater prominence to women's role in the workforce, although rarely on an equal footing to men's (Pearson, 1992b). As Mayo notes, feminists have played an increasingly influential role in 'challenging the gender-blind assumptions of development strategies and community-development programmes' (1994, p. 114) in both rural and urban contexts throughout the third world.

Mindful of the existence of significant differences between women's experiences in Singapore and South Korea, Pearson cautions against 'making simple generalizations about third world women workers, even in countries whose industrialization strategies have been relatively similar' (1992b, p. 242). At a very general level, it is the case that the female labour force participation rate has risen and that 'economic and social development has been toward slight, but perceptible, reductions in the gender gap in health, educational, and economic status' (Joekes, 1987, p. 21). Such trends may be considered likely to continue in those countries which are able to generate steady growth, but for those societies unable to sustain such development strategies the future is bleaker. Newly industrializing countries such as South Korea may have succeeded in bringing about an economic and social transformation over the last four decades, but the global context in which the foundations of their industrialization were laid has been replaced by a very different world economy. The prospect held out to the 'third world' in the 1950s of 'catching up' with the rich industrialized nations has receded over time for most of them as their living standards have fallen further and further behind (Adams, 1993). On a world scale, the 'development gap' has widened rather than narrowed, exacerbated in recent years by the international debt crisis, while the various processes which make up 'globalization' work to undermine the integrity of attempts to secure national development. Analysis of the reproduction of national and international inequalities requires understanding of the increasingly complex interconnectedness of the various parts of the global system, and the next chapter is devoted to this task.

7

From Three Worlds to Globalization: Economic Restructuring, Democratization and Cultural Change in a Global Context

The expectation that in the modern world societies would follow convergent paths of development has not by and large been borne out by events in the post-Second World War period. The widening gap between rich and poor nations is merely the most stark expression of the more general phenomenon of continued difference and divergence both between modern capitalist, former state socialist and underdeveloped countries and also among members of each of these three 'worlds'. As was seen in Chapter 4, within the first world of modern capitalist societies Esping-Andersen (1990) found it possible to identify three distinct welfare-state regimes, while Chapter 5 recorded the variety of routes out of state socialism which have been followed, and Chapter 6 highlighted the fragmentation of the 'third world' as the newly industrializing countries parted company with their poorer neighbours in the South. Yet behind these divergent trajectories lie certain common forces which link the various paths together. It has been noted already in Chapter 6 that dependency theory emphasized the link between the development of some parts of the world with the underdevelopment of other areas, and several writers have continued to advance this line of argument. Mies, for example, suggests that 'we cannot treat the "First" and "Third" world as separate entities, but have to identify the relations that exist between the two', and she goes on to claim that underdevelopment results from the way in which 'the rich and powerful Western industrial countries are getting more and more "overdeveloped"' (1986, p. 39). Minh-ha (1993) makes a similar point about the link between 'underdeveloped' countries and the 'over-industrialized' West. These ideas have fed into current analyses of globalization, which stress that although the analytical distinction between the three worlds is becoming ever more difficult to sustain, it remains imperative that the connections which link the various parts of the modern global system are not lost to view.

The economic dimension of international interconnectedness has been recognized for some time, for example in the debates on late industrialization which were discussed in Chapter 2. More recently, attention has focused on the links between the industrialization of parts of the underdeveloped world and the 'de-industrialization' of advanced capitalist economies, and it has been suggested that such changes signal the emergence of a new international division of labour (Fröbel *et al.*, 1980), although there are competing interpretations of precisely what implications these developments have (Cohen, 1987; Jenkins, 1987). Few participants in this debate see the shifting location of industrial production from the North of the global system to the South as working unambiguously to the latter's advantage. It has been argued, for example, that change in 'the territorial division of labor between the core and the periphery enables a larger proportion of core workers to have cleaner and more skilled jobs' (Chase-Dunn, 1989, p. 42), while what is relocated to the third world is predominantly 'routine, monotonous and dangerous work' (Held, 1989, p. 193). It is also possible to regard the expansion of the power exercised by transnational corporations as a key development in the globalization of production (Sklair, 1995), against which force national governments may be considered to be increasingly impotent. A different perspective on the progressively more complex global economy is the view that it is moving beyond the control of any organizations, whether private or public, and it is certainly the case that globalization has thrown up a number of seemingly intractable international economic problems (such as the debt crisis [George, 1992]) which have highlighted the limited powers of existing agencies.

Global forces have also been unfolding in the political sphere, stimulating extensive discussion about whether world-wide trends towards democratic arrangements can be discerned. Hippler's observation that 'Almost everyone today is in favour of democracy'

(1995, p. vii) echoes the point made in the previous chapter about the universal popularity of the goal of 'development', and it carries the same implication that there is a need for caution in dealing with contested concepts. The process of decolonization in much of Africa, Asia and the Caribbean in the period since 1945 opened up the possibility of a transition to more democratic political arrangements, and while this transition has rarely been a smooth one, it has remained an objective which is aspired to widely in underdeveloped societies, despite the unfavourable economic context in which governments there operate (Held, 1993; Munck, 1994; Pinkney, 1993; Potter, 1992). Democratization of the former state socialist societies as they undergo demilitarization can also be interpreted as part of a global trend (McGrew, 1992b; Shaw, 1991), although this is a process which is occurring in often inauspicious economic conditions, as was noted in Chapter 5. Gordon White's (1993) analysis of contemporary China also casts doubt on the idea that a fixed relationship between economic development and democratization can be identified, offering support to Munck's general conclusion that any link between democracy and development is 'contingent and historically-bound' (1994, p. 37). Neither does the process of democratization come to an end with the establishment of constitutions which enshrine the citizen's right to participate in multi-party elections; as Melucci argues in his analysis of 'the democratization of everyday life' (1989, Ch. 8) in complex and fragmenting post-industrial societies, there is constant pressure to extend the boundaries of democratic accountability.

It is important to consider not only the economic and political faces of globalization, but also its cultural dimension. The attempt to attain economic development and democracy may be interpreted as part of the more general pursuit of modernity, including modern culture. Sklair has highlighted the crucial role played by what he calls 'the culture-ideology of consumerism' (1995, Ch. 5) in the increasing incorporation of the third world into the global economic system, while Worsley has argued that democratization can be understood as the assertion by members of cultural communities of their 'right to self-expression and self-determination' (1990, p. 93). These various forces do not necessarily push societies in the same direction, and there is no uniform pattern of global culture towards which things are moving. Just as economic development and democracy have taken on contrasting forms in different contexts, so too in the realm of culture has global interconnectedness promoted diversity as much as it has homogeneity. As Waters observes, 'Globalization is the direct consequence of the expansion of European culture across the planet via settlement, colonization and cultural mimesis', but it does not follow 'that every corner of the planet must become Westernized and capitalist' (1995, p. 3). Rather, it is the case that the modern world is marked by cultural confrontation at points where global economic and political forces bring diverse cultures into contact, a situation which has in turn generated growing demands for consideration of alternative conceptions of development and a radical questioning of the whole idea of becoming modern (Hettne, 1995). The global system thus constitutes an arena in which the protagonists of competing economic, political and cultural forces struggle to decide nothing less than the future course of social development.

Change and continuity in global economic relations

The second half of the twentieth century has witnessed unprecedented change in many respects, not least in the sphere of production. The speed of the growth of the global economy is illustrated by a few key indicators: 'Between 1950 and 1985 world output of goods increased fivefold, and exports ninefold. Manufacturing output rose seven times and exports sixteen times' (Kidron and Segal, 1991, p. 125). Against the background of the prolonged expansion which characterized the 'great boom' (Armstrong *et al.*, 1984) of the period from 1950 to the mid-1970s, it was plausible to entertain the possibility of progressive development occurring in the 'third world' at the same time as growing affluence was enjoyed in the industrialized nations. In the countries undergoing it, decolonization was interpreted as a change which promised economic as well as political independence, and 'For virtually all of these countries the first priority became rapid industrialisation which they saw as the only means of eliminating the poverty, ignorance and disease which they felt to be the most significant legacy of the colonial system' (Brett, 1985, p. 183). But while rising levels of production and world trade appeared to some commentators to allow newly industrializing countries to forge a path of development which other third world countries could follow, the sustainability of this perspective was increasingly brought into question. The failure of the majority of third world countries to narrow the economic gap between themselves and the advanced industrial nations and to escape dependency led to growing confrontation between the North and the South, with the latter demanding more than the 'grudging concessions' (Adams, 1993, p. 67) which the former had made. The concept of a 'third world' of poor countries embodied a critique of the structured inequality of international economic arrangements and a demand for a more just alternative (Harris, 1987), and by the 1970s this demand was being pursued more forcefully than in previous decades in the hope of securing a systematic redistribution of global resources.

Demands from the third world for the establishment of a New International Economic Order arose out of the desire to translate the promise of development into more concrete results. As time passed, it became increasingly clear that the fruits of the great expansion of the global economy were not being distributed evenly but rather were being channelled disproportionately to the richer countries. The decades of the 1950s and 1960s may have appeared to those in the West as the 'golden years' (Hewitt, 1992, p. 224), but from the South a less sanguine attitude appeared appropriate. Absolute output levels were increasing, but the third world's share of industrial production actually fell from 14 per cent to 12.2 per cent of the global total during the period 1948 to 1966, the slight rise in the share produced in the newly industrializing countries being more than offset by the fall elsewhere in the third world (Jenkins, 1992). At the same time, the terms of trade moved relentlessly against third world countries which relied on the export of primary commodities in order to purchase manufactured imports (Hewitt, 1992), and the overall effect of the development of the global economic system was that the gap between the rich world and the poor continued to widen (Brett, 1985). The proposed New International Economic Order held out 'the prospect of ameliorating some of the structural impediments to Third World advancement' by advocating a range of reforms to the international economic system, including 'commodity agreements, more preferential trade arrangements, increased aid, debt relief, controls over multinational corporations, and the democratization of all the key international financial institutions' (McGrew, 1992c, p. 259). The underlying implication was that a far greater degree of political intervention would be necessary if the growth in international inequality which had accompanied the expansion of the global economy were to be modified.

These proposals did usher in some changes, but they did not bring about the broader shift in the conception of 'development' for which there had been hope (South Commission, 1990). McGrew's general conclusion regarding the New International Economic Order is that 'this challenge to the dominance of the Western industrialized states with respect to the management of the global economy failed to deliver any significant "victories" for the Third World' (1992c, p. 259), which instead experienced a period of drift and mounting problems (Amin, 1990a). The fortunes of the newly industrializing countries and the rest of the third world in terms of their share of global industrial production continued to diverge (Jenkins, 1992), and the situation of those countries which continue to depend heavily on the export of primary products has been made increasingly desperate by the fact that 'The real prices for these commodities dropped by more than 40% through the 1980s' (Hewitt, 1992, p. 234). The global economic system remains massively unequal, and the failure of political efforts to redress this situation merely underlines the influence of 'the underlying balance of economic forces' (Adams, 1993, p. 137) and the power of the core elements in the system to reproduce their dominant position. Expressed another way, globalization has reinforced the tendency for development to be uneven. Within the third world, it would be difficult to imagine paths more divergent than those followed over recent decades by the newly industrializing countries on the one hand and the distressed and indebted states of sub-Saharan Africa on the other, the former increasingly integrated into the global economy, the latter becoming more peripheral and marginalized (Kennedy, 1993). In the urgent search for an explanation of this process, theories of how the development of the world economy is propelled by capitalist forces have been highly influential.

The analysis of the modern global system as a capitalist world-economy is the central theme of Wallerstein's work, which has been described as 'The most influential sociological argument for considering the world as a single economic system' (Waters, 1995, p. 22). Wallerstein's starting point was his observation that 'by a host of indicators, the economic gap between the more- and the less-developed countries seems to be increasing rather than narrowing despite the presumed efforts of multitudes of groups and governments' (1976, p. 277). As Wallerstein (1979) himself acknowledges, his ideas overlap with Frank's account of third world dependency (which was discussed in Chapter 6), not least because of their common insistence that the current situation must be seen in long-term historical perspective. For Wallerstein, present patterns of global interdependence have been evolving over the course of several centuries with the emergence of the modern capitalist world-economy which spread outwards from Europe, ultimately to cover the entire globe. From the sixteenth century onwards, 'there grew up a world-economy with a single division of labor within which there was a world market' (1979, p. 16). Within this world-economy what Wallerstein calls 'core', 'semiperipheral' and 'peripheral' areas became identifiable 'by about

1640' (1979, p. 18), with core areas increasing their dominance by their ability to appropriate the surplus of the whole world-economy. The semiperiphery occupies an intermediate position in Wallerstein's model, helping to secure the stability of the system overall by being 'both exploited and exploiter' (1979, p. 23), thereby inhibiting unity among those exploited by the minority of the world's population in the core states. The subsequent industrialization of the core states strengthened their position and extended their global reach, ushering in a new stage of the development of the capitalist world-economy with the now-familiar world division of labour from which third world countries have found it difficult to escape.

The debates generated by Wallerstein's writings have been touched on already in Chapter 1, where the question was raised of precisely what comparisons the core/periphery model allows. Wallerstein's position is that it is erroneous to treat societies or nation states as autonomous entities because 'there is no such thing as "national development"' independent of global forces, and he argues instead that 'the proper entity of comparison is the world system' (1979, p. 4). Only by comparing different elements of the world-economy as integrated parts of the same system can it be recognized that 'The early economic development of Western Europe was made possible by their utilization of cheap colonial labor in the Western Hemisphere and Asia' (1976, pp. 279–80), a process which cannot be repeated by developing countries in the twentieth century since they find themselves in a completely different global situation. Several evaluations have questioned the analytical purchase of Wallerstein's schema. Hulme and Turner's view that 'Wallerstein's semiperiphery encompasses a bewilderingly wide range of countries in terms of economic strength and political background' (1990, p. 52) is typical of the judgements of several commentators for whom the division of the world into three basic categories is insufficiently subtle to capture the complexity of the situations of countries which make up the global system, and for whom it is unhelpful to treat all of these countries as generically 'capitalist' simply by virtue of their involvement in the world-economy (Booth, 1994; Goodman and Redclift, 1981; Hettne, 1995; Sklair, 1995; Worsley, 1980). This criticism is linked to the observation that Wallerstein's focus obscures the extent to which the economic processes on which he concentrates can themselves be affected by political and non-class forces (Spybey, 1992; Sztompka, 1993). These criticisms of Wallerstein's world-system theory indicate that its tendency to overgeneralize limit its usefulness in comparative sociology, but this claim has been contested (Chase-Dunn, 1989), and the broad insights which have been made possible by this perspective deserve elaboration.

The dynamic nature of the capitalist world-economy makes it likely that global development will be subject to periods of instability and structural change. Wallerstein's (1979) identification of the 'contradictions' present in the system help to make sense of the difficulties which have been encountered in relation to both the narrowing of the development gap by the minority of third world states which constitute the newly industrializing countries and the more general polarization of global fortunes in the period since 1945. Wallerstein's historical studies suggest that the development of what came to be called the 'new international division of labour' (Fröbel *et al.*, 1980) marks merely the latest stage in the expansion of the capitalist world-economy. Earlier periods have witnessed the movement of states such as Japan from periphery to semiperiphery and core status, while other states have made converse transitions, and the trend towards the relocation of industrial production from industrial capitalist societies to parts of the third world by no means heralds a transformation of the global economy. The emergence of the newly industrializing countries as significant exporters of manufactured goods has not been without cost to the core states in terms of the increasing vulnerability of their hegemonic position within the system, however, and Wallerstein suggests that 'the cost of "cooption" rises ever higher' (1979, p. 35) with each new state from the periphery that gains access to the privileges of the core.

If the uneasy integration of the newly industrializing countries into the global economy illustrates one of the fundamental contradictions of the capitalist world-economy identified by Wallerstein, the continued impoverishment of much of the rest of the third world is an example of the other. The capitalist accumulation process dictates that 'in the short run the maximization of profit requires maximizing the withdrawal of surplus from immediate consumption of the majority' (1979, p. 35), and while in the longer term global development would benefit from a more equitable distribution of resources, the means to achieve this within the framework of a capitalist world-economy are absent. In the period since Wallerstein identified this contradiction, it is the short run pressures which have won out, demonstrated most starkly in the continued transfer of resources from poor to rich countries in order to meet international debt obligations which are widely recognized to be crippling for those forced to pay them (S. George, 1988, 1992; V. George, 1988). The 1980s were truly a 'lost decade' for the less developed countries of sub-Saharan Africa, where

levels of indebtedness grew to be equivalent to the size of their gross
domestic product and debt repayments claimed over a fifth of their
export revenues while per capita income fell by nearly one fifth
(Adams, 1993; Gibson and Tsakalotos, 1992; Vickers, 1991). Some
other parts of the third world fared even worse than this over the same
period, while in the developed world per capita incomes rose by 20 per
cent (Adams, 1993), trends which for Amin (1990b) demonstrate a
link between global economic expansion and the polarization of
wealth and power.

A key issue between Wallerstein and his critics is that of precisely
how the global economic system operates, as this has a crucial bearing
on conceptions of the possibility of social change. Wallerstein treats
global polarization as 'not an anomaly but a continuing basic
mechanism of the operation of the world economy', and he argues
that not only is it impossible 'for all states to "develop" simultaneously',
but it is also the case that there are only 'limited possibilities of
transformation within the capitalist world-economy' (1979, pp. 73,
66). For people attempting to bring about development and social
change, such a message is 'a profoundly demobilizing counsel of
despair' (Worsley, 1984, p. 22), implying as it does the power of
economic forces to foreclose alternative arrangements. What Wallerstein's perspective overlooks, Worsley argues, is that 'What is produced
and who gets what... are culturally and not just economically
determined' (1980, p. 333). A similar point is made in Sklair's analysis
of the global system in which he observes that world-system theorists
have tended to concentrate too much on the search for cheap labour by
transnational corporations, thereby failing 'to connect economic with
political and cultural–ideological transnational practices' (1995,
p. 40). Sztompka too criticizes Wallerstein's theory for its 'strong
economistic bias' (1993, p. 91), which led to the overemphasis on class
relations as sources of change and the neglect of the cultural
dimension of globalization.

It is incontrovertible that production has become progressively
internationalized and that transnational corporations have grown
enormously in power over the second half of the twentieth century. By
the mid 1980s, 600 transnational corporations generated 'half the
world's industrial output, a quarter of all physical goods and a fifth of
all income' (Kidron and Segal, 1991, p. 81); transnational corporations thus 'dominate virtually every sector of global industrial,
economic and financial activity' (McGrew, 1992c, p. 268). It would
nevertheless be an oversimplification to presume from this that
transnational corporations' interests always prevail in the global

economy (Jenkins, 1987). Sklair has argued against the idea that 'third world governments and institutions stand idly by while the bearers of transnational practices wreak havoc on their societies' (1995, p. 266), noting that it is rather the case that third world states are integrally involved with transnational corporations in shaping the changing international division of labour. As Chase-Dunn recognizes, 'The power of the transnational firms should not be overestimated' in the light of their 'dependence on individual states' (1989, p. 75). The modification of the logic of global capitalism by national political and cultural influences is illustrated by the diversity of employment practices operated by transnational corporations in different countries. In particular, research into the arrangements relating to women's incorporation into the industrial workforce as transnational corporations promote export-oriented industrialization in the third world reveals great variation (Mitter, 1986; Pearson, 1994). These findings, together with the continued concentration of global industrial production in the advanced capitalist economies, tend to confound the somewhat mechanical predictions of a new international division of labour in which transnational corporations progressively move their operations from the North of the global system to the South (Braham, 1992; Cohen, 1987; Hoogvelt, 1992; Wield and Rhodes, 1988).

That Wallerstein's identification of abstract contradictions at the heart of the capitalist world-economy does not necessarily allow predictions about the future course of its development to be made with any great precision is further illustrated by the way in which the debt crisis has unfolded (Hettne, 1995). While debt repayments constitute 'a continuing South-to-North resource flow on a scale far outstripping any the colonial period could command' (George, 1992, p. xvii), the system within which these transfers occur is not subject to overall control (Strange, 1986). George (1992) has pointed out that the rich creditor countries of the industrialized North have not been able to avoid the impact of what she calls 'the debt boomerang', and have themselves suffered from the debt crisis through lost jobs, environmental damage, the drugs trade, public subsidies to banks, migration pressures and international conflict. It is, of course, in the debtor countries that the effects of international indebtedness are felt most acutely, but even here the operation of economic forces in the process of 'restructuring' has to be understood in its wider social and political contexts (S. George, 1988). As Hettne has put it, 'Societies are not only economic systems, but populated with people who refuse to disappear when they become superfluous, either as producers or consumers'

(1995, p. 110). The economics of indebtedness undoubtedly narrows the options of third world states, but while some governments 'may be responsive to the interests of transnational capital', others are more responsive to 'the interests of a political class dependent on popular or sectional support to maintain its position of power' (Sklair, 1995, p. 5). Put another way, the discussion of the debt crisis involves 'talking not economics but politics' (S. George, 1988, p. 253), and the complex relationships between debt, development and democracy may be reworked in a number of different ways. George argues that debt does not rule out the possibility of democratic development, and in doing so revisits the classical sociological debate about the link between economic and social change.

The tortured link between development and democracy

The problematic relationship between the two revolutions which ushered industrialism and democracy into nineteenth-century Europe was a crucial issue of contention for the classical sociologists (Nisbet, 1967, Ch. 2). Moore's analysis of the social origins of democratic and non-democratic political arrangements (discussed in Chapter 2) returned to this theme, and concluded that where industrialization had occurred in the twentieth century, it had done so under the auspices of authoritarian governments, the 'democratic' route being no longer appropriate to changed global conditions. Other thinkers at this time also put forward the view that democracy was 'an *outcome* of socioeconomic development, not a condition of it' (Leftwich, 1995, p. 429, emphasis in original), reflecting a similar confidence in the evolution of progressively expanded citizenship to that which informed Marshall's classic model, which was examined in Chapter 4. More recently, the idea of a long-term tendency towards democracy appears to be given support by what Lewis calls 'processes of global democrati-zation' (1992, p. 49), reflecting the movement of much of the former state socialist world and many societies of the South towards more democratic politics along the lines of the systems found in the West, together with the further development of these systems in industrial capitalist states. Yet while certain changes, such as the extension of global communications, may have worked to promote the spread of democracy, other faces of globalization are more antithetical to democratization, making commentators cautious about pronouncing on the overall relationship between development and democracy in the contemporary world.

Hopes that the second half of the twentieth century would witness the democratization of the third world were not entirely groundless, but they were sociologically naive. Colonial rule was generally highly centralized and exclusive, and it left post-colonial societies with a legacy of bureaucratic administration 'from the top downwards' which generated 'popular predisposition to leave social initiatives to government and to external forces' (Worsley, 1967, p. 132). Colonial regimes also left behind them military institutions and class structures which were often inimical to democratic development, together with further problems relating to ethnic divisions exacerbated by the arbitrariness of colonial boundaries (Alavi, 1982; Leys, 1975; Webster, 1990). Pinkney's general view is that 'there was little basis for any expectation of the triumph of democracy once the countries of the third world became nominally independent' (1993, p. 60), and the successful establishment of durable democratic regimes has been very much the exception rather than the rule (Hadenius, 1992). Explanations of this situation framed in terms of late development and the consequences of dependency in the capitalist world-economy have wide currency, but Rueschemeyer *et al.*'s study concludes that 'the empirical cross-national evidence does not support these radical claims' (1992, p. 71). Economic explanations are also insufficient to account for the broad move towards democracy in the context of the debt-induced austerity programmes of the 1980s and 1990s which have been a widespread feature of the modern global system (Leftwich, 1995; Potter, 1992).

One of the reasons behind the renewed interest in the politics of development was the build up of pressure for democratic reforms in several newly industrializing countries, such as South Korea and Taiwan (Sklair, 1995). As was noted in Chapter 6, industrialization in these countries had been overseen by authoritarian governments, but the very success of building a modern industrial economy promoted the growth of a civil society which challenged existing political arrangements. In South Korea, for example, capitalist industrialization proceeded to bring about a situation in which 'the authoritarian state gradually came under increasing pressure from the growing power of the capital-owning and middle classes, who found the economic and social controls of the authoritarian state increasingly irksome' (Potter, 1993, p. 363). Yet there is, as Potter points out, 'nothing automatic about (late) capitalist development of this kind leading in a democratic direction' (1993, p. 364), and he goes on to compare events in South Korea with those in Indonesia, which has seen a similar economic transformation without equivalent political change. His conclusion that in South Korea higher rates of urbanization enabled the growth of a more powerful working class than that found in predominantly rural Indonesia fits in with the more general argument of Rueschemeyer *et al.* (1992) that it is the role of subordinate classes, and in particular the working class, which is the crucial determinant of the relationship between capitalist development and democracy.

Rueschemeyer *et al.* reach their conclusions about the long-term instability of non-democratic regimes in capitalist societies on the basis of extensive comparisons within and between the countries of the advanced capitalist world and those of the third world. The broad thrust of their case is that capitalism promotes democracy because it 'brings the subordinate class or classes together in factories and cities where members of those classes can associate and organize more easily; it improves the means of communication and transportation facilitating nationwide organization; in these and other ways it strengthens civil society and facilitates subordinate class organization' (1992, pp. 271–2). In the nature of the questions it addresses and the range of its coverage, the analysis put forward by Rueschemeyer *et al.* is reminiscent of Moore's study, which they attempt to build on through their criticism of the neglect in *Social Origins* of the international context in which political change takes place. By challenging Moore's 'exclusive focus on domestic developments', Rueschemeyer *et al.* are able to suggest that 'the reactionary path to political modernity has some potential for leading – by tortuous detours – to democratic political forms' (1992, p. 25). The external imposition of democratic constitutions on post-1945 Germany and Japan demonstrates that late developing capitalist countries are not necessarily locked permanently into authoritarian political arrangements. More recent moves towards democracy in southern Europe, Latin America and elsewhere provide additional illustrations in support of the contention that 'modern capitalist dictatorship is unstable and... further economic development will result in greater pressures for democratization' (1992, p. 292), although this argument is qualified by the observation that the difficulties of securing sustained economic growth in the third world are also likely to make democratic regimes there unstable.

The broad proposition that economic development leads to political pressures for democracy leaves unsolved the problem of how to explain the 'wave of democratization' (Potter, 1992, p. 273) which spread through much of Africa, Asia and Latin America in the 1980s and 1990s. Leftwich's argument that 'there is no necessary relationship between democracy and development' rests in part on the recognition that growth rates and political systems do not correlate at all strongly, and it is particularly instructive that 'some Third World democracies have had stagnant or even negative average annual growth records over the last 25 years' (1995, pp. 431–2). Additions to the ranks of democratic states among poorer nations may be accounted for in part by the tendency of economic difficulties to weaken the ideological bases of authoritarian regimes. Attempts to legitimize authoritarian rule by claiming that it fosters material prosperity have been discredited by the numerous counterinstances which led the World Bank to pronounce that 'Dictatorships have proven disastrous for development in many economies' (quoted in Munck, 1994, p. 25). Against the background of international debt, structural adjustment and austerity programmes, democratization may be supported not only by subordinate classes but also by powerful groups who see it as a means of 'spreading and sharing responsibilities, and defusing the mobilization of discontent' (Potter, 1993, p. 364), of 'legitimising the disempowerment of the people' (Aké, 1995, p. 78). At the same time, legitimations of state socialism as a course of development alternative to that of integration into the capitalist world-economy have been thrown onto the defensive by the recent events in Eastern Europe, where efforts to de-Stalinize the system from above finally ran their course, further strengthening pressure across the globe for the democratization of political arrangements.

Disillusionment with state-directed, 'top-down' strategies of development has sponsored the search for more democratic and participatory processes able to incorporate 'action from below' (Johnson, 1992; Mackintosh, 1992). A strong parallel exists between these ideas as they relate to the situation in the third world and the literature on democratization in former state socialist societies discussed in Chapter 5, not least because of their characterization of the centralized state as oppressive and their emphasis on the need for it to be counterbalanced by a dynamic civil society. Democratization is far from being a uniform process, however, and its progress in different countries has been influenced by local as well as global forces. As Shaw shows, the movement towards democracy in Eastern Europe is integrally connected to the process of demilitarization, and the difficulties and national peculiarities of this transition make it probable that wherever democratization involves a challenge to militarism, its course will be 'uneven and contradictory' (1991, p. 209). Similarly, the fact that China has embarked upon the path of what Gordon White calls 'economic de-Stalinisation' does not dictate that it will have the same outcome as the reform of Eastern European state socialism; whatever form democratization there takes, it is bound to be 'distinctively Chinese' (1993, pp. 246, 256), given its contrasting starting point.

Awareness of the complex connection between the development of capitalism and the growth of pressures for democratization can be traced back at least as far as Weber (Scaff, 1989), whose wariness of universal explanations continues to be widely shared. In this spirit, Lewis' survey of democracy in modern societies concludes that in comparison to the situation in societies with long parliamentary traditions, democracy's 'instability is likely to be that much greater in countries like those in Eastern Europe and parts of South-East Asia which have become involved in recent processes of global democratization' (1992, p. 49). Lewis makes a similar point about the greater uncertainties surrounding the return to democracy in those Latin American countries which have alternated between democratic and more authoritarian forms of government, a view echoed in Roberts' observation that 'The re-emergence of democracy in Latin America in the 1980s and 1990s has... occurred in unpropitious circumstances' (1995, p. 210). The austere economic situation of Latin America might be thought likely to induce a rapid return to authoritarianism there, but Roberts suggests that while democratization may be hampered by the reduction of national control over economic forces due to globalization, other changes internal to these societies have broadened the bases of political participation and brought the extension of citizenship. As Roberts notes, the growth of citizenship in Latin America over the last 40 years has not conformed to the pattern set out by Marshall, nor to the alternative top-down models, described by Mann (1987), which were developed in Europe. Rather, it has been much more strongly influenced by the urban poor's 'vigorous, if piecemeal, grass roots organization' and popular pressures from below to include 'issues of age, gender and ethnicity' (Roberts, 1995, pp. 187, 211) in new and extended definitions of citizenship.

The key role played by women in the evolution of citizenship in Latin America is a good illustration of Mayo's point that there are lessons 'for the First World to draw from the experiences of the Third World, and especially so in relation to community participation and community development' (1994, p. 112). The very different constellation of civil, political and social rights in Latin America from that found in European welfare states emphasizes the diversity of political arrangements which are labelled 'democratic' and the range of ways in which 'participation' is understood (Whitehead, 1993). One of the central difficulties with the concept of democratization has been the problem of defining and operationalizing it (Hadenius, 1992;

Rueschemeyer *et al.*, 1992), and the tendency of conventional studies to treat democracy as 'an abstract western ideal inextricably bound up with a particular notion of (capitalist) development' (Munck, 1994, p. 36) highlights the need to transcend 'Eurocentrism', that is, treating Europe as 'the standard by which development in other parts of the world is measured' (Hettne, 1995, p. 258). Pinkney is right to stress that 'the forces which have established and maintained democracy in the West are different from those which have done so in the Third World' (1993, p. 168), just as they are different again from those operating in former state socialist societies, and globalization works in many ways to sustain and deepen these differences.

At a general level, it is the case that globalization has eroded the power of all nation states to control economic activity within their borders, but it has not done so evenly. While it may be that 'Issues of economic and social development for the vast majority of the world's population reveal anything but self-determination and autonomy' (Lash and Urry, 1994, p. 320), it does not follow that the potential for democratic forces to exercise restraint on global economic forces is equally constrained in rich and poor countries. As Held points out, 'The loss of control of national economic programmes is... not uniform across economic sectors or societies' (1991, p. 215), and he goes on to specify a number of ways in which nation states may, either individually or as part of larger groupings, modify the power of transnational economic networks. The emergence of international trading blocs is one example of political attempts to regulate international market forces, producing 'a regionalized world system' (Hettne, 1995, p. 116) in which the power of the core states and the marginality of the periphery is readily apparent. Global economic processes have not totally undermined the power of states to express democratic sentiments, as 'States may have surrendered some rights and freedoms, but in the process they have gained and extended others' (Held, 1991, p. 223). Held recognizes that by no means all states have been able to secure 'the curtailment of the power of multinational corporations to constrain and influence the political agenda' (1991, p. 234), illustrating the point that democratization can vary enormously according to the context in which it unfolds.

Global influences have had a crucial bearing on the way in which democracy has developed in contemporary capitalist societies. In Melucci's account of the evolution of what he calls 'the democracy of everyday life' (1989, p. 174), it is argued that the familiar distinction between state and civil society has become increasingly blurred in the complex and fragmenting societies of the post-industrial age. For

Melucci, the unitary state characteristic of earlier, organized capitalist societies has dissolved and 'has been replaced from above, by a tightly interdependent system of transnational relationships, as well as subdivided, from below, into a multiplicity of partial governments' (1989, p. 171). The emergence of new social movements has been central to this shift, since the proliferation of different groups within complex societies poses a growing challenge to conventional legitimations of state activity as 'neutral' and 'rational' (1989, p. 175). Melucci acknowledges that this argument carries echoes of the ideas of Habermas (discussed in Chapter 4), but he places greater emphasis than does Habermas on the way in which 'Democracy in complex societies requires conditions which enable individuals and social groups to affirm themselves and to be recognized for what they are or wish to be' (1989, p. 172). Democratization is pushed further as diverse groups, aware of global heterogeneity, assert their right to be different and in doing so challenge narrow and uniform conceptions of citizenship and belonging. The contribution of the feminist movement to democratization might be cited as an example of this point (Rueschemeyer and Rueschemeyer, 1990), and the changing position of women is seen by Hutton as generating pressure for 'the democratisation of the welfare-state' (1996, p. 306). At the same time, other aspects of globalization work to bring about 'a levelling of differences, turning peripheral cultures into insignificant "folk cultures" which are appendices of the few "centres" responsible for producing and diffusing cultural codes' (Melucci, 1989, p. 177). Expressed another way, globalization's effects in the sphere of politics are contradictory, promoting 'democratization and *de*-democratization, modernity and *counter*-modernity' (Beck, 1992, p. 192, emphases in original), and it is against this background that speculation about the emergence of a global society needs to be set.

The flawed critique of globalization as Westernization

Doubts about whether integration into the capitalist world-economy and democratization constitute social 'progress' are echoed by concerns over the effects of globalization in the cultural sphere. Latouche has noted that, contrary to some of the more fanciful predictions of earlier generations of forecasters, the spread from the West of modern, economic influences across the globe 'has by no means brought about a universal equalising of real living standards' (1993, p. 199); indeed, the reverse is more the case. In similar vein, Melucci raises the question of where democratization is leading by observing that the challenge to conventional politics by new social movements involves 'their proclamation of the end of linear progress'; the assertion of their difference is an indication of the way in which 'Change in complex societies becomes discontinuous' (1989, p. 168). Likewise, the expectation that modernization would promote a world of increasing homogeneity organized along rational lines has been confounded by the persistence of cultural diversity and the growing strength of movements opposed to core Western values. That global-ization ushers in changes which are contested can be seen in proposals for third world countries to 'de-link' from the capitalist world-economy (Amin, 1990b), the resurgence of alternative political and cultural agendas such as those of Islamic fundamentalism (Amin, 1990b, Ch. 6; Ray, 1993, Ch. 7; Spybey, 1992, Ch. 12), and the active promo-tion in some quarters of 'demodernization' (Hettne, 1995, p. 66).

Wallerstein's historical research tracing the position of Europe at the core of the development of the capitalist world-economy is a powerful illustration of McGrew's general point that 'the dominant processes of globalization have intimate connections with processes of Westernization' (1992c, p. 263). Modernization theory's simple equation of social progress with the spread of Western institutions and norms is now effectively defunct, but Hettne's identification of 'Eurocentric bias' (1995, p. 67) in development thinking extends far beyond this and leads ultimately to the need to re-think the fundamental categories which are employed in understanding the world. One immediate casualty of this re-examination is the notion of Western superiority over Southern backwardness, which is conjured by treating the first and third worlds as the top and bottom elements of a hierarchy. Rooted in dissatisfaction with the way in which 'Western theorists have too often tended to generalize from a Eurocentric base', the central thrust of Asante's writings on 'Afrocentricity' is 'to dispense with the notion that, in all things, Europe is teacher and Africa is pupil' (1993, p. 555). Similar expressions of 'the voice of the other' (Hettne, 1995, Ch. 2) have come from elsewhere in the third world. The logic of such arguments is towards 'multicentricity' or 'polycentrism', incorpo-rating a range of alternative paths of development emerging out of relations of global interdependence rather than dependence (Amin, 1990a). At the same time, in the West the expanded contact with other cultures brought about by globalization has had the effect of undermining the presumed certainties on which ideas of Western superiority were based, making it increasingly difficult to specify the essential elements of what it means to be Western (Robins, 1990).

While the processes of globalization and Westernization are closely interconnected, there are good reasons to be wary of equating them. To begin with, attempts to develop an account of globalization as Westernization run into the difficulty of the progressive blurring of the West's geographical boundaries as commodities, people and ideas cross those boundaries with greater frequency. Among the most widely recognized effects of globalization is that social relationships are less and less bound by spatial location, a point central to Waters' definition of globalization as '*A social process in which the constraints of geography on social and cultural arrangements recede and in which people become increasingly aware that they are receding*' (1995, p. 3, emphasis in original). It has been acknowledged for a long time that the interconnectedness of local and global social relationships makes problematic the idea of societies as discrete, bounded entities, but recent years have witnessed changes which have brought about further and faster erosion of the effectiveness of territorial boundaries, reflecting the intensification of 'time–space compression' (Harvey, 1989, p. 240). These changes have allowed an expanded flow of traffic (in its broadest sense) across frontiers in both directions, and while the movement in one direction might be understood as Westernization, as 'the export of western commodities, values, priorities, ways of life', globalization also involves processes which import to Western societies 'the encounter of colonial centre and colonized periphery' (Robins, 1990, p. 197). Robins notes that this encounter is particularly striking in the context of the large-scale migration from the third world to former colonial metropolises, which has produced the cultural flux associated with the presence of '"the rest" in "the West"' (Hall, 1992, p. 306). Other examples of the 'Third World in the First World' (Minh-ha, 1993, p. 608; Peters, 1988) and the converse scenario of countries such as South Africa being the 'First World in the Third World' (Mayo, 1994, p. 128) reveal the more general difficulty of specifying to and from which locations in the global system the process of Westernization runs.

Globalization may be regarded as synonymous with Westernization in the sense that its defining features have their historical origins in the West, but it would be a mistake to see it as a process which promotes global homogeneity through the imposed reproduction of Western patterns elsewhere in the world. As Giddens states, globalization 'is more than a diffusion of Western institutions across the world, in which other cultures are crushed' (1990, p. 175). It was noted in the previous two sections of this chapter that the expansion of the world-economy has produced important variations in patterns of development which have, on the whole, not followed European paths, while in the political sphere Westernization understood as the adoption of arrangements akin to those practised in Europe has been the exception rather than the rule. In the realm of culture, it is similarly the case that the countries of the periphery have not imitated the core in any mechanical fashion, while there has also been extensive appropriation of ideas and practices by the West from the rest of the world (McGrew, 1992a; Sztompka, 1993; Waters, 1995). In the period since the Second World War, Europe has 'ceased to be the explicit yardstick of modernity', not least because of the declining power of European states to impose their ideas on other parts of the world, but this shift is more profound than 'The end of exporting European modernity by gunboat' (Therborn, 1995, pp. 360, 362). Power in the global system has shifted away from Europe (and from other Western countries such as the USA), partly because of the rise of East Asian economies, but more importantly because the nature of power in the global system has changed, making what takes place increasingly beyond anyone's control.

The analysis of the future course of globalization reveals that complex and contradictory forces are unfolding. The graphic suggestion that 'living in the modern world is more like being aboard a careering juggernaut... rather than being in carefully controlled and well-driven motor car' (Giddens, 1990, p. 53) is founded on the assumption that the several dimensions of globalization are influenced by distinct pressures and are not subject to overall synchronization or direction. Political pressures for democratization may be at odds with changes in the world-economy which limit the power of nation states, and cultural changes have the potential to add further to what might be termed 'the new world chaos' in which 'forces operating beyond human control... are transforming the world' (Waters, 1995, pp. 120, 3). From this point of view, globalization may be seen as disorganized capitalism (which was discussed in Chapter 3) writ large. Not all commentators interpret globalization in this way, however. Just as there are writers who are critical of the theory of disorganized capitalism for its neglect of continuities in the power of the capitalist class to shape wider social developments, so too there are theorists for whom it is important to highlight capitalism as the crucial driving force within globalization. For example, Sklair (1994, 1995) has argued that the role of the transnational capitalist class has been pivotal in what he regards as the two key shifts in the contemporary world, the spread of transnational corporations and the globalization of the mass media, both of which have promoted consumerism as the centrepiece of modern global culture.

It is beyond dispute that globalization is unfolding within the context of a global system dominated by transnational corporations which have acquired awesome power. As Sklair notes, 'The largest TNCs have assets and annual sales far in excess of the gross national products of most of the countries in the world' (1994, p. 166). In their promotion of the global expansion of capitalism in which the spread of 'the culture-ideology of consumerism' plays a crucial role, transnational corporations are assisted by 'globalizing state bureaucrats' in key political positions and 'capitalist-inspired politicians and professionals' (1994, pp. 175–7). Sklair's analysis suggests that the power of transnational corporations to influence political and cultural as well as economic aspects of global change make it appropriate to speak of their distorting effect on development. This allows the distinction to be made between 'capitalist "development"' and alternative definitions of development framed in terms of 'economic growth plus criteria of distribution of the social product, democratic politics and the elimination of class, gender and ethnic privileges' (1994, p. 165), although Sklair is under no illusions about the difficulties of securing the latter type of social change in the face of the power of transnational corporations such as Coca-Cola and McDonald's. Furthermore, he recognizes that while some critics of prevailing patterns of development interpret them in terms of 'Americanization' (1995, p. 186), others see the need to go beyond the critique of Westernization to raise the more radical possibility of going beyond industrial society.

Globalization focuses attention once more on the central questions of classical sociology relating to the nature of modern societies and the direction of social change, although the writings of the classical sociologists offer no more than a starting point for their analysis (Robertson, 1992; Waters, 1995). A curious feature of much of the more recent literature addressing these questions makes the link with the classical debates by suggesting that current developments have gone beyond earlier stages without specifying precisely how things have moved on. Chapter 3 considered various theories of the shift from industrialism to post-industrialism and Fordism to post-Fordism, while Chapter 5's discussion of post-communist societies examined writers who employ the similar technique of characterizing the present in terms of former arrangements which have been superseded. In the analysis of third world societies, there is extensive resort to concepts such as 'post-colonialism' (Alavi, 1972; Corbridge, 1994) and 'post-development' (Escobar, 1995; Latouche, 1993), the latter term having a wider usage in the critique of any theory of social change which 'depicts a historical process as endowed with a specific logic, meaning or form, and as progressing in predetermined fashion according to some "iron laws" of history' (Sztompka, 1993, p. 296). This idea is echoed in the notion of 'postmodernization' (Crook *et al.*, 1992) and the associated claim that a transition from modernity is underway. Sceptical of any theory of social change formulated around universal concepts such as 'progress' or 'development', post-modernists raise fundamental doubts not only about the direction of social change, but also about the very idea of attempting to predict the future. The implications for comparative sociology of these revitalized classical debates about the nature of modernity and social change will be the subject of the next chapter.

8

Comparative Sociology and Theories of Social Change: Progress, Unpredictability and Visions of the Future

There is a widespread sense that the contemporary world is undergoing a profound transition, perhaps as profound as Polanyi's (1957) 'great transformation' which marked the emergence of modernity and which sponsored the birth of the discipline of sociology. It is certainly the case that the global reach of economic, political and cultural forces has had an intensely destabilizing effect throughout what Horowitz called the 'three worlds of development' (1972), resulting in the need to reconsider the very terminology of first, second and third worlds coined in the period following the Second World War (Worsley, 1984). Chapters 3 and 4 charted the various processes unfolding within industrial capitalist societies, which are becoming in some senses 'post-industrial' and which are in important respects increasingly diverse. The second world of state socialist societies examined in Chapter 5 has undergone even more dramatic changes, to the extent that 'when communism was abandoned in Eastern Europe and the former Soviet Union, the rationale for the Second World appeared to have vanished' (Sklair, 1995, p. 11). From the outset, the heterogeneity of the countries grouped together in the third world made the category inherently problematic, and the further differentiation of these countries during the second half of the twentieth century has added to doubts about its analytical usefulness, as has been noted in Chapters 6 and 7. If comparative sociology is to fulfil its promise and to have continued relevance in the twenty-first century, it will be necessary to reassess this inherited framework of analysis and go beyond the three worlds.

Underlying the division of the globe into three worlds was the dichotomous distinction between traditional and modern societies, a distinction which served as the linchpin of modernization theory. Divisions between the first and second worlds were impossible to ignore in the context of their military rivalry during the Cold War, but whatever differences of economic and political system existed between them, their common achievement of industrial development set them apart from the underdeveloped world, where it appeared that 'the countries which were now coming into being were different in kind' (Worsley, 1984, pp. 306–7). As was noted in Chapter 5, state socialism shared with industrial capitalism the goal of material abundance, the aspiration to secure standards of material welfare akin to those in the 'age of high mass consumption' to which Rostow's (1960) modernization sequence ultimately led. The desirability of becoming modern in order to achieve this goal has been brought into question with the emergence of oppositional social movements such as environmentalists, 'The *post-materialists* who search for and defend values that have been eroded by the modern project' (Hettne, 1995, p. 66, emphasis in original). It may not (yet) be appropriate to consider rich countries as having reached 'post-material society, in which the primary needs of the population are to a large extent satisfied' (Melucci, 1989, p. 177), but the prospect of social change taking a radically different course once scarcity is overcome has been anticipated for some time, as has the related idea of a transition to 'post-modern society' (Kumar, 1995). This and other concepts involving 'post' as a prefix give a 'sense of marking time, of living in an interregnum' (Bell, 1974, p. 51). Bell also writes of modernism becoming 'exhausted' (1976, p. 84) and suggests that its contradictions are serious enough to threaten social disintegration through the decline of modernism's moral order.

The theme of modernity having run its course informs analyses of other societies besides industrial capitalist ones. Bauman's work on state socialism contains the claim that 'The postmodern challenge proved to be highly effective in speeding up the collapse of communism' (1992, p. 171). Bauman considers modernity to be 'an obsessive march forward' (1991, p. 10), and while this may involve different countries taking different routes, they are all informed by the philosophy of progress, by the sense that social change has an overall direction, moving towards a future which is somehow better. The concept of progress and the related concept of social evolution have been matters of contention within sociology since the classics debated their place in explanations of the course of social change (Kumar, 1978; Pollard, 1971; Salomon, 1995), and scepticism about whether they have a legitimate place in sociological analysis extends far beyond post-modernist theorists (Füredi, 1992). For example, doubt about the idea that social change is structurally determined is one factor leading Giddens to the view that 'Human history does not have an evolutionary "shape", and positive harm can be done by attempting to compress it into one' (1984, p. 236). Against this, Giddens is also wary of exaggerating historical disjunctions and is of the opinion that 'Rather than entering a period of post-modernity, we are moving into one in which the consequences of modernity are becoming more radicalised and universalised than before' (1990, p. 3). A key issue at stake here is that of identifying how social change comes about. There is, as Collins has observed, 'no reason why societies must solve their problems; history is full of failures to do so' (1981, p. 49), and it follows that theories which rely on identified contradictions working themselves out in a law-like fashion will probably provide poor bases for analysis and prediction.

Theories of social evolution and progress are hamstrung by their narrowness of vision, both historical and geographical. Interpretations of human history from the vantage point of the current time suffer from 'presentism' (Bauman, 1991, p. 5), a tendency to exaggerate the importance of current achievements and to offer distorted accounts of both the past and the future. Likewise, as Caldwell notes in his critical comments on 'Europocentrism', 'It *is* difficult for people in the West to shake off the illusion, ingrained over generations, that the world revolves round the rich white countries – their actions, initiatives, decisions and directions' (1977b, p. ix, emphasis in original). These problems are not restricted to progressive theories, however, because any theory of social change needs to address the question of perspective, and all attempts by comparative sociologists to develop analytical frames are hampered by insufficient distance from their subject matter. For example, Esping-Andersen's work on social stratification in post-industrial society is qualified by the recognition that 'A project which addresses an unfolding, not yet clearly visible, process can hardly ever be precise, let alone definitive', and he goes on to point out that 'the reigning modern theories of *industrial* society were forged long after the fact' (1993a, p. 1, emphasis in original). A generation earlier, Moore acknowledged the strength of the argument 'that we are too close to communist revolutions to judge them properly', experience teaching us that 'the liberating effects of past revolutions took a long time to appear' (1967, p. 507), although Moore is not prevented by this from anticipating communism's transcendence. It is less true for Moore than for his contemporaries that 'In these now uncannily distant times the audacious communist project seemed to make a lot of sense and was taken quite seriously by its friends and foes alike' (Bauman, 1992, p. 168). Further examples could be cited to show the need for 'sociological imagination', for 'the capacity to shift from one perspective to another' (Mills, 1970, p. 232), if the practitioners of comparative sociology are to locate their times and places in frameworks which are durable.

The crisis of modernity and the idea of post-modernity

Much of what has been discussed in previous chapters could be used to illustrate what Bauman (1991) refers to as the ambivalence of modernity. Modernization promised material plenty through industrialization, but this has been a far from universal experience. Some societies, such as the newly industrializing countries, have managed to join the ranks of the developed economies, and Latouche comments sardonically that in Taiwan, South Korea, Hong Kong and Singapore 'That means about 70 million lucky beneficiaries. But the trickle-down effect operates poorly in Brazil, and not at all in India. There are still billions of people for whom the end of the Third World has spelt nothing but the end of a great hope' (1993, pp. 38–9). At the same time, where it has occurred, material prosperity has not necessarily brought the satisfaction expected of it, as writers such as Berger *et al.* have noted in their analysis of how pressure for 'demodernization' may be generated out of 'modernity and its discontents' (1973, Ch. 8). Modernity generates negative as well as positive reactions not only because of the co-existence of affluence and poverty, but also because the attempt to secure freedom from old social, political and physical constraints has frequently been accompanied by the generation of new ones. Weighing up the overall balance sheet, it can be said that 'Modern society brings progress in the form of material abundance. Less certainly it brings increasing control of the natural and social environment. But its scientific and technological achievements are bought at high cost to spiritual and emotional life' (Kumar, 1988, p. 33). The gist of this assessment of modernity was already present in Weber's critique of the idea of progress, as was noted in Chapter 1, although much of the contemporary writing on this subject has sought to go beyond his core theme of rationalization.

Modernity's ambivalence has given rise to several competing visions of the future. According to Sztompka, the most optimistic of these sees the benefits outweighing the costs, and predictions from this standpoint anticipate that 'modernity will simply evolve in the same direction, reaching more mature, perfected forms' (1993, p. 81). In stark contrast to this scenario, Sztompka notes, stands 'the main thrust of recent social theory' which posits that societies are in the process of moving 'towards some qualitatively new type of society to emerge out of the ashes of modernity' (1993, pp. 82–3). Lyotard's 'incredulity towards metanarratives' (1990, p. 330) encompasses doubts about theories of progress which presume modernity's ability to satisfy material aspirations, but more fundamentally it challenges the status of claims to scientific knowledge on which the whole project of building a rational society was based. Post-modernism's scepticism about interpretations of history framed in terms of inevitability has been employed to 'deconstruct' many conventional theories such as those of development (Crush, 1995; Escobar, 1995) and democratization (Munck, 1994), but while these exercises are in tune with the growing emphasis on difference and diversity which has come to characterize much of social science, their implications for what comparative sociologists can say about the future remain contested (Booth, 1994). By heightening doubts about the degree to which contemporary societies are organized and controlled, and the extent to which they change along predictable lines, post-modernism has made it possible to envisage a wider range of alternative futures than those set down in the inflexible schema of stages of development found in progressive perspectives. At the same time, its emphasis on historical discontinuity serves to warn of the pitfalls liable to befall those who attempt social forecasting in the age characterized as being 'after progress' (Smart, 1992, p. 24).

That the potential exists for patterns of social change to be partially interpreted is not in dispute. Foucault's extensive writings in the diverse fields of the history of madness, punishment and sexuality contain ample demonstrations of the way in which social arrangements come to be judged through specific rationalities rather than a universal rationality, the different standpoints being inevitable in Foucault's view because of the link between rationality and the exercise of power (Garland, 1990, Ch. 6; Smart, 1988). In his work on the history of punishment, for example, Foucault suggests that it is necessary to be sceptical of accounts framed in terms of progressive reform, since apparent liberalization in this sphere may mask the development of new and more subtle, sophisticated and oppressive mechanisms of social control. Moreover, prisons have failed to eliminate crime over the past two centuries, but this has to be seen in the context of their 'success' in contributing to the rise of 'the disciplinary society' (1979, p. 217), in which all citizens are subjected to increasing surveillance and control. Once established, institutions quickly come to be regarded as 'natural' (1979, p. 233), and faith in the capacity of rational criticism to bring about the humanitarian reform of their operation is misplaced because it overlooks the intricate interconnectedness of what Foucault terms 'power-knowledge' and avoids the necessary question, '*What* is this Reason that we use?' (quoted in Rabinow, 1986, p. 14, emphasis in original). That there are more than passing resemblances between Foucault's work and Weber's theory of rationalization has been widely noted, even if some scholars, such as Dean (1994), are keen play down the extent to which the two perspectives coincide.

Several commentators suggest that Foucault shares Weber's suspicion of theories which conceptualize society as a coherent and integrated system following a pre-determined course. Both Weber and Foucault insist that it is vital to analyze 'social relations and social institutions without positing any essential or unified conception of the social whole' (Garland, 1990, p. 178). In contrast to the rigid patterns of social change set down in evolutionary theories, 'What both Weber and Foucault proffer... is a heroic refusal to sentimentalize the past in any way or to shirk the necessity of facing the future as dangerous but open' (Rabinow, 1986, p. 27). The reassertion of the openness of the future to which Foucault's writings have contributed has prompted a renewed interest in 'alternative futures', a project given greater urgency by the perception of the present state of modernity as characterized by 'increasing levels of inequality and exploitation, an accelerating deterioration in the quality of life, and a growing ecological crisis' (Smart, 1992, p. 108). Others have drawn from Foucault more pessimistic 'visions of social control' with the prospect of the emergence of 'the classified society' (Cohen, 1985, p. 191) as surveillance and regulation employing increasingly refined classifications of the population creep into more and more areas. The surveillance associated with the growth of centralized welfare bureaucracies may be considered a paradoxical effect of the expansion of citizenship (Abercrombie *et al.*, 1986), part of what for Hall *et al.* is a tendency for modern societies to be marked by 'a growth of organizations... seeking greater regulation and surveillance of social life' (1992, p. 3). While Giddens (1982) has contested the validity of extending Foucault's analysis of prisons to other institutions such as schools and workplaces, the prospect of an emergent 'surveillance society' (Lyon, 1994) remains a powerful image.

The strength of the forces driving modern societies towards ever-finer classifications and greater regulation and control prompts Bauman to observe that 'modernity is about the production of order' (1991, p. 15), although he goes on to point out that this is a goal which is bound to be frustrated. One of the key reasons for this is that modern societies are composed of 'a cluster of institutions, each with its own pattern of change and development' (Hall *et al.*, 1992, p. 3). Organized capitalism, state socialism and some strategies of development in the third world were in their different ways attempts to secure the integration of these diverse elements within a unified system subject to overall regulation and direction, but the difficulties encountered have necessitated fundamental reviews of these projects, as previous chapters have shown. Recent experience has highlighted that there is no simple, deterministic relationship between the economic, political and cultural elements of modernity, and that while a process of rationalization may be underway in each of these spheres, 'rationalization of fragments of the system does not lead to the rationality of the system as a totality' (Bauman, 1987, p. 188); rather, Bauman argues, it reinforces the tendency of modern societies to fragment. These developments make it increasingly implausible to suppose that social change is under overall control or direction, whether by the state, capitalist forces or any other agency, and it is against this backdrop that perceptions of modernity being in crisis have hardened.

These arguments do not convince everyone of the conclusion that a qualitative change from modern society to post-modern society has been effected. Harvey, for example, sees post-modernity as a particular 'historical condition', but one very much shaped by the forces of capitalism against the background of 'The crisis of overaccumulation that began in the late 1960s' (1989, p. 327). For Harvey, post-Fordism and post-modernity should not be conflated. In similar vein, albeit from a rather different starting point, Giddens has argued that 'We have not moved beyond modernity but are living precisely through a phase of its radicalisation' (1990, p. 51). This 'radicalised modernity', 'high modernity' or 'late modernity' (Giddens, 1990, pp. 149, 163; 1991, p. 3) is not a simple continuation of modernity as it is conventionally understood, since the forces of globalization have not only accelerated processes of social change, but have also forced the recognition that 'Modernity is essentially a post-traditional order' (Giddens, 1991, p. 20). Globalization has wrought profound changes in each of 'the four basic institutional dimensions of modernity' that Giddens identifies, which become 'disembedded' (1990, pp. 59, 79) as a result of the dynamic processes unfolding in the world capitalist economy, the international division of labour, the nation state system and the world military order. While these various changes add up to the modern world being a 'runaway world' beyond overall control, Giddens also argues that 'the unifying features of modern institutions are just as central to modernity – especially in the phase of high modernity – as the disaggregating ones' (1991, pp. 16, 27), by implication criticizing the overemphasis on disunity, disorganization and fragmentation contained in theories of post-modern society.

A further and more important point at issue between post-modernist theorists and Giddens is the question of how far it is possible to identify patterns of history as they unfold. Giddens is dismissive of 'the idea that no systematic knowledge of human action or trends of social development is possible' (1990, p. 47). On the basis of his identification of the institutional dimensions of modernity, Giddens claims that it is conceivable to imagine a movement beyond modernity towards an institutionally complex 'post-modern system' (1990, p. 163) characterized by the replacement of the world capitalist-system by a post-scarcity system, the humanization of technology, multi-layered democratic participation and demilitarization. These 'contours of a post-modern order' appear markedly utopian, as Giddens recognizes, particularly when they are set against the more sombre possibilities of economic collapse, ecological disaster, the growth of totalitarian power and nuclear conflict, the 'high-consequence risks of modernity' (1990, pp. 164, 171). Giddens' critique of the post-modernist assertion that modernity is exhausted and has run its course does not share the confidence of writers such as Habermas (1990) and Callinicos (1989) about the sustainability of the project of modernity, but it does contain a sense of how the institutions of modernity are likely to have a continuing effect on the alternatives confronting contemporary societies.

Approaching the question in this fashion leads to the conclusion that the options available in the modern world are necessarily narrower than those implicit in post-modern characterizations of the future as 'open'. In the extreme, the post-modern perspective suggests that anything is possible, and under the influence of the post-modern critique of generalization in social theory, 'The search for determinate linkages between social relations which characterized nineteenth-century sociology, and in particular nineteenth-century evolutionism, has largely collapsed into what may be called "accidentalism"' (Holton and Turner, 1989, p. 111). At the same time, from Giddens' point of view, the range of possible futures is necessarily broader than that implicit in the perspective advanced in the 1980s that, as Bauman described the position, 'the modern world faces a situation without good choices' (1987, p. 124). This narrow choice between alienating consumer capitalism and repressive state socialism has narrowed further following the revolutionary changes in Eastern Europe to leave those in the industrialized world, again employing Bauman's characterization, 'living without an alternative' (1992, Ch. 8). The comparable argument that 'poverty in the Third World forecloses any option other than capitalism' (Crow, 1988, p. 348) is, as Crow emphasizes, one that rules out the possibility of alternative development strategies and in doing so treats the undeniably real constraints as determining forces.

Historians of social theory will recognize as familiar many of the issues raised by these contemporary debates. The posited supersession of modernity has parallels with claims by Bell (1976) and others to have detected a movement from industrialism and capitalism towards post-industrial society, one response to which was that it exaggerated the degree of change and underplayed the extent of continuity involved (Kumar, 1995). Similarly, it was noted above that some theorists prefer to operate with the concept of neo-Fordism rather than post-Fordism (Allen, 1992b), while others employ the term 'neo-colonialism' rather than 'post-colonialism' (Leys, 1975) in order to make essentially the same point. Situations which strike some observers as 'new times' (Hall and Jacques, 1989) are perceived by others to involve greater continuity (McDowell, 1992), but to construct debates around the opposition of continuity and change is to operate with a false dichotomy, as Burke (1992) has observed. Part of the difficulty here for the practice of comparative sociology is that of identifying the level at which analysis is pitched and, as Runciman has indicated, this methodological question needs to be settled from the outset before judgements can be made about whether resemblances between cases are 'sufficient to outweigh the differences' (1989, p. 59). In this respect, post-modernism may be understood as a reaction against the overgeneralized theories of progress, industrial society and capitalist society which were guilty of treating differences insensitively. For current practitioners of comparative sociology, which Sklair describes as 'the attempt to generate universal propositions on the basis of systematic comparisons of a variety of different societies' (1995, p. 1), post-modernism stands as a timely reminder of the dangers of mis-recognizing similarities and differences.

Beyond evolutionary logics and the resolution of contradictions

The difficulties inherent in making decisions about how best to compare societies are well illustrated by the theory of industrial society as a generic type. It has already been noted in Chapter 1 that the idea of a long-term, evolutionary movement whereby societies converge on a common set of social arrangements was influential among comparative sociologists in the 1950s and 1960s, although the roots of this perspective can be traced back much earlier (Kerr, 1983; Kumar, 1978). At the most abstract level, Parsons developed a 'paradigm of evolutionary change' in which he distinguished between 'three very broad evolutionary levels... *primitive*, *intermediate* and *modern*' (1966, pp. 21, 26, emphasis in original). Parsons immediately qualified this schema by identifying sub-divisions within the broad categories, and by noting that evolution was neither continuous nor 'a simple linear process' (1966, p. 26), but its ranking of societies according to their degree of structural differentiation captured the spirit of a generation of scholars' thinking. Modernity's central values were specified as those of 'economic development, education, political independence and some form of democracy', and Parsons anticipated not only that they would be consolidated in the advanced societies, but also that they would have growing influence globally through 'the trend toward modernization in the non-Western world' (1977, p. 228). Overall, he felt justified in claiming that it was 'only a slight exaggeration to say that all contemporary societies are more or less modern' (1977, p. 229), and that what stood out was the similarity between them, not their differences.

Numerous critical responses to generalized theories of modern society as industrial society have been advanced, and at their core is an awareness of the insensitivity to difference from which theorizing at this level of abstraction suffers. Parsons has famously been taken to task by C. Wright Mills for his tendency to conduct analysis at the level of 'grand theory', which falls down because it prevents social scientists from moving between different levels of abstraction, something Mills regarded as 'a signal mark of the imaginative and systematic thinker' (1970, p. 43). The criticism of grand theory is made all the more telling in this context by the fact that Mills himself planned (but was unable to complete before his death in 1962) a work of between six and nine volumes to be entitled 'Comparative Sociology'. Mills' aim was, as his biographer Horowitz puts it, 'to capture in one fell swoop the meaning of the modern world', yet at the same time he recognized the need for 'a multilinear rather than a unilinear theory of history' in which 'Each major world region has its own historic and irreducible form of development' (1983, pp. 305, 324). Mills was aware of the pitfalls of ethnocentrism, observing in his draft notes that 'since World War I, Russia has demonstrated to the world an alternative form of industrialization' (quoted in Horowitz, 1983, p. 327), an observation which pre-dates the elaboration of this theme by Moore which was examined in Chapter 2. Mills was equally conscious of the need to avoid perspectives dominated by the concerns of the present, and he took seriously the distinction between the 'modern era' and the prospective 'postmodern era' or 'Fourth epoch' which might emerge out of the incompatibilities of contemporary society. In contrast to Mills' claim that the most advanced countries of his day were witnessing 'The *post-modern* climax' (1970, p. 202, emphasis in original) to developments in economic, political and military spheres, Parsons was prepared to dismiss reference to post-modern society as 'premature' (1977, p. 241), unable as he was to envisage the possibility of an alternative to a further century or more of modern evolution.

The critique of grand theory which Mills advanced was part of a broader, two-pronged attack on the theoretical and methodological shortcomings of unimaginative sociology, as he was equally critical of 'abstracted empiricism' (1970, Ch. 3), the conduct of research in which sight is lost of what are the important questions to ask. Mills' preference when studying a social institution or arrangement was for questions such as 'What kinds of men and women does it tend to create?' (1967, p. 349). Methods would need to be the servants and not the agenda-setters if such questions were to be answered satisfactorily by sociologists engaging in research which was 'fully comparative on a worldwide scale', and if the 'comparative accounting' (Mills, quoted in Horowitz, 1983, pp. 314, 324) which he envisaged was to extend beyond available statistical data on societies to wider issues such as their rationality and the extent of the freedom they allow to their citizens. It is a constant theme in Mills' writing that 'Rationally organized social arrangements are not necessarily a means of increased freedom' (1970, p. 187), and his conviction of the need to establish empirically the nature of the relationship between economic and political institutions reflects the enduring influence of Weber's ideas on his work (Eldridge, 1983). It also indicates his distance from models of societies as systems in which elements such as the development of capitalism and democracy are related in a logical and deterministic fashion.

Subsequent developments in debates in comparative sociology have tended to bear out the strength of the case outlined by Mills. Giddens has commented that 'Parsons's view that half a million years of human history culminate in the social and political system of the United States' is 'faintly ridiculous', and he suggests that for practical purposes Parsons' schema is 'empty' (1984, pp. 273–4). Even if they are stripped of their more obvious normative bias, evolutionary theories are confronted by extensive doubt about whether 'we can usefully classify societies, as we can biological organisms, in terms of ascending levels of complexity' (Giddens, 1989, p. 637), with modern industrial societies being the most complex. It has been suggested that Mills shared this evolutionary belief and detected the 'convergence of the Soviet Union and the United States as centralized, bureaucratized societies' (Bell, 1976, p. 113), but such an assessment overlooks his awareness of 'important differences between politics and culture in the Soviet Union and the United States' (Mills, 1960, p. 34). More generally, Mills observes that capitalist and communist societies have different trajectories, and his realization that 'how they are run differs profoundly' allows him to recognize that their 'parallel development' (1960, p. 30) does not mean that they operate with the same rationality. Other writers on state socialism have also pointed to the distinctive rationality according to which the system was operated (Clarke *et al.*, 1993; Marcuse, 1971, Ch. 3), and the role of political factors in reproducing this difference between state socialist and capitalist societies despite their both being industrial societies has long been identified as a weak point of convergence theory (Goldthorpe, 1971).

Theorists of industrial society have gone some way to acknowledging that the sphere of politics places limits on the convergence of industrial societies. Kerr's examination of the growing evidence on the subject led him to the conclusion that 'The political structure... does not always follow the economic structure', and he notes that 'National history, historical accidents and geographic location seem to play a more major role in determining the political structure than does the economic structure' (1983, p. 64). This reassessment by one of the leading convergence theorists fits the changing mood among comparative sociologists about the need to 'bring the state back in' to analyses, although others have gone further in exploring 'differences among and within Western advanced industrial-capitalist nations... "newly-industrializing" capitalist nations or among the "state-socialist" countries' (Skocpol, 1985, p. 21). Previous chapters have examined the role of political factors in bringing about differences between countries which excessively general theories place in the same category. The recognition of the diversity of capitalist societies and also of their welfare states was a central theme of Chapters 3 and 4, while Chapter 5 identified the continued existence of heterogeneity within state socialist societies, and Chapters 6 and 7 noted the active divergence within the countries of the third world. Each of these could be given as examples of how what Therborn calls 'processes of social steering' affect 'actual social development' (1995, pp. 334, 347), and in each case politics and the state have a crucial bearing on how societies are 'steered' between alternative courses.

Kerr's revision and reformulation of his ideas in the light of the growing evidence of societies' diversity stopped some way short of abandoning the convergence framework and the idea of a 'logic of industrialism' altogether. One reason for this is his belief in the tendency of the 'cultural contradictions inherent in industrialism' (1983, p. 107) to generate pressure for change, and while this aspect of his argument draws directly on Bell's (1976) analysis of capitalism's 'cultural contradictions', it resonates more generally with the idea that contradictions in sets of social relationships necessarily work themselves out. Holmwood and Stewart (1991) have noted that this type of argument is employed widely in social theory, and their doubts about the effectiveness of explanations in which it is thought sufficient simply to identify 'contradictions' are borne out by the failure of the situations analyzed in this way to evolve as anticipated. The contradictions underlying the 'legitimation crisis' of advanced capitalist societies identified by Habermas (1976) have no more worked themselves in the way anticipated than have Offe's (1984) 'contradictions of the welfare state' or Wallerstein's 'six contradictions of the capitalist world economy' (1990, p. 42). Of course, by no means all analyses that employ the concept of contradiction do so in such a deterministic fashion. Sassoon's discussion of women's position in relation to the contradictions of the welfare state reaches the conclusion that, 'Despite the tensions and contradictions caused by the lack of "fit" between traditional institutions and women's new role, the outcome is unclear. It is certainly not inevitable that these institutions will be transformed to meet the new situation' (1987, p. 174). In similar fashion, McDowell's examination of the contradictions surrounding the implications for women of the shift to post-Fordism anticipates that the outcome will not be pre-determined but will be shaped by the 'struggle' and the 'scope for new alliances' (1992, p. 192) which are generated.

Such analyses are more in tune with the case put by Giddens (1981, Ch. 10) that the casual use of the concept of contradiction common in both functionalist and Marxist investigations needs to be shorn of its evolutionary connotations by dropping the assumption that contradictions necessarily lead to change. He proposes that it is more fruitful to conceive of contradictions as 'structural fault-lines that tend to produce clusterings of conflicts' (1981, p. 238). This reformulation allows the focus to be shifted away from the contradictions of systems and more onto the ways in which people within those systems engage in struggles over possible futures. Giddens' critique concentrates on the Marxist use of the concept of contradiction, but essentially the same criticisms can be made of functionalist writers such as Smelser who, in his account of social evolution during industrialization, 'never really asks *who* suffers or *who* profits from such contradictions, *who* tries to solve them' (Mouzelis, 1991, p. 57, emphases in original). By adopting the approach to the study of social change which focuses on conflicts and struggles rather than the logical resolution of contradictory forces, the framework of stages of development passed through in a mechanical and deterministic fashion can be replaced by a perspective which highlights alternatives and at the same time acknowledges the possibility that contradictions will remain unresolved. To illustrate this point, reference could be made to the fact that numerous analyses of the contradictions of state socialist regimes have been advanced (Callinicos, 1991; Clarke *et al.*, 1993; Fejtö, 1974; Kennedy, 1989; Lane, 1990), despite which the details of the course of the system's demise through Czechoslovakia's 'tender revolution' (Sayer, 1991, p. viii) and similar events elsewhere in Eastern Europe in the recent past were still largely unanticipated.

The struggles to which Giddens, Mouzelis and others direct our attention may or may not be class struggles, but in all cases analyses of these struggles in terms of conflicts between beneficiaries of change and groups which lose out are highly instructive for comparative sociologists. Such analyses have been referred to throughout this book. In the examination of change in contemporary capitalist societies, the question posed by Westergaard (1995) of 'Who gets what?' pointed to 'the hardening of class inequality', while McDowell's question of whether the shift to post-Fordism brings 'gains or losses for women' (1992, p. 188) is equally illuminating of how these societies stand in comparative perspective. Just as pertinent are the contrasts between the 'winners and losers after the collapse of state socialism' which Ferge (1993) draws; while some individuals have undoubtedly gained since the 1989 revolutions, Eastern Europe in general has experienced 'a fall of living standards for the majority of the population' (Therborn, 1995, p. 300). Latouche would interpret this situation as just one more example of the mistakenness of the pervasive belief in what he calls 'the myth of a world of winners' (1993, Ch. 2). The divergent experiences of winners and losers among the rural population studied by Scott meant that there were 'two green revolutions' (1985, p. 140), that celebrated in the accounts of the large-scale farmer and that lamented by the landless labourer. As Hettne has pointed out, the harsh reality is that 'The process of globalization has winners and losers' (1995, p. 110), and this is true both of the nations of the developing world (Kennedy, 1993, Ch. 10) and more generally. The 'victims of development' in Seabrook's (1993) analysis are not exclusively located in poor countries, just as it was the purpose of George's (1992) study of the debt crisis to show 'how third world debt harms us all'. What Latouche refers to as 'the scandal of the losers' is that the contemporary global system includes an emergent 'Fourth World' of diverse groups which are united by their shared status as 'victims of progress' (1993, pp. 78, 42), expressed in terms of their common exclusion from the benefits promised by modernity.

Latouche's view is that the upward mobility of the newly industrializing countries and the downward mobility of the poorest countries means that 'There is no longer a Third World' (1993, p. 38). The same judgement, that changes have brought about 'The end of the Third World', is reached by Harris (1987), albeit with less pessimistic overtones. Harris argues that 'we can always perceive the losses in what is declining, rarely the gains in what is rising' (1987, p. 202). It is certainly the case that situations of rapid social change throw established classifications into a state of flux, and that new perspectives take time to crystallize. Mills was making this point when he wrote that people 'come only grudgingly to a consciousness of epochal change', and he drew the obvious conclusion of the need for 'a certain imagination' (quoted in Horowitz, 1983, p. 327) before the full significance of changes can be grasped. The question of perspective is thus crucial in the process of re-thinking that is currently underway in the light of the truly global changes discussed in previous chapters. The formulation of new concepts such as 'fourth world' (Hoogvelt, 1982; Jary and Jary, 1991; Todaro, 1989) indicates the need for re-thinking but does not solve the problem. Hettne rightly comments that these 'concepts are examples of the growing awareness that the third world is disappearing but do not amount to a (much needed) systematic categorization of the developing world' (1995, p. 265). This, Hettne says, is particularly the case if the concept of the fourth world is treated only as a 'statistical category' (1995, p. 288). Indeed, the re-thinking required needs to go much further in that the re-examination of the concept of the third world, if it is to be systematic, needs also to include the related concepts of first world and second world in the process.

The changing agenda of the unfolding future

Fifty years on from its construction, the classification of the global system into first, second and third worlds is breaking down. Developed in the context of the Cold War preoccupation with East–West divisions and confrontation, the concept of the third world was an assertion of the right of poor nations to be heard. McNeill has observed that 'The "Third World" of new nations and uncommitted peoples was... a reality in the postwar decades, modifying the simple polarity of the cold war' (1983, p. 363), but the ability of third world states to achieve and sustain unity was hampered by political divisions between them and was subject to erosion because of the processes of economic differentiation between newly industrializing countries and others closer to the margins of the global economic order. Further blows to the viability of the three worlds classification have been delivered by the proliferation of different types of capitalism within the first world, examined in Chapters 3 and 4, and the collapse of the second world of state socialism which was charted in Chapter 5. At the level of ideas, the last fifty years have seen 'the making and unmaking of the third world' (Escobar, 1995) and of the 'Third-Worldism', which Booth describes as 'the belief that the study of less developed societies calls for *special* methods and theoretical perspectives, the validity of which is restricted to developing country contexts' (1994, pp. 37–8, emphasis in original). No longer able to separate the first, second and third worlds, comparative sociology is being forced to become more truly global in its purview, as Hettne (1995), Sklair (1995) and others have been prominent in arguing.

Moving beyond the analytical framework of the three worlds promises to open up all sorts of new avenues for comparative sociologists to pursue. Collins has argued that the broad move away from the 'ethnocentric evolutionist developmentalism' which dominated theories of social change at mid-century has allowed subsequent years to be 'a golden age for historical and macrocomparative sociology', not least because of the preparedness of writers 'to drastically revise received positions' (1981, pp. 1–2). For all its problems, dependency theory's imaginative leap linking first world development with third world underdevelopment opened the way to conceptions of the situation alternative to those contained in modernization theory, and globalization is in turn leading to further reassessments of established frameworks of analysis, as Chapter 7 showed. Similarly, the challenge to the idea that the countries of the third world are somehow 'behind' the industrialized North allows questions to be posed about how the study of the third world can inform the analysis of industrialized societies. Various themes running through the analyses of capitalist, state socialist and underdeveloped societies include the presence of an informal economy alongside the formal economy, the importance of the relationship between civil society and the state, and the tendency of the process of polarization to unfold both within and between societies. Of course, the informal economies of the first, second and third worlds are not identical (Firlit and Chłopecki, 1992; Latouche, 1993; Scott, 1994), and the same point could be made about other comparisons that are drawn, but for the purposes of comparative sociology what is important is that the matter is placed on the research agenda.

At the same time as it promises to liberate the sociological imagination, taking analysis beyond the three worlds is a process fraught with difficulties. Latouche has suggested that the various groups which make up the fourth world 'are the laboratories of a possible future' as alternatives to the modernist project are sought, but their exclusion by 'the grand society' (1993, pp. 42, 48) may also breed indifference. Thomas has noted that 'Looking at the problems of the Third World shows the continuing need to ask "Is there an alternative?"', and that current changes in the global system carry with them the danger of 'Western attention being drawn away from the Third World' (1992, p. 5). If Hall is correct in his proposition that, contrary to dependency theory, 'Advanced capitalism does not "depend" upon the Third World' (1986, p. 245), then the loss of the term 'Third World' which Minh-ha regards as empowering of 'non-whites in their solidarist struggle against all forms of Western dominance' (1993, p. 608) risks compounding economic marginalization with loss of political voice. As Worsley has pointed out, classifications such as that of the three worlds are not 'merely academic exercises'; rather, they have practical consequences and 'real-life implications' (1984, p. 311), not least through the effect which they have on perceptions of alternatives. Although it was made in the rather different context of discussing the effects of the collapse of state socialism in Eastern Europe, Scase's comment that 'In the closing decade of the twentieth century, there remains no viable alternative to capitalism' (1992, p. 83) nevertheless raises the awesome prospect of the old three worlds model being replaced by one in which the spread of global capitalism has ruled out other futures, at least for the time being.

It was noted in Chapter 7 that theories of the capitalist world-economy have been criticized for exaggerating the constraints on what sorts of society are possible in the modern world, and in this context it is instructive to consider Wallerstein's comment that 'we must begin to do research on the historical choices that are before us in the future' (1991, p. 270). Wallerstein argues that an essential part of the 'unthinking' of the legacy of nineteenth-century sociology is the rejection of 'the belief in inevitable progress', proposing instead a model of change involving 'nonlinear processes which eventually reach bifurcation points, whereupon slight fluctuations have large consequences' (1991, p. 270). There are resemblances here to Weber's famous suggestion that at certain moments interventions may have the effect of 'switchmen' in redirecting 'the tracks along which action has been pushed' (1970c, p. 280), and although Wallerstein would dispute with Weber the precise nature of the forces involved in these interventions, Weber would accept Wallerstein's conclusion that the outcomes of such situations are 'indeterminate' but not 'beyond the reach of rational research' (1991, p. 270). The two theorists would also be in strong agreement that historical research is indispensable to any assessments of the range of possible futures which are open.

The style of comparative sociology being discussed here is by no means easy to emulate. Collins has said of Weber's wide-ranging comparative work *Economy and Society* that 'The sheer knowledge of history that is summed up in sentences (or even parts of sentences) is usually intellectually overwhelming... the sensation of dealing with the Weberian style of comparison is dizzying' (1986b, p. 130). By contrast, the fixed stages of development characteristic of evolutionary theories are crude and misleading. Kumar has described how theories of industrial society are in many ways ahistorical, involving 'a serious misconception about when, and how quickly, the industrial society came into being' (1978, p. 131). Such rigid models distort perceptions, by among other things, detecting 'discontinuities and novelties where there are in fact basic continuities with the past' (1978, p. 131), and Smith has charted how their demise has coincided with the revival of historical sociology which is, 'At its best, rational, critical and imaginative' (1991, p. 1). Smith includes in this latter category the work of Moore which was examined in Chapter 2, not least because an important part of Moore's purpose was to investigate and analyze historical alternatives. In the examination of change in the contemporary world, a similar approach would lead to caution when confronted by 'The proliferation of labels, such as "postmodernist", "post-materialist", "post-fordist" or "post-industrial"', which are, as Esping-Andersen observes, too often mistakenly treated as 'substitutes for analysis' (1990, p. 222). If sociologists in their assessment of alternatives are to be able 'to distinguish between open doors and brick walls' (Smith, 1991, p. 1), then empirically sensitive historical investigations are an essential part of the process.

The work of illustrious forerunners in the field of comparative sociology is not above critical reassessment and refinement, of course. For example, Moore justified his focus in *Social Origins* on large countries by asserting that because 'smaller countries depend economically and politically on big and powerful ones', it followed that 'the decisive causes of their politics lie outside their own boundaries' (1967, p. x). This can be considered a misjudgement in the light of the way in which small countries may be pioneers of new social arrangements and are not necessarily dependent. One of the features common to the social-democratic welfare-state regimes examined in Chapter 4 is their relatively small size, and studies of other aspects of industrial capitalist societies have also drawn the conclusion that the distinctiveness of small countries is important (Katzenstein, 1985; Stephens, 1979). Chapter 5 highlighted the way in which Hungary experimented with many of the reforms which were later adopted in other state socialist societies, while the success of the newly industrializing countries in pioneering export-oriented industrialization, which was noted in Chapter 7, has frequently been attributed to their relatively small size, amongst other factors. Moore's work has also been questioned in relation to his concentration on processes internal to the countries he studied, as was remarked in the discussion of global influences on democratization in Chapter 7, and this echoes the point made in Chapter 1 that globalization requires analyses framed in terms of autonomous 'societies' to be re-evaluated.

Ultimately, what stands out about the writings of comparative sociologists such as Moore is not their shortcomings but their insights. Moore's contribution to the debate in comparative sociology about the range of different types of social arrangements which are possible at any one time highlights the need to explain how 'the suppression of historical alternatives' (1978, Ch. 11) comes about. As was seen in Chapter 2, Moore is aware that people are not automatically radicalized by being socially disadvantaged, and because of this it is necessary to do more than simply analyze social structures in terms of 'winners' and 'losers'. Part of the reason for this may be that people who engage in radical action to change the world do not always end up as 'winners'. An example of this paradox was observed in Chapter 5 in relation to the Polish industrial workers whose involvement in the

Solidarity movement helped to bring about an end to state socialism there, but who are 'now bound to be the first to bear the most severe hardships of the economic transformation – intensification of labour, sharpening of work discipline, loss of job security, unemployment and all' (Bauman, 1992, p. 163). Similarly, it was noted in Chapter 2 that the American Civil War resulted in the abolition of the slave system in the southern states there, but the sober statistic that in the thirty years following 1865 more than 10,000 African–American men were murdered by lynch mobs (O'Connell-Davidson and Layder, 1994, p. 81) indicates the dangers of reading too much in to the replacement of slavery by 'free' capitalism. As Moore appreciated, such outcomes make the comparison of different types of society far from clear-cut.

The value of Moore's emphasis on the moral dimension of comparative sociology is further illustrated by Geertz's (1976) comparison between the divergent paths of development in Japan and Java, which stresses the need to place contrasting economic rationalities in their broader social and historical contexts. Geertz's study of how Dutch colonialism siphoned off the growth potential of the Javanese economy and prevented the possibility of a course of development similar to Japan's leads him to the conclusion that 'The real tragedy of colonial history in Java after 1830 is not that the peasantry suffered. It suffered much worse elsewhere... The tragedy is that it suffered for nothing' (1976, p. 54). Geertz's research also reveals how misleading it is to treat Japan as model of a 'developed' society which Indonesia (in which present-day Java is located) could emulate, since 'Japanese economic history is Javanese with a few crucial parameters changed' (Geertz, 1976, p. 52), differences which are sufficiently pivotal to rule out the possibility of Indonesia subsequently following the Japanese path of industrialization. Theories of development which hold out the prospect of the third world coming to be like the first world have not understood the lessons of such findings, and confirm the wisdom of Moore's observation that if people in the future 'are ever to break the chains of the present, they will have to understand the forces that forged them' (1967, p. 508). The responsibilities of comparative sociologists to avoid repeating the mistakes of previous generations are in this respect of no small importance.

It is not yet clear precisely what frameworks of analysis will emerge to replace the problematic three worlds model, but it is certain that there will be no consensus on how to go beyond the three worlds. To begin with, there is far from unanimity on the appropriate level at which analysis should be conducted. In his discussion of Weber's comparative sociology, Wrong has observed that 'Most sociologists can be located at different points on a continuum between the poles of generalizing and individualizing interpretation and conceptualization; there is unlikely ever to be agreement on a "correct" location' (1981, p. 54). In turn, as Wrong notes, this reflects the great range of questions which are asked by comparative sociologists, not only because of their different theoretical orientations, but also because of their different purposes. Given the infinite diversity of social developments, perhaps all that can be specified about the form of 'a critical theory of contemporary society' is that it must seek 'To investigate the roots of these developments and examine their historical alternatives' (Marcuse, 1972, p. 10). Inevitably, the discussion of alternatives raises the vexed question of the place of value judgements in sociological analysis, touching as it does on deeply held views about the capacity of people to live by standards different from those of the present. There are, too, deep methodological divides between different perspectives, as comparative sociologists negotiate the best ways of transcending the quantitative–qualitative dichotomy. And, finally, there is the point that comparative sociology is an exercise in imagination, in which we try to make sense of our world through our awareness of alternatives. Imagine!

Bibliography

Abbott, P. and Sapsford, R. (1987) *Women and Social Class* (London: Tavistock).

Abercrombie, N., Hill, S. and Turner, B. (1984) *The Dominant Ideology Thesis* (London: George Allen and Unwin).

Abercrombie, N., Hill, S. and Turner, B. (1986) *Sovereign Individuals of Capitalism* (London: Allen and Unwin).

Abrams, P. (1982) *Historical Sociology* (Shepton Mallet: Open Books).

Adams, N. (1993) *Worlds Apart: The North–South Divide and the International System* (London: Zed Books).

Agger, B. (1989) *Fast Capitalism* (Urbana, Ill.: University of Illinois Press).

Aké, C. (1995) 'The Democratisation of Disempowerment in Africa' in J. Hippler (ed.) *The Democratisation of Disempowerment: The Problem of Democracy in the Third World* (London: Pluto), 70–89.

Alavi, H. (1972) 'The state in post-colonial societies – Pakistan and Bangladesh', *New Left Review*, **74**:59–81.

Alavi, H. (1982) 'State and Class Under Peripheral Capitalism' in H. Alavi and T. Shanin (eds) *Introduction to the Sociology of 'Developing Societies'* (London and Basingstoke: Macmillan), 289–307.

Alber, J. (1988) 'Continuities and changes in the idea of the welfare state', *Politics and Society*, **16**(4):451–68.

Albert, M. (1993) *Capitalism against Capitalism* (London: Whurr).

Alexander, J. and Sztompka, P. (eds) (1990) *Rethinking Progress: Movements, Forces and Ideas at the End of the Twentieth Century* (London: Unwin Hyman).

Allen, J. (1992a) 'Fordism and Modern Industry' in J. Allen, P. Braham and P. Lewis (eds) *Political and Economic Forms of Modernity* (Cambridge: Polity Press), 229–60.

Allen, J. (1992b) 'Post-Industrialism and Post-Fordism' in S. Hall, D. Held and T. McGrew (eds) *Modernity and its Futures* (Cambridge: Polity Press), 169–204.

Amin, A. (1994) 'Post-Fordism: Models, Fantasies and Phantoms of Transition' in A. Amin (ed.) *Post-Fordism: A Reader* (Oxford: Basil Blackwell), 1–39.

Amin, S. (1990a) *Maldevelopment: Anatomy of a Global Failure* (London: Zed Books).

Amin, S. (1990b) *Delinking: Towards a Polycentric World* (London: Zed Books).

Amsden, A. (1985) 'The State and Taiwan's Economic Development' in P. Evans, D. Rueschemeyer and T. Skocpol (eds) *Bringing the State Back In* (Cambridge: Cambridge University Press), 78–106.

Armstrong, P., Glyn, A. and Harrison, J. (1984) *Capitalism Since World War II: The Making and Breakup of the Great Boom* (London: Fontana).

Asante, M. (1993) 'The Afrocentric Idea' in C. Lemert (ed.) *Social Theory: The Multicultural and Classic Readings* (Boulder: Westview Press), 554–7.

Bakker, I. (1988) 'Women's Employment in Comparative Perspective' in J. Jenson, E. Hagen and C. Reddy (eds) *Feminization of the Labour Force* (Cambridge: Polity Press), 17–44.

Baldwin, P. (1990) *The Politics of Social Solidarity: Class Bases of the European Welfare State 1875–1975* (Cambridge: Cambridge University Press).

Barnett, T. (1988) *Sociology and Development* (London: Hutchinson).

Bauman, Z. (1982) *Memories of Class: The Pre-history and After-life of Class* (London: Routledge & Kegan Paul).

Bauman, Z. (1987) *Legislators and Interpreters: On Modernity, Post-modernity and Intellectuals* (Cambridge: Polity Press).

Bauman, Z. (1991) *Modernity and Ambivalence* (Cambridge: Polity Press).

Bauman, Z. (1992) *Intimations of Postmodernity* (London: Routledge).

Beck, U. (1992) *Risk Society: Towards a New Modernity* (London: Sage).

Bell, D. (1974) *The Coming of Post-Industrial Society: A Venture in Social Forecasting* (Harmondsworth: Penguin).

Bell, D. (1976) *The Cultural Contradictions of Capitalism* (London: Heinemann).

Bello, W. (1995) 'Export-led Development in East Asia: A Flawed Model' in R. Ayres (ed.) *Development Studies* (Dartford: Greenwich University Press), 342–54.

Bendix, R. (1966) *Max Weber: An Intellectual Portrait* (London: Methuen).

Berger, P., Berger, B. and Keller, H. (1973) *The Homeless Mind: Modernization and Consciousness* (New York: Random House).

Berliner, J. (1966) 'The Economics of Overtaking and Surpassing' in H. Rosovsky (ed.) *Industrialization in Two Systems: Essays in Honor of Alexander Gerschenkron* (London: John Wiley and Sons), 159–85.

Bernstein, H. (1982) 'Industrialization, Development and Dependence' in H. Alavi and T. Shanin (eds) *Introduction to the Sociology of 'Developing Societies'* (London and Basingstoke: Macmillan), 218–35.

Bernstein, H. (1988) 'Development 1: Variations on Capitalism' in B. Crow, M. Thorpe, H. Bernstein *et al. Survival and Change in the Third World* (Cambridge: Polity Press), 67–82.

Bernstein, H. (1992) 'Agrarian Structures and Change: India' in H. Bernstein, B. Crow and H. Johnson (eds) *Rural Livelihoods: Crises and Responses* (Oxford: Oxford University Press), 51–64.

Beveridge, W. (1942) *Social Insurance and Allied Services* (London: HMSO).

Bialer, S. (1983) 'The Question of Legitimacy' in D. Held, J. Anderson, B. Gieben *et al.* (eds) *States and Societies* (Oxford: Martin Robertson), 418–30.

Booth, D. (ed.) (1994) *Rethinking Social Development: Theory, Research and Practice* (Harlow: Longman).

Boserup, E. (1970) *Women's Role in Economic Development* (London: George Allen and Unwin).

Bottomore, T. (1985) *Theories of Modern Capitalism* (London: George Allen and Unwin).

Bottomore, T. (1992) 'Citizenship and Social Class, Forty Years On' in T. Marshall and T. Bottomore *Citizenship and Social Class* (London: Pluto Press), 55-93.

Bottomore, T. and Brym, R. (eds) (1989) *The Capitalist Class: An International Study* (Hemel Hempstead: Harvester Wheatsheaf).

Braham, P. (1992) 'The Divisions of Labour and Occupational Change' in J. Allen, P. Braham and P. Lewis (eds) *Political and Economic Forms of Modernity* (Cambridge: Polity Press), 275–314.

Brett, E. (1985) *The World Economy since the War: The Politics of Uneven Development* (Basingstoke: Macmillan).

Brown, P. and Scase, R. (eds) (1991) *Poor Work: Disadvantage and the division of Labour* (Buckingham: Open University Press).

Bryant, C. and Mokrzycki, E. (1994) 'Introduction: Theorizing the Changes in East-Central Europe' in C. Bryant and E. Mokrzycki (eds) *The New Great Transformation? Change and Continuity in East-Central Europe* (London: Routledge), 1–13.

Bryson, L. (1992) *Welfare and the State* (Basingstoke: Macmillan).

Burawoy, M. (1985) *The Politics of Production: Factory Regimes Under Capitalism and Socialism* (London: Verso).

Burawoy, M. (1988) 'Piece Rates, Hungarian Style' in R. Pahl (ed.) *On Work: Historical, Comparative and Theoretical Approaches* (Oxford: Basil Blackwell), 210–28.

Burawoy, M. and Lukács, J. (1989) 'What is Socialist about Socialist Production? Autonomy and Control in a Hungarian Steel Mill' in S. Wood (ed.) *The Transformation of Work? Skill, Flexibility and the Labour Process* (London: Unwin Hyman), 295–316.

Burke, P. (1992) *History and Social Theory* (Cambridge: Polity Press).

Burrows, R. and Loader, B. (eds) (1994) *Towards a Post-Fordist Welfare State?* (London: Routledge).

Byres, T. and Crow, B. (1988) 'New Technology and New Masters for the Indian Countryside' in B. Crow, M. Thorpe, H. Bernstein *et al. Survival and Change in the Third World* (Cambridge: Polity Press), 163–81.

Byrne, D. (1989) *Beyond the Inner City* (Milton Keynes: Open University Press).

Caldwell, M. (1977a) *The Wealth of Some Nations* (London: Zed Books).

Caldwell, M. (1977b) 'Foreword' to U. Melotti, *Marx and the Third World* (London and Basingstoke: Macmillan), vii–x.

Callinicos, A. (1989) *Against Postmodernism: A Marxist Critique* (Cambridge: Polity Press).

Callinicos, A. (1991) *The Revenge of History: Marxism and the East European Revolutions* (Cambridge: Polity Press).

Charles, N. (1993) *Gender Divisions and Social Change* (Hemel Hempstead: Harvester Wheatsheaf).

Chase-Dunn, C. (1989) *Global Formation: Structures of the World Economy* (Oxford: Basil Blackwell).

Clarke, S., Fairbrother, P., Burawoy, M. and Krotov, P. (1993) *What About the Workers? Workers and the Transition to Capitalism in Russia* (London: Verso).

Cochrane, A. (1993) 'Comparative Approaches and Social Policy' in A. Cochrane and J. Clarke (eds) *Comparing Welfare States: Britain in International Context* (London: Sage), 1–18.

Cochrane, A. and Clarke, J. (eds) (1993) *Comparing Welfare States: Britain in International Context* (London: Sage).

Cohen, R. (1987) *The New Helots: Migrants and the International Division of Labour* (Aldershot: Gower).

Cohen, Stanley (1985) *Visions of Social Control: Crime, Punishment and Classification* (Cambridge: Polity Press).

Cohen, Stephen (1986) *Rethinking the Soviet Experience: Politics and History Since 1917* (Oxford: Oxford University Press).

Collins, R. (1981) *Sociology Since Midcentury: Essays in Theory Cumulation* (New York: Academic Press).

Collins, R. (1986a) *Weberian Sociological Theory* (Cambridge: Cambridge University Press).

Collins, R. (1986b) *Max Weber: A Skeleton Key* (London: Sage).

Corbridge, S. (1994) 'Post-Marxism and Post-colonialism: The Needs and Rights of Distant Strangers' in D. Booth (ed.) *Rethinking Social Development: Theory, Research and Practice* (Harlow: Longman), 90–117.

Corbridge, S. (ed.) (1995) *Development Studies: A Reader* (London: Edward Arnold).

Corrigan, P. and Sayer, D. (1985) *The Great Arch: English State Formation as Cultural Revolution* (Oxford: Basil Blackwell).

Corrigan, P., Ramsay, H. and Sayer, D. (1978) *Socialist Construction and Marxist Theory: Bolshevism and its Critique* (London: Basingstoke).

Crompton, R. (1993) *Class and Stratification: An Introduction to Current Debates* (Cambridge: Polity Press).

Crook, S., Pakulski, J. and Waters, M. (1992) *Postmodernization: Change in* J. Hall (ed.) *States in History* (Oxford: Basil Blackwell), 177–210.

Crow, B. (1988) 'Conclusion: The Invidious Dilemmas of Capitalist Development' in B. Crow, M. Thorpe, H. Bernstein *et al. Survival and Change in the Third World* (Cambridge: Polity Press), 331–48.

Crow, B., Thorpe, M. and Bernstein, H. *et al.* (1988) *Survival and Change in the Third World* (Cambridge: Polity Press).

Crush, J. (ed.) (1995) *Power of Development* (London: Routledge).

Culpitt, I. (1992) *Welfare and Citizenship: Beyond the Crisis of the Welfare State?* (London: Sage).

Dahrendorf, R. (1959) *Class and Class Conflict in Industrial Society* (London: Routledge & Kegan Paul).

Davis, H. and Scase, R. (1985) *Western Capitalism and State Socialism: An Introduction* (Oxford: Basil Blackwell).

Deacon, B. (1994) 'Global Social Policy Actors and the Shaping of Post-communist Social Policy' in A. De Swann (ed.) *Social Policy Beyond Borders: The Social Question in Transnational Perspective* (Amsterdam: Amsterdam University Press), 59–81.

Dean, H. and Taylor-Gooby, P. (1992) *Dependency Culture: The Explosion of a Myth* (Hemel Hempstead: Harvester Wheatsheaf).

Dean, M. (1994) *Critical and Effective Histories: Foucault's Methods and Historical Sociology* (London: Routledge).

De Swaan, A. (1988) *In Care of the State: Health Care, Education and Welfare in Europe and the USA in the Modern Era* (Cambridge: Polity Press).

De Swann, A. (1994a) 'Introduction' in A. De Swann (ed.) *Social Policy Beyond Borders: The Social Question in Transnational Perspective* (Amsterdam: Amsterdam University Press), 1–6.

De Swann, A. (1994b) 'Perspectives for Transnational Social Policy in Europe: Social Transfers from West to East' in A. De Swann (ed.) *Social Policy Beyond Borders: The Social Question in Transnational Perspective* (Amsterdam: Amsterdam University Press), 101–15.

Deyo, F. (1989) *Beneath the Miracle: Labor Subordination in the New Asian Industrialism* (Berkeley: University of California Press).

Dominelli, L. (1991) *Women Across Continents: Feminist Comparative Social Policy* (Hemel Hempstead: Harvester Wheatsheaf).

Dore, R. (1987) 'Late Capitalism, Corporatism and Other -isms' in W. Outhwaite and M. Mulkay (eds) *Social Theory and Social Criticism: Essays for Tom Bottomore* (Oxford: Basil Blackwell), 114–23.

Doyal, L. and Gough, I. (1991) *A Theory of Human Need* (Basingstoke: Macmillan).

Durkheim, E. (1970) *Suicide: A Study in Sociology* (London: Routledge & Kegan Paul).

Durkheim, E. (1982) *The Rules of Sociological Method* (London and Basingstoke: Macmillan).

Edgell, S. (1993) *Class* (London: Routledge).

Edgell, S. and Duke, V. (1991) *A Measure of Thatcherism: A Sociology of Britain* (London: Harper Collins).

Edwards, C. (1992) 'Industrialization in South Korea' in T. Hewitt, H. Johnson and D. Wield (eds) *Industrialization and Development* (Oxford: Oxford University Press), 97–127.

Eldridge, J. (1983) *C. Wright Mills* (London: Tavistock).

Eldridge, J., Cressey, P. and MacInnes, J. (1991) *Industrial Sociology and Economic Crisis* (Hemel Hempstead: Harvester Wheatsheaf).

Emmons, T. (1968) 'The Peasant and the Emancipation', in W. Vucinich (ed.) *The Peasant in Nineteenth-Century Russia* (Stanford: Stanford University Press).

Escobar, A. (1995) *Encountering Development: The Making and Unmaking of the Third World* (Princeton, NJ: Princeton University Press).

Esping-Andersen, G. (1990) *The Three Worlds of Welfare Capitalism* (Cambridge: Polity Press).

Esping-Andersen, G. (1993a) 'Introduction' in G. Esping-Andersen (ed.) *Changing Classes: Stratification and Mobility in Post-Industrial Societies* (London: Sage), 1–6.

Esping-Andersen, G. (1993b) 'Post-industrial Class Structures: An Analytical Framework' in G. Esping-Andersen (ed.) *Changing Classes: Stratification and Mobility in Post-Industrial Societies* (London: Sage), 7–31.

Esping-Andersen, G., Assimakopoulou, Z. and van Kersbergen, K. (1993) 'Trends in Contemporary Class Structuration: A Six-nation Comparison' in G. Esping-Andersen (ed.) *Changing Classes: Stratification and Mobility in Post-Industrial Societies* (London: Sage), 32–57.

Evans, P., Rueschemeyer, D. and Skocpol, T. (eds) (1985) *Bringing the State Back In* (Cambridge: Cambridge University Press).

Featherstone, M. (1990) 'Global Culture: An Introduction' in M. Featherstone (ed.) *Global Culture: Nationalism, Globalization and Modernity* (London: Sage), 1–14.

Fejtö, F. (1974) *A History of the People's Democracies: Eastern Europe since Stalin* (Harmondsworth: Penguin).

Ferge, Z. (1979) *A Society in the Making: Hungarian Social and Societal Policy 1945–75* (Harmondsworth: Penguin).

Ferge, Z. (1989) 'Social Policy and the Economy' in M. Bulmer, J. Lewis and D. Piachaud (eds) *The Goals of Social Policy* (London: Unwin Hyman), 267–87.

Ferge, Z. (1993) 'Winners and losers after the collapse of state socialism' in R. Page and J. Baldock (eds) *Social Policy Review* 5 (Canterbury: Social Policy Association), 270–87.

Firlit, E. and Chłopecki, J. (1992) 'When Theft is Not Theft' in J. Wedel (ed.) *The Unplanned Society: Poland During and After Communism* (New York: Columbia University Press), 95–109.

Fogel, R. (1989) *Without Consent or Contract: The Rise and Fall of American Slavery* (New York: W. Norton & Co.).

Fogel, R. and Engerman, S. (1974) *Time on the Cross: The Economics of American Negro Slavery* (London: Wildwood House).

Foster-Carter, A. (1985) *The Sociology of Development* (Ormskirk: Causeway Press).

Foucault, M. (1979) *Discipline and Punish: The Birth of the Prison* (Harmondsworth: Penguin).

Frank, A. (1967) *Capitalism and Underdevelopment in Latin America: Historical Studies of Chile and Brazil* (New York: Monthly Review Press).

Frank, A. (1969) *Latin America: Underdevelopment or Revolution* (New York: Monthly Review Press).

Frank, A. (1978) *Dependent Accumulation and Underdevelopment* (Basingstoke: Macmillan).

Frank, A. (1984) *Critique and Anti-Critique: Essays on Dependence and Reformism* (Basingstoke: Macmillan).

Frisby, D. and Sayer, D. (1986) *Society* (London: Tavistock).

Fröbel, F., Heinrichs, J. and Kreye, O. (1980) *The New International Division of Labour: Structural Unemployment in Industrialized Countries and*

Industrialization in Developing Countries (Cambridge: Cambridge University Press).

Fukuyama, F. (1989) 'The end of history', *The National Interest*, **16**:3–18.

Fukuyama, F. (1992) *The End of History and the Last Man* (London: Penguin).

Funk, N. and Mueller, M. (eds) (1993) *Gender Politics and Post-Communism: Reflections from Eastern Europe and the Former Soviet Union* (London: Routledge).

Füredi, F. (1992) *Mythical Past, Elusive Future: History and Society in an Anxious Age* (London: Pluto Press).

Garfinkel, A. (1981) *Forms of Explanation: Rethinking the Questions in Social Theory* (New Haven: Yale University Press).

Garland, D. (1990) *Punishment and Modern Society: A Study in Social Theory* (Oxford: Clarendon Press).

Geertz, C. (1976) 'Java and Japan Compared' in H. Bernstein (ed.) *Underdevelopment and Development: The Third World Today* (Harmondsworth: Penguin), 44–56.

George, S. (1988) *A Fate Worse than Debt* (Harmondsworth: Penguin).

George, S. (1992) *The Debt Boomerang: How Third World Debt Harms Us All* (London: Pluto).

George, V. (1988) *Wealth, Poverty and Starvation: A World Perspective* (Hemel Hempstead: Harvester Wheatsheaf).

Gerschenkron, A. (1962) *Economic Backwardness in Historical Perspective* (Cambridge, Mass.: Harvard University Press).

Gerth, H. and Mills, C. W. (1970) 'Introduction' in H. Gerth and C. W. Mills (eds) *From Max Weber: Essays in Sociology* (London: Routledge & Kegan Paul), 3–74.

Gibson, H. and Tsakalotos, E. (1992) 'The International Debt Crisis: Causes, Consequences and Solutions' in T. Hewitt, H. Johnson and D. Wield (eds) *Industrialization and Development* (Oxford: Oxford University Press), 41–65.

Giddens, A. (1971) *Capitalism and Modern Social Theory: an Analysis of the Writings of Marx, Durkheim and Max Weber* (Cambridge: Cambridge University Press).

Giddens, A. (1981) *A Contemporary Critique of Historical Materialism, volume 1: Power, Property and the State* (London and Basingstoke: Macmillan).

Giddens, A. (1982) *Profiles and Critiques in Social Theory* (London and Basingstoke: Macmillan).

Giddens, A. (1984) *The Constitution of Society: Outline of the Theory of Structuration* (Cambridge: Polity Press).

Giddens, A. (1985) *The Nation-State and Violence* (Cambridge: Polity Press).

Giddens, A. (1989) *Sociology* (Cambridge: Polity Press).

Giddens, A. (1990) *The Consequences of Modernity* (Cambridge: Polity Press).

Giddens, A. (1991) *Modernity and Self-Identity: Self and Society in the Late Modern Age* (Cambridge: Polity Press).

Giddens, A. (1992) 'Introduction' in A. Giddens (ed.) *Human Societies* (Cambridge: Polity Press), 1–2.

Giddens, A. (1994) *Beyond Left and Right: The Future of Radical Politics* (Cambridge: Polity Press).

Ginsburg, N. (1992) *Divisions of Welfare: A Critical Introduction to Comparative Social Policy* (London: Sage).

Goldthorpe, J. (1971) 'Social Stratification in Industrial Society' in K. Thompson and J. Tunstall (eds) *Sociological Perspectives* (Harmondsworth: Penguin), 331–47.

Goldthorpe, J. (1984) 'The End of Convergence: Corporatist and Dualist Tendencies in Modern Western Societies' in J. Goldthorpe (ed.) *Order and Conflict in Contemporary Capitalism: Studies in the Political Economy of Western European Nations* (Oxford: Clarendon Press), 315–43.

Goldthorpe, J. (1987) 'Problems of Political Economy after the Postwar Period' in C. Maier (ed.) *Changing Boundaries of the Political: Essays on the Evolving Balance Between the State and Society, Public and Private in Europe* (Cambridge: Cambridge University Press), 363–407.

Goodman, D. and Redclift, M. (1981) *From Peasant to Proletarian: Capitalist Development and Agrarian Transitions* (Oxford: Basil Blackwell).

Gould, A. (1993) *Capitalist Welfare Systems: A Comparison of Japan, Britain and Sweden* (London: Longman).

Grant, W. (1985) 'Introduction' in W. Grant (ed.) *The Political Economy of Corporatism* (Basingstoke: Macmillan), 1–31.

Gray, F. (1989) 'Steered by the State?' in M. Ball, F. Gray and L. McDowell *The Transformation of Britain: Contemporary Social and Economic Change* (London: Fontana), 303–29.

Gurnah, A. and Scott, Alan (1992) *The Uncertain Science: Criticism of Sociological Formalism* (London: Routledge).

Habermas, J. (1976) *Legitimation Crisis* (London: Heinemann).

Habermas, J. (1990) 'Modernity versus Postmodernity' in J. Alexander and S. Seidman (eds) *Culture and Society: Contemporary Debates* (Cambridge: Cambridge University Press), 342–54.

Hadenius, A. (1992) *Democracy and Development* (Cambridge: Cambridge University Press).

Hall, J. (1986) *Powers and Liberties: The Causes and Consequences of the Rise of the West* (Harmondsworth: Penguin).

Hall, J. (1993) 'Consolidations of Democracy' in D. Held (ed.) *Prospects for Democracy: North, South, East, West* (Cambridge: Polity Press), 271–90.

Hall, S. (1989) 'The Meaning of New Times' in S. Hall and M. Jacques (eds) *New Times: The Changing Face of Politics in the 1990s* (London: Lawrence and Wishart), 116–34.

Hall, S. (1992) 'The Question of Cultural Identity' in S. Hall, D. Held and T. McGrew (eds) *Modernity and its Futures* (Cambridge: Polity Press), 273–316.

Hall, S. and Jacques, M. (1989) 'Introduction' in S. Hall and M. Jacques (eds) *New Times: The Changing Face of Politics in the 1990s* (London: Lawrence and Wishart), 11–20.

Hall, S., Held, D. and McLennan, G. (1992) 'Introduction' in S. Hall, D. Held and T. McGrew (eds) *Modernity and its Futures* (Cambridge: Polity Press), 1–11.

Halsey, A. (1988) 'Introduction: Statistics and Social Trends in Britain' in A. Halsey (ed.) *British social Trends since 1900: A Guide to the Changing Social Structure of Britain* (Basingstoke: Macmillan), 1–35.

Hamilton, M. and Hirszowicz, M. (1993) *Class and Inequality: Comparative Perspectives* (Hemel Hempstead: Harvester Wheatsheaf).

Harris, N. (1987) *The End of the Third World: Newly Industrializing Countries and the Decline of an Ideology* (Harmondsworth: Penguin).

Harrison, D. (1988) *The Sociology of Modernization and Development* (London: Unwin Hyman).

Harvey, D. (1989) *The Condition of Postmodernity* (Oxford: Basil Blackwell).

Held, D. (1989) 'The Decline of the Nation State' in S. Hall and M. Jacques (eds) *New Times: The Changing Face of Politics in the 1990s* (London: Lawrence and Wishart) 191–204.

Held, D. (1991) 'Democracy, the Nation-State and the Global System' in D. Held (ed.) *Political Theory Today* (Cambridge: Polity Press), 197–235.

Held, D. (1993) 'Democracy: From City-States to a Cosmopolitan Order' in D. Held (ed.) *Prospects for Democracy: North, South, East, West* (Cambridge: Polity Press), 13–52.

Held, D. and Krieger, J. (1983) 'Accumulation, Legitimation and the State: the Ideas of Claus Offe and Jürgen Habermas' in D. Held, J. Anderson, B. Gieben *et al.* (eds) *States and Societies* (Oxford: Martin Robertson), 487–97.

Hettne, B. (1995) *Development Theory and the Three Worlds*, 2nd edn (London: Longman).

Hewitt, T. (1992) 'Developing Countries – 1945 to 1990' in T. Allen and A. Thomas (eds) *Poverty and Development in the 1990s* (Oxford: Oxford University Press), 221–37.

Higgins, J. (1981) *States of Welfare: Comparative Analysis in Social Policy* (Oxford: Basil Blackwell).

Hinrichs, K., Offe, C. and Wiesenthal, H. (1988) 'Time, Money, and Welfare-state Capitalism' in J. Keane (ed.) *Civil Society and the State: New European Perspectives* (London: Verso), 221–43.

Hippler, J. (1995) 'Preface' in J. Hippler (ed.) *The Democratisation of Disempowerment: The Problem of Democracy in the Third World* (London: Pluto), vii–ix.

Holmwood, J. and Stewart, A. (1991) *Explanation and Social Theory* (Basingstoke: Macmillan).

Holton, R. and Turner, B. (1989) *Max Weber on Economy and Society* (London: Routledge).

Hoogvelt, A. (1982) *The Third World in Global Development* (Basingstoke: Macmillan).

Hoogvelt, A. (1992) 'The New International Division of Labour' in A. Giddens (ed.) *Human Societies: A Reader* (Cambridge: Polity Press), 281–5.

Horowitz, I. (1972) *Three Worlds of Development: The Theory and Practice of International Stratification*, 2nd edn (New York: Oxford University Press).

Horowitz, I. (1983) *C. Wright Mills: An American Utopian* (New York: Free Press).

Hulme, D. and Turner, M. (1990) *Sociology and Development: Theories, Policies and Practices* (Hemel Hempstead: Harvester Wheatsheaf).

Hutton, W. (1996) *The State We're In* (London: Vintage).

Independent Commission on International Development Issues (1980) *North-South: A Programme for Survival* (London: Pan).

Ingalls, G. and Martin, W. (1988) 'Defining and Identifying NICs' in J. Norwine and A. Gonzalez (eds) *The Third World: States of Mind and Being* (London: Unwin Hyman), 82–98.

Inkeles, A, and Sasaki, M. (1996) 'Preface' in A. Inkeles and M. Sasaki (eds) *Comparing Nations and Cultures: Readings in a Cross-Disciplinary Perspective* (Englewood Cliffs, NJ: Prentice Hall), xi–xv.

Jary, D. and Jary, J. (1991) *Collins Dictionary of Sociology* (Glasgow: Harper Collins).

Jenkins, R. (1987) *Transnational Corporations and Uneven Development: The Internationalization of Capital and the Third World* (London: Methuen).

Jenkins, R. (1992) 'Industrialization and the Global Economy' in T. Hewitt, H. Johnson and D. Wield (eds) *Industrialization and Development* (Oxford: Oxford University Press), 13–40.

Jenkins, R. (1994) 'Capitalist Development in the NICs' in L. Sklair (ed.) *Capitalism and Development* (London: Routledge), 72–86.

Jenson, J., Hagen, E. and Reddy, C. (eds) (1988) *Feminization of the Labour Force* (Cambridge: Polity Press).

Jessop, B. (1987) 'The Future of Capitalism' in R. Anderson, J. Hughes and W. Sharrock (eds) *Classic Disputes in Sociology* (London: Allen and Unwin), 36–66.

Jessop, B. (1992) 'Fordism in Britain and Germany' in J. Allen, P. Braham and P. Lewis (eds) *Political and Economic Forms of Modernity* (Cambridge: Polity Press), 268–74.

Joekes, S. (1987) *Women in the World Economy* (Oxford: Oxford University Press).

Johnson, H. (1992) 'Rural Livelihoods: Action from Below' in H. Bernstein, B. Crow and H. Johnson (eds) *Rural Livelihoods: Crises and Responses* (Oxford: Oxford University Press), 274–300.

Johnson, N. (1987) *The Welfare State in Transition: The Theory and Practice of Welfare Pluralism* (Brighton: Wheatsheaf Books).

Jones, H. (1990) *Social Welfare in Third World Development* (Basingstoke: Macmillan).

Kalberg, S. (1994) *Max Weber's Comparative–Historical Sociology* (Cambridge: Polity Press).

Katzenstein, P. (1985) 'Small Nations in an Open International Economy: The Converging Balance of State and Society in Switzerland and Austria' in P. Evans, D. Rueschemeyer and T. Skocpol (eds) *Bringing The State Back In* (Cambridge: Cambridge University Press), 227–51.

Keane, J. (1984) *Public life and late capitalism: Toward a socialist theory of democracy* (Cambridge: Cambridge University Press).

Keane, J. (1988) 'Introduction' in J. Keane (ed.) *Civil Society and the State: New European Perspectives* (London: Verso), 1–31.

Kennedy, P. (1989) *The Rise and Fall of the Great Powers: Economic Change and Military Conflict from 1500 to 2000* (London: Fontana).

Kennedy, P. (1993) *Preparing for the Twenty-first Century* (London: Fontana).

Kerr, C. (1983) *The Future of Industrial Societies: Convergence or Continuing Diversity?* (Cambridge, Mass.: Harvard University Press).

Kerr, C., Dunlop, J., Harbison, F. and Myers, C. (1973) *Industrialism and Industrial Man: The Problems of Labour and Management in Economic Growth*, 2nd edn (Harmondsworth: Penguin).

Kidron, M. and Segal, R. (1991) *The New State of the World Atlas*, 4th edn (London: Simon and Schuster).

Kiely, R. (1995) *Sociology and Development: The Impasse and Beyond* (London: UCL Press).

Kilminster, A. (1992) 'Socialist Models of Development' in T. Allen and A. Thomas (eds) *Poverty and Development in the 1990s* (Oxford: Oxford University Press), 238–52.

Konrad, G. (1992) 'Anti-Politics' in J. Allen, P. Braham and P. Lewis (eds) *Political and Economic Forms of Modernity* (Cambridge: Polity Press), 56–8.

Konrad, G. and Szelenyi, I. (1979) *The Intellectuals on the Road to Class Power: A Sociological Study of the Role of the Intelligentsia in Socialism* (Brighton: Harvester Press).

Korpi, W. (1989) 'Can we Afford to Work?' in M. Bulmer, J. Lewis and D. Piachaud (eds) *The Goals of Social Policy* (London: Unwin Hyman), 297–310.

Kotkin, S. (1992) *Steeltown, USSR: Soviet Society in the Gorbachev Era* (Berkeley: University of California Press).

Krejčí, J. (1994) *Great Revolutions Compared: The Outline of a Theory*, 2nd edn (Hemel Hempstead: Harvester Wheatsheaf).

Kumar, K. (1978) *Prophecy and Progress: The Sociology of Industrial and Post-Industrial Society* (Harmondsworth: Penguin).

Kumar, K. (1988) *The Rise of Modern Society: Aspects of the Social and Political Development of the West* (Oxford: Basil Blackwell).

Kumar, K. (1995) *From Post-Industrial to Post-Modern Society: New Theories of the Contemporary World* (Oxford: Basil Blackwell).

Laite, J. (1984) 'The Social Realities of Development' in R. Anderson and W. Sharrock (eds) *Applied Sociological Perspectives* (London: George Allen and Unwin), 190–214.

Lane, C. (1981) *The Rites of Rulers: Ritual in Industrial Society – the Soviet case* (Cambridge: Cambridge University Press).

Lane, C. (1988) 'Industrial Change in Europe: The Pursuit of Flexible Specialisation in Britain and West Germany', *Work, Employment and Society*, 2(2):141–68.

Lane, D. (1985a) *State and Politics in the USSR* (Oxford: Basil Blackwell).

Lane, D. (1985b) *Soviet Economy and Society* (Oxford; Basil Blackwell).

Lane, D. (1989) 'Social change, division and control in the USSR' in R. Scase (ed.) *Industrial Societies: Crisis and Division in Western Capitalism and State Socialism* (London: Unwin Hyman), 168–92.

Lane, D. (1990) *Soviet Society Under Perestroika* (London: Unwin Hyman).

Lash, S. and Urry, J. (1987) *The End of Organized Capitalism* (London: Sage).

Lash, S. and Urry, J. (1994) *Economies of Signs and Space* (London: Sage).

Latouche, S. (1993) *In the Wake of the Affluent Society: An Exploration of Post-development* (London: Zed Books).

Layder, D. (1994) *Understanding Social Theory* (London: Sage).

Leftwich, A. (1995) 'Governance, Democracy and Development in the Third World' in S. Corbridge (ed.) *Development Studies: A Reader* (London: Edward Arnold), 427–38.

Leira, A. (1992) *Welfare States and Working Mothers: The Scandinavian Experience* (Cambridge: Cambridge University Press).

Lewis, P. (1983) 'Legitimacy and the Polish Communist State' in D. Held, J. Anderson, B. Gieben *et al.* (eds) *States and Societies* (Oxford: Martin Robertson), 431–56.

Lewis, P. (1992) 'Democracy in Modern Societies' in J. Allen, P. Braham and P. Lewis (eds) *Political and Economic Forms of Modernity* (Cambridge: Polity Press), 13–51.

Lewis, P. (1993) 'Democracy and its Future in Eastern Europe' in D. Held (ed.) *Prospects for Democracy: North, South, East, West* (Cambridge: Polity Press), 291–311.

Leys, C. (1975) *Underdevelopment in Kenya: The Political Economy of Neo-Colonialism* (London: Heinemann).

Lipton, M. (1977) *Why Poor People Stay Poor: A Study of Urban Bias in World Development* (London: Temple Smith).

Lister, R. (1990) *The Exclusive Society: Citizenship and the Poor* (London: Child Poverty Action Group).

Littlejohn, G. (1984) *A Sociology of the Soviet Union* (London: Macmillan).

Llosa, M. V. (1995) 'Foreword to "The Other Path: The Invisible Revolution in the Third World" by Hernando de Soto' in S. Corbridge (ed.) *Development Studies: A Reader* (London: Edward Arnold), 288–95.

Lloyd, P. (1979) *Slums of Hope? Shanty Towns of the Third World* (Manchester: Manchester University Press).

Lloyd, P. (1982) *A Third World Proletariat?* (London: George Allen and Unwin).

Long, N. (1992) 'From Paradigm Lost to Paradigm Regained?' in N. Long and A. Long (eds) *Battlefields of Knowledge: The Interlocking of Theory and Practice in Social Research and Development* (London: Routledge), 16–43.

Long, N. and Long, A. (eds) (1992) *Battlefields of Knowledge: The Interlocking of Theory and Practice in Social Research and Development* (London: Routledge).

Lyon, D. (1994) *The Electronic Eye: The Rise of Surveillance Society* (Cambridge: Polity Press).

Lyotard, J.-F. (1990) 'The Postmodern Condition' in J. Alexander and S. Seidman (eds) *Culture and Society: Contemporary Debates* (Cambridge: Cambridge University Press), 330–41.

McClelland, D. (1967) *The Achieving Society* (New York: Free Press).

McCrone, D., Elliott, B. and Bechhofer, F. (1989) 'Corporatism and the New Right' in R. Scase (ed.) *Industrial Societies: Crisis and Division in Western Capitalism and State Socialism* (London: Unwin Hyman), 44–63.

McDowell, L. (1992) 'Gender Divisions in a Post-Fordist Era: New Contradictions or the Same Old Story?' in L. McDowell and R. Pringle (eds) *Defining Women: Social Institutions and Gender Divisions* (Cambridge: Polity Press), 181–92.

McEachern, D. (1990) *The Expanding State: Class and Economy in Europe since 1945* (London: Harvester Wheatsheaf).

McGrew, A. (1992a) 'A Global Society?' in S. Hall, D. Held and T. McGrew (eds) *Modernity and its Futures* (Cambridge: Polity Press), 61–102.

McGrew, A. (1992b) 'The State in Advanced Capitalist Societies' in J. Allan, P. Braham and P. Lewis (eds) *Political and Economic Forms of Modernity* (Cambridge: Polity Press), 65–114.

McGrew, A. (1992c) 'The Third World in the New Global Order' in T. Allen and A. Thomas (eds) *Poverty and Development in the 1990s* (Oxford: Oxford University Press), 255–72.

Mackintosh, M. (1992) 'Questioning the State' in M. Wuyts, M. Mackintosh and T. Hewitt (eds) *Development Policy and Public Action* (Oxford: Oxford University Press), 61–89.

McNeill, W. (1983) *The Pursuit of Power: Technology, Armed Force, and Society since A.D. 1000* (Oxford: Basil Blackwell).

Macpherson, C. (1962) *The Political Theory of Possessive Individualism: Hobbes to Locke* (Oxford: Oxford University Press).

Makkai, T. (1994) 'Social Policy and Gender in Eastern Europe' in D. Sainsbury (ed.) *Gendering Welfare States* (London: Sage), 188–205.

Mann, M. (1986) *The Sources of Social Power, volume I: A History of Power from the Beginning to A.D. 1760* (Cambridge: Cambridge University Press).

Mann, M. (1987) 'Ruling class strategies and citizenship', *Sociology*, 21(3):339–54.

Mann, M. (1988) *States, War and Capitalism* (Oxford: Basil Blackwell).

Mann, M. (1993) *The Sources of Social Power, volume II: The Rise of Classes and Nation-States, 1760–1914* (Cambridge: Cambridge University Press).

Marcuse, H. (1971) *Soviet Marxism: A Critical Analysis* (Harmondsworth: Penguin).

Marcuse, H. (1972) *One Dimensional Man* (London: Abacus).

Marshall, G., Rose, D., Newby, H. and Vogler, C. (1988) *Social Class in Modern Britain* (London: Unwin Hyman).

Marshall, T. (1992) 'Citizenship and Social Class' in T. Marshall and T. Bottomore *Citizenship and Social Class* (London: Pluto Press), 3–51.

Marx, K. (1973) *Surveys from Exile* (Harmondsworth: Penguin).

Marx, K. (1982) 'Pathways of Social Development: A Brief Against Suprahistorical Theory' in H. Alavi and T. Shanin (eds) *Introduction to the Sociology of 'Developing Societies'* (Basingstoke: Macmillan), 109–11.

May, T. (1993) *Social Research: Issues, Methods and Process* (Buckingham: Open University Press).

Mayo, M, (1994) *Communities and Caring: The Mixed Economy of Welfare* (Basingstoke: Macmillan).

Melotti, U. (1977) *Marx and the Third World* (London and Basingstoke: Macmillan).

Melucci, A. (1989) *Nomads of the Present: Social Movements and Individual Needs in Contemporary Society* (London: Radius).

Merton, R. (1967) 'Foreword' in R. Marsh, *Comparative Sociology: A Codification of Cross-Societal Analysis* (New York: Harcourt Brace), v–vi.

Mies, M. (1986) *Patriarchy and Accumulation on a World Scale: Women in the International Division of Labour* (London: Zed Books).

Mills, C. W. (1960) *The Causes of World War Three* (New York: Ballantine Books).

Mills, C. W. (1967) *Power, Politics and People* (London: Oxford University Press).

Mills, C. W. (1970) *The Sociological Imagination* (Harmondsworth: Penguin).

Mingione, E. (1991) *Fragmented Societies: A Sociology of Economic Life Beyond the Market Paradigm* (Oxford: Basil Blackwell).

Minh-ha, T. (1993) 'Infinite Layers/Third World?' in C. Lemert (ed.) *Social Theory: The Multicultural and Classic Readings* (Boulder, Colorado: Westview Press), 605–9.

Mishra, R. (1984) *The Welfare State in Crisis: Social Thought and Social Change* (Brighton: Wheatsheaf).

Mishra, R. (1990) *The Welfare State in Capitalist Society: Policies of Retrenchment and Maintenance in Europe, North America and Australia* (Hemel Hempstead: Harvester Wheatsheaf).

Mitter, S. (1986) *Common Fate, Common Bond: Women in the Global Economy* (London: Zed Books).

Moore, B. (1942) 'The relation between social stratification and social control', *Sociometry*, 5(3):230–50.

Moore, B. (1945) 'A comparative analysis of the class struggle', *American Sociological Review*, 10(1):31–7.

Moore, B. (1962) *Political Power and Social Theory* (New York: Harper and Row).

Moore, B. (1967) *Social Origins of Dictatorship and Democracy: Lord and Peasant in the Making of the Modern World* (Harmondsworth: Penguin).

Moore, B. (1972) *Reflections on the Causes of Human Misery and upon Certain Proposals to Eliminate Them* (London: Allen Lane).

Moore, B. (1978) *Injustice: The Social Bases of Obedience and Revolt* (London and Basingstoke: Macmillan).

Moore, B. (1984) *Privacy: Studies in Social and Cultural History* (Armonk, NY: Sharpe).

Morris, L. (1994) *Dangerous Classes: The Underclass and Social Citizenship* (London: Routledge).

Morris, M. (1979) *Measuring the Condition of the World's Poor: The Physical Quality of Life Index* (Oxford: Pergamon).

Mouzelis, N. (1991) *Back to Sociological Theory: The Construction of Social Orders* (Basingstoke: Macmillan).

Munck, R. (1994) 'Democracy and Development: Deconstruction and Debates' in L. Sklair (ed.) *Capitalism and Development* (London: Routledge), 21–39.

Newman, O. (1981) *The Challenge of Corporatism* (London: Macmillan).

Nisbet, R. (1965) *Emile Durkheim* (Englewood Cliffs, NJ: Prentice Hall).

Nisbet, R. (1967) *The Sociological Tradition* (London: Heinemann).

Nove, A. (1989) *Stalinism and After: The Road to Gorbachev* (London: Unwin Hyman), 3rd edn.

O'Connell-Davidson, J. and Layder, D. (1994) *Methods, Sex and Madness* (London: Routledge).

Offe, C. (1984) *Contradictions of the Welfare State* (London: Hutchinson).

Offe, C. (1985) *Disorganized Capitalism: Contemporary Transformations of Work and Politics* (Cambridge: Polity Press).

Offe, C. (1993) 'Interdependence, Difference and Limited State Capacity' in G Drover and P. Kerans (eds) *New Approaches to Welfare Theory* (Cheltenham: Edward Elgar), 235–41.

Øyen, E. (1990) 'The Imperfection of Comparisons' in E. Øyen (ed.) *Comparative Methodology: Theory and Practice in International Social Research* (London: Sage), 1–18.

Pahl, R. (1984) *Divisions of Labour* (Oxford: Basil Blackwell).

Pahl, R. (ed.) (1988) *On Work: Historical, Comparative and Theoretical Approaches* (Oxford: Basil Blackwell).

Pahl, R. (1989) 'From "Informal Economy" to "Forms of Work": Cross-National Patterns and Trends' in R. Scase (ed.) *Industrial Societies: Crisis and Division in Western Capitalism and State Socialism* (London: Unwin Hyman), 90–119.

Pakulski, J. (1990) 'Poland: Ideology, Legitimacy and Political Domination' in N. Abercrombie, S. Hill and B. Turner (eds) *Dominant Ideologies* (London: Unwin Hyman), 38–64.

Parkin, F. (1982) *Max Weber* (London: Tavistock).

Parsons, T. (1966) *Societies: Evolutionary and Comparative Perspectives* (Englewood Cliffs, NJ: Prentice Hall).

Parsons, T. (1977) *The Evolution of Societies* (Englewood Cliffs, NJ: Prentice Hall).

Pawson, R. (1989) *A Measure for Measures: A Manifesto for Empirical Sociology* (London: Routledge).

Payne, G. (1987) *Mobility and Change in Modern Society* (Basingstoke: Macmillan).

Pearson, R. (1992a) 'Gender matters in development' in T. Allen and A. Thomas (eds) *Poverty and Development in the 1990s* (Oxford: Oxford University Press), 291–312.

Pearson, R. (1992b) 'Gender Issues in Industrialization' in T. Hewitt, H. Johnson and D. Wield (eds) *Industrialization and Development* (Oxford: Oxford University Press), 222–47.

Pearson, R. (1994) 'Gender Relations, Capitalism and Third World Industrialization' in L. Sklair (ed.) *Capitalism and Development* (London: Routledge), 339–58.

Peet, R. (1991) *Global Capitalism: Theories of Societal Development* (London: Routledge).

Pelczynski, Z. (1988) 'The Rebirth of Civil Society' in J. Keane (ed.) *Civil Society and the State: New European Perspectives* (London: Verso), 361–80.

Peters, E. (1988) 'World (Third?) within a world (First?): Canadian Indian people' in J. Norwine and A. Gonzalez (eds) *The Third World: States of Mind and Being* (London: Unwin Hyman), 243–52.

Phillips, A. (1993) 'Must Feminists Give up on Liberal Democracy?' in D. Held (ed.) *Prospects for Democracy: North, South, East, West* (Cambridge: Polity Press), 93–111.

Pierson, C. (1991) *Beyond the Welfare State? The New Political Economy of Welfare* (Cambridge: Polity Press).

Pinkney, R. (1993) *Democracy in the Third World* (Buckingham: Open University Press).

Polanyi, K. (1957) *The Great Transformation: The Political and Economic Origins of our Time* (Boston, Mass.: Beacon Press).

Pollard, S. (1971) *The Idea of Progress: History and Society* (Harmondsworth: Penguin).

Potter, D. (1992) 'The Democratization of Third World States' in T. Allen and A. Thomas (eds) *Poverty and Development in the 1990s* (Oxford: Oxford University Press), 273–90.

Potter, D. (1993) 'Democratization in Asia' in D. Held (ed.) *Prospects for Democracy: North, South, East, West* (Cambridge: Polity Press), 355–79.

Preston, P. (1982) *Theories of Development* (London: Routledge & Kegan Paul).

Preston, P. (1985) *New Trends in Development Theory: Essays in Development and Social Theory* (London: Routledge & Kegan Paul).

Pusey, M. (1987) *Jürgen Habermas* (London: Tavistock).

Rabinow, P. (1986) 'Introduction' in P. Rabinow (ed.) *The Foucault Reader* (Harmondsworth: Penguin), 3–29.

Ragin, C. (1987) *The Comparative Method: Moving Beyond Qualitative and Quantitative Strategies* (Berkeley: University of California Press).

Rakovski, M. (1983) 'Capitalist and Socialist States: a Critique of the Convergence Thesis' in D. Held, J. Anderson, B. Gieben *et al.* (eds) *States and Societies* (Oxford: Martin Robertson), 395–410.

Ray, L. (1993) *Rethinking Critical Theory: Emancipation in the Age of Global Social Movements* (London: Sage).

Riley, D. (1992) 'Citizenship and the Welfare State' in J. Allan, P. Braham and P. Lewis (eds) *Political and Economic Forms of Modernity* (Cambridge: Polity Press), 179–210.

Ritzer, G. (1993) *The McDonaldization of Society: An Investigation into the Changing Character of Contemporary Social Life* (Thousand Oaks: Pine Forge Press).

Roberts, B. (1995) *The Making of Citizens: Cities of Peasants Revisited* (London: Arnold).

Roberts, K., Cook, F., Clark, S. and Semeonoff, E. (1977) *The Fragmentary Class Structure* (London: Heinemann).

Robertson, R. (1992) *Globalization: Social Theory and Global Culture* (London: Sage).

Robins, K. (1990) 'Global Local Times' in J. Anderson and M. Ricci (eds) *Society and Social Change: A Reader* (Milton Keynes: The Open University), 196–205.

Rodinson, M. (1977) *Islam and Capitalism* (Harmondsworth: Penguin).

Rogers, B. (1981) *The Domestication of Women: Discrimination in Developing Societies* (London: Tavistock).

Rose, M. (1985) *Re-working the Work Ethic: Economic Values and Socio-Cultural Politics* (London: Batsford).

Rostow, W. (1960) *The Stages of Economic Growth: A Non-communist Manifesto* (Cambridge: Cambridge University Press).

Rueschemeyer, D. and Rueschemeyer, M. (1990) 'Progress in the Distribution of Power: Gender Relations and Women's Movements as a Source of Change' in J. Alexander and P. Sztompka (eds) *Rethinking Progress: Movements, Forces and Ideas at the End of the Twentieth Century* (London: Unwin Hyman), 106–22.

Rueschemeyer, D., Stephens, E. and Stephens, J. (1992) *Capitalist Development and Democracy* (Cambridge: Polity Press).

Runciman, W. G. (1989) *A Treatise on Social Theory, volume II: Substantive Social Theory* (Cambridge: Cambridge University Press.

Rupnik, J. (1988) 'Totalitarianism Revisited' in J. Keane (ed.) *Civil Society and the State: New European Perspectives* (London: Verso), 263–89.

Sainsbury, D. (ed.) (1994) *Gendering Welfare States* (London: Sage).

Salomon, A. (1995) 'The Religion of Progress' in S. Lyman (ed.) *Social Movements: Critiques, Concepts, Case-Studies* (Basingstoke: Macmillan), 27–46.

Sassoon, A. (1987) 'Women's New Social Role: Contradictions of the Welfare State' in A. Sassoon (ed.) *Women and the State: The Shifting Boundaries of Public and Private* (London: Hutchinson), 158–88.

Savage, M., Barlow, J., Dickens, P. and Fielding, T. (1992) *Property, Bureaucracy and Culture: Middle-Class Formation in Contemporary Britain* (London: Routledge).

Sayer, D. (1991) *Capitalism and Modernity: An Excursus on Marx and Weber* (London: Routledge).

Scaff, L. (1989) *Fleeing the Iron Cage: Culture, Politics and Modernity in the Thought of Max Weber* (Berkeley: University of California Press).

Scase, R. (ed.) (1977) *Industrial Society: Class, Cleavage and Control* (London: George Allen and Unwin).

Scase, R. (1989) 'Introduction' in R. Scase (ed.) *Industrial Societies: Crisis and Division in Western Capitalism and State Socialism* (London: Unwin Hyman), 1–15.

Scase, R. (1992) *Class* (Buckingham: Open University Press).

Scott, Alan (1990) *Ideology and the New Social Movements* (London: Unwin Hyman).

Scott, Alison (1986) 'Women and industrialization: examining the "female marginalisation" thesis', *Journal of Development Studies*, 22(4):649–80.

Scott, Alison (1994) *Divisions and Solidarities: Gender, Class and Employment in Latin America* (London: Routledge).

Scott, H. (1984) *Working Your Way to the Bottom: The Feminization of Poverty* (London: Pandora).

Scott, James (1985) *Weapons of the Weak: Everyday Forms of Peasant Resistance* (New Haven: Yale University Press).

Scott, John (1979) *Corporations, Classes and Capitalism* (London: Hutchinson).

Scott, John (1991) *Who Rules Britain?* (Cambridge: Polity Press).

Seabrook, J. (1993) *Victims of Development: Resistance and Alternatives* (London: Verso).

Seers, D. (1995) 'What Are we Trying To Measure?' in R. Ayres (ed.) *Development Studies* (Dartford: Greenwich University Press), 3–20.

Sen, A. (1995) 'Food and Freedom' in S. Corbridge (ed.) *Development Studies: A Reader* (London: Edward Arnold), 90–108.

Shanin, T. (1984) *Late Marx and the Russian Road: Marx and 'the Peripheries of Capitalism'* (London: Routledge & Kegan Paul).

Shanin, T. (1990) *Defining Peasants: Essays Concerning Rural Societies, Expolary Economies, and Learning from them in the Contemporary World* (Oxford: Basil Blackwell).

Shaw, M. (1991) *Post-Military Society: Militarism, Demilitarization and War at the End of the Twentieth Century* (Cambridge: Polity Press).

Sheehan, J. (1980) "Barrington Moore on Obedience and Revolt', *Theory and Society*, 9 (5): 723–34.

Sklair, L. (1994) 'Capitalism and Development in Global Perspective' in L. Sklair (ed.) *Capitalism and Development* (London: Routledge), 165–85.

Sklair, L. (1995) *Sociology of the Global System*, 2nd edn (Hemel Hempstead: Harvester Wheatsheaf).

Skocpol, T. (1979) *States and Social Revolutions: A Comparative Analysis of France, Russia and China* (Cambridge: Cambridge University Press).

Skocpol, T. (1984) 'Sociology's Historical Imagination' in T. Skocpol (ed.) *Vision and Method in Historical Sociology* (Cambridge: Cambridge University Press), 1–21.

Skocpol, T. (1985) 'Bringing the State Back In: Strategies of Analysis in Current Research' in P. Evans, D. Rueschemeyer and T. Skocpol (eds) *Bringing the State Back In* (Cambridge: Cambridge University Press), 3–37.

Skocpol, T. (1992) *Protecting Soldiers and Mothers: The Political Origins of Social Policy in the United States* (Cambridge, Mass.: Belknap Press of Harvard University Press).

Skocpol, T. (1994) *Social Revolutions in the Modern World* (Cambridge: Cambridge University Press).

Skocpol, T. (1995) *Social Policy in the United States: Future Possibilities in Historical Perspective* (Princeton, NJ: Princeton University Press).

Smart, B. (1988) *Michel Foucault* (London: Routledge).

Smart, B. (1992) *Modern Conditions, Postmodern Controversies* (London: Routledge).

Smith, D. (1983) *Barrington Moore: Violence, Morality and Political Change* (Basingstoke: Macmillan).

Smith, D. (1991) *The Rise of Historical Sociology* (Cambridge: Polity Press).

Smith, P. (1992) 'Industrialization and Environment' in T. Hewitt, H. Johnson and D. Wield (eds) *Industrialization and Development* (Oxford: Oxford University Press), 277–302.

South Commission (1990) *The Challenge to the South* (Oxford: Oxford University Press).

Spybey, T. (1992) *Social Change, Development and Dependency: Modernity, Colonialism and the Development of the West* (Cambridge: Polity Press).

Stacey, M. (1969) 'The myth of community studies', *British Journal of Sociology*, 20(2):134–47.

Stephens, J. (1979) *The Transition from Capitalism to Socialism* (London: Macmillan).

Strange, S. (1986) *Casino Capitalism* (Oxford: Basil Blackwell).

Sułek, A. (1992) 'Farewell to the Party' in J. Wedel (ed.) *The Unplanned Society: Poland During and After Communism* (New York: Columbia University Press), 249–61.

Szabó, M. (1992) 'Social Movements, Mobilization and Democratization in Hungary' in J. Allen, P. Braham and P. Lewis (eds) *Political and Economic Forms of Modernity* (Cambridge: Polity Press), 175–7.

Szelenyi, I. (1988) *Socialist Entrepreneurs: Embourgeoisement in Rural Hungary* (Cambridge: Polity Press).

Sztompka, P. (1993) *The Sociology of Social Change* (Oxford: Basil Blackwell).

Tåhlin, M. (1993) 'Class Inequality and Post-Industrial Employment in Sweden' in G. Esping-Andersen (ed.) *Changing Classes: Stratification and Mobility in Post-Industrial Societies* (London: Sage), 80–108.

Taylor, B. (1990) *Imagine No Possessions: Towards a Sociology of Poverty* (Hemel Hempstead: Harvester Wheatsheaf).

Therborn, G. (1986) *Why Some Peoples Are More Unemployed Than Others: The Strange Paradox of Growth and Unemployment* (London: Verso).

Therborn, G. (1989) 'The two-thirds, one-third society' in S. Hall and M. Jacques (eds) *New Times: The Changing Face of Politics in the 1990s* (London: Lawrence and Wishart), 103–15.

Therborn, G. (1995) *European Modernity and Beyond: The Trajectory of European Societies 1945–2000* (London: Sage).

Thomas, A. (1992) 'Introduction' in T. Allen and A. Thomas (eds) *Poverty and Development in the 1990s* (Oxford: Oxford University Press), 1–9.

Thompson, P. and McHugh, D. (1990) *Work Organisations: A Critical Introduction* (Basingstoke: Macmillan).

Tilly, C. (1984) *Big Structures, Large Processes, Huge Comparisons* (New York: Russell Sage Foundation).

Tiryakian, E. (1986) 'On the Significance of De-differentiation' in S. Eisenstadt and H. Helle (eds) *Macro-Sociological Theory: Perspectives on Sociological Theory*, volume 1 (London: Sage), 118–34.

Todaro, M. (1989) *Economic Development in the Third World*, 4th edn (London: Longman).

Townsend, P. (1993) *The International Analysis of Poverty* (Hemel Hempstead: Harvester Wheatsheaf).

Townsend, P., Corrigan, P. and Kowarzik, U. (1987) *Poverty and Labour in London* (London: Low Pay Unit).

Toye, J. (1995) 'Is the Third World Still There?' in R. Ayres (ed.) *Development Studies* (Dartford: Greenwich University Press), 35–49.

Turner, B. (1981) *For Weber: Essays on the Sociology of Fate* (London: Routledge & Kegan Paul).

Turner, B. (1986) *Citizenship and Capitalism: The Debate Over Reformism* (London: Allen and Unwin).

Turner, B. (1990) 'Outline of a theory of citizenship', *Sociology*, 24(2):189–217.

Twine, F. (1994) *Citizenship and Social Rights: The Interdependence of Self and Society* (London: Sage).

Urry, J. (1981) *The Anatomy of Capitalist Societies: The Economy, Civil Society and the State* (London and Basingstoke: Macmillan).

Vattimo, G. (1994) 'The Postmodern: A Transparent Society?' in *The Polity Reader in Social Theory* (Cambridge: Polity Press), 367–72.

Vickers, J. (1991) *Women and the World Economic Crisis* (London: Zed Books).

Wallerstein, I. (1976) 'The State and Social Transformation: Will and Possibility' in H. Bernstein (ed.) *Underdevelopment and Development: The Third World Today* (Harmondsworth: Penguin), 277–83.

Wallerstein, I. (1979) *The Capitalist World-Economy* (Cambridge: Cambridge University Press).

Wallerstein, I. (1990) 'Culture as the Ideological Battleground of the Modern World System' in M. Featherstone (ed.) *Global Culture* (London: Sage), 31–55.

Wallerstein, I. (1991) *Unthinking Social Science: The Limits of Nineteenth-Century Paradigms* (Cambridge: Polity Press).

Wallerstein, I. (1994) 'Development: Lodestar or Illusion?' in L. Sklair (ed.) *Capitalism and Development* (London: Routledge), 3–20.

Wallerstein, I. and Smith, J. (1992) 'Households as an Institution of the World-economy' in J. Smith and I. Wallerstein (eds) *Creating and Transforming Households: The Constraints of the World-economy* (Cambridge: Cambridge University Press) 3–23.

Wallman, S. (1985) 'Structures of Informality: Variation in Local Style and the Scope for Unofficial Economic Organisation in London' in B. Roberts, R. Finnegan and D. Gallie (eds) *New Approaches to Economic Life* (Manchester: Manchester University Press) 184–97.

Ward, G. (1991) *The Civil War* (London: Bodley Head).

Warde, A. (1990) 'The Future of Work' in J. Anderson and M. Ricci (eds) *Society and Social Science: A Reader* (Milton Keynes: The Open University), 86–94.

Warren, B. (1980) *Imperialism: Pioneer of Capitalism* (London: Verso).

Waters, M. (1995) *Globalization* (London: Routledge).

Weber, M. (1930) *The Protestant Ethic and the Spirit of Capitalism* (London: George Allen and Unwin).

Weber, M. (1970a) 'Politics as a Vocation' in H. Gerth and C. Wright Mills (eds) *From Max Weber: Essays in Sociology* (London: Routledge & Kegan Paul), 77–128.

Weber, M. (1970b) 'Science as a vocation' in H. Gerth and C. Wright Mills (eds) *From Max Weber: Essays in Sociology* (London: Routledge & Kegan Paul), 129–56.

Weber, M. (1970c) 'The Social Psychology of the World Religions' in H. Gerth and C. W. Mills (eds) *From Max Weber: Essays in Sociology* (London: Routledge & Kegan Paul), 267–301.

Weber, M. (1978) *Economy and Society* (Berkeley: University of California Press).

Weber, M. (1981) *General Economic History* (New Brunswick: Transaction Books).

Webster, A. (1990) *Introduction to the Sociology of Development*, 2nd edn (Basingstoke: Macmillan).

Wedel, J. (ed.) (1992) *The Unplanned Society: Poland During and After Communism* (New York: Columbia University Press).

Westergaard, J. (1995) *Who Gets What? The Hardening of Class Inequality in the Late Twentieth Century* (Oxford: Polity Press).

Whimster, S. and Lash, S. (1987) 'Introduction' in S. Whimster and S. Lash (eds) *Max Weber, Rationality and Modernity* (London: Allen and Unwin), 1–31.

White, G. (1993) *Riding the Tiger: The Politics of Economic Reform in Post-Mao China* (Basingstoke: Macmillan).

White, S. (1993) 'Eastern Europe after Communism' in S. White, J. Batt and P. Lewis (eds) *Developments in East European Politics* (Basingstoke: Macmillan), 2–15.

Whitehead, L. (1993) 'The Alternatives to "Liberal Democracy": A Latin American Perspective' in D. Held (ed.) *Prospects for Democracy: North, South, East, West* (Cambridge: Polity Press), 312–29.

Wield, D. and Rhodes, E. (1988) 'Divisions of Labour or Labour Divided?' in B. Crow, M. Thorpe, H. Bernstein *et al. Survival and Change in the Third World* (Cambridge: Polity Press), 288–309.

Wield, D., Johnson, H. and Hewitt, T. (1992) 'Conclusions' in T. Hewitt, H. Johnson and D. Wield (eds) *Industrialization and Development* (Oxford: Oxford University Press), 303–15.

Wiener, J. (1975) 'The Barrington Moore Thesis and its Critics', *Theory and Society*, (2):301–30.

Williams, F. (1994) 'Social Relations, Welfare and the Post-Fordism Debate', in R. Burrows and B. Loader (eds) *Towards a Post-Fordist Welfare State?* (London: Routledge), 49–73.

Williams, R. (1983) *Keywords: A Vocabulary of Culture and Society* (London: Flamingo).

Wilson, G. (1992) 'Technology in Development' in T. Allen and A. Thomas (eds) *Poverty and Development in the 1990s* (Oxford: Oxford University Press), 313–330.

Winkler, J. (1977) 'The Corporatist Economy' in R. Scase (ed.) *Industrial Society: Class, Cleavage and Control* (London: George Allen and Unwin), 43–58.

Wittfogel, K. (1957) *Oriental Despotism: A Comparative Study of Total Power* (New Haven: Yale University Press).

Wood, A. (1990) *Stalin and Stalinism* (London: Routledge).

Wood, S. (1989) 'The Transformation of Work?' in S. Wood (ed.) *The Transformation of Work? Skill, Flexibility and the Labour Process* (London: Unwin Hyman), 1–43.

Wood, S. (1991) 'Japanization and/or Toyotaism?', *Work, Employment and Society*, 5(4):567–600.

Worsley, P. (1967) *The Third World*, 2nd edn (London: Wiedenfeld and Nicolson).

Worsley, P. (1980) 'One world or three? A critique of the world-system theory of Immanuel Wallerstein', *Socialist Register*, 298–338.

Worsley, P. (1984) *The Three Worlds: Culture and World Development* (London: Wiedenfeld and Nicolson).

Worsley, P. (1987) 'Development' in P. Worsley (ed.) *The New Introducing Sociology* (Harmondsworth: Penguin), 48–83.

Worsley, P. (1990) 'Models of the Modern World System' in M. Featherstone (ed.) *Global Culture: Nationalism, Globalization and Modernity* (London: Sage), 83–95.

Wright, E. (1989) 'A General Framework for the Analysis of Class Structure' in E. Wright *et al. The Debate on Classes* (London: Verso), 3–43.

Wrong, D. (1981) 'Max Weber and Contemporary Sociology' in B. Rhea (ed.) *The Future of the Sociological Classics* (London: George Allen and Unwin), 39–59.

Young, M. (1988) *The Metronomic Society: Natural Rhythms and Human Timetables* (London: Thames and Hudson).

Zohar, D. and Marshall, I. (1994) *The Quantum Society: Mind, Physics and a New Social Vision* (London: Flamingo).

Index